Wolfram Elsner (Ed.)

Arms, War, and Terrorism in the Global Economy Today

Bremer Schriften zur Konversion

herausgegeben von

Prof. Dr. Wolfram Elsner

Band 13

LIT

Wolfram Elsner (Ed.)

Arms, War, and Terrorism in the Global Economy Today

Economic Analyses and Civilian Alternatives

LIT

The editor is grateful to the U.S. and European chapters of Economists Allied for Arms Reduction (ECAAR, now: Economists for Peace and Security – EPS) for sponsoring the Joint Seminars where the papers of this volume were presented. He is also grateful to the German ECAAR chapter for sponsoring the print of this volume.

Bibliographic information published by the Deutsche Nationalbibliothek
The Deutsche Nationalbibliothek lists this publication in the Deutsche Nationalbibliografie; detailed bibliographic data are available in the Internet at http://dnb.d-nb.de.

ISBN 3-8258-0045-8

A catalogue record for this book is available from the British Library

© LIT VERLAG Dr. W. Hopf Hamburg 2007
Grindelberg 15a
D-20144 Hamburg

Auslieferung:
LIT Verlag Fresnostr. 2, D-48159 Münster
Tel. +49 (0) 2 51/620 32 - 22, Fax +49 (0) 2 51/922 60 99, e-Mail: lit@lit-verlag.de

Distributed in the UK by: Global Book Marketing, 99B Wallis Rd, London, E9 5LN
Phone: +44 (0) 20 8533 5800 – Fax: +44 (0) 1600 775 663
http://www.centralbooks.co.uk/acatalog/search.html

Distributed in North America by:

Transaction Publishers
New Brunswick (U.S.A.) and London (U.K.)

Transaction Publishers
Rutgers University
35 Berrue Circle
Piscataway, NJ 08854

Phone: +1 (732) 445 - 2280
Fax: + 1 (732) 445 - 3138
for orders (U. S. only):
toll free (888) 999 - 6778
e-mail:
orders@transactionspub.com

Contents

Introduction and Overview
    Wolfram Elsner   1

PART I: ECONOMICS AND CONFLICT, WAR, AND TERRORISM   9

1. *Michael D. Intriligator* - Economics and the Problems of Armed Conflict, War, and Peace   11

2. *Fanny Coulomb, Liliane Bensahel, Jacques Fontanel* - The Concepts of Economic War and Economic Conflicts in a Global Market Economy   39

PART II: MILITARY SPENDING AND ARMS EXPORTS -THE MACROECONOMIC AND SECTORAL PICTURES   59

3. *Jurgen M. Brauer* - United States Military Expenditure   61

4. *Gulay Gunluk-Senesen* - Accounting for Arms in Input-Output and National Income Accounts   79

PART III: THE EVOLUTION OF THE INTERNATIONAL ARMS INDUSTRIES AND THE INCREASING ROLE OF THE FINANCIAL MARKETS   95

5. *J. Paul Dunne, Maria Garcia Alonso, Paul Levine, Ron P. Smith* - The Evolution of the International Arms Industry   97

6. *Luc Mampaey, Claude Serfati* - Armaments Groups and the Financial Markets: An "Unlimited Warfare" Convention in the Making?   121

PART IV: THE MACRO-REGIONAL CASE OF THE GREEK-TURKISH CONFLICT AND THE "GREATER MIDDLE EAST" 149

7. *Andrew Michael* – Reasons for Turkey's Military Presence in Cyprus and Its Potential Effects on Regional Stability 151

8. *Christos Kollias, Susana-Maria Paleologou* - Military Tension and Defence Spending Dynamics Between Greece and Turkey 169

9. *Galip Isen* - The "Broader" Middle East and North Africa: Transcending Beyond the Traditional *Realpolitik*-Security Mechanisms 181

PART V: PROBLEMS OF TERRORISM, AND PERSPECTIVES ON A MORE PEACEFUL DEVELOPMENT 209

10. *Clark C. Abt* - Countering Global Terrorist Use of Biological and Nuclear Weapons by Civil Means 211

11. *Wolfram Elsner* - Heterodox Economics and Radical Non-Intervention - Theses 261

12. *Lucy Law Webster* - Overcoming War and Empire by Incentivizing Justice and Democracy 265

About the Authors 273

INTRODUCTION AND OVERVIEW

Wolfram Elsner

After the end of the Cold War, the world has experienced the tendency towards a more mono-polar international power structure, with a single superpower that has concentrated and employs the most dominant financial, political and military resources. However, this seems not to have provided more international justice, lawfulness, security, and peacefulness, nor reduced international conflict as compared to the earlier bipolar world system, a system of mutual threat, but also mutual bargaining and partial cooperation. Viewed from some time distance, the bipolar world system seems to have provided considerable free room for action and development for a great number of nations, and the competition between the two politico-economic systems seemed to have worked largely in favour of the countries and populations that were wooed from both sides. De-colonisation, the containment of imperialist interventionism and the establishment of the movement of independent 'third' countries that gained a major voice in the global system, were secular processes feasible under that global structure. Compared to that earlier system, freedom under the auspices of one single dominating economic, financial and military power, and one political and cultural model with global claims, and the power to enforce them, seems to have its drawbacks. Against the background of the new mono-polar global power structure, and in contrast to some earlier promises of a peaceful, re-united, 'one' world, a new intensity and new kinds of conflicts have emerged that have made the world in fact less secure.

With this, it has also become evident that defence-related issues, long given minor attention in economics, have surfaced as a central mechanism and force in the current stage of globalisation. Increase in military expenditures at the world level, the multiplication and continuation of wars in many parts of the world, new generations of sophisticated technological weapons, and increased interest for defence stocks at the financial markets, indicate that a new type of relation between defence and economy had set in at the turn of the century.

Arms production and the disposal of arms of all kinds in all corners of the world have not decreased but increased, conflicts about natural resources, labour force and productions sites, and sales markets have not reduced, and war and pre-emptive intervention, with or without the UN, even have become an allegedly legitimate way of defending the superpower's and its following powers' interests and perceived security. The claims and the military reach of the largest political, military and economic powers have become truly global, ambitions, strategic planning, military presence and intervention today include the 'Greater Middle East' and central and east Asia (the latter formerly being 'remote', stable, peaceful, although somewhat 'closed' areas of the world, clearly allocated, though, to one of the two major power systems). In fact, war and military intervention has become a potential scenario in virtually every corner of the world.

The globalisation of the economy, finance, politics and culture, its consequences on the global strategic planning and reach for resources, labour and markets, its consequences on potential conflict and on political and military intervention, its consequences in terms of arms production, new wars, pre-emptive or not, and – finally – the implications of this complex of interdependent factors on mechanisms and systems of terrorism and counterterrorism have now been widely analysed in recent years. Four years after 'September 11' and two years after the US intervention in Iraq, the scientific community has reacted and a whole series of 'second-thought' analyses on war and terrorism has been launched in the scientific literature recently[1].

While there is ample analysis of globalisation, conflict, intervention, the new wars, and a new imperialism and 'empire' in economic books now, specific analyses of the nexusses between

- economic theory
- and conflict, war, and terrorism,
- military spending, arms production and financial markets,
- macro- and sectoral economic implications of military spending and arms production,

as well as on civilian alternatives from an 'economically enlightened' perspective seem still to be lacking.

---

[1] See e.g. B.S. Frey, Dealing with Terrorism—Stick or Carrot? Cheltenham (UK), Northampton (MA, USA): E. Elgar, 2005; H.W. Richardson, P. Gordon, J.E. Moore II (Eds.), The Economic Costs and Consequences of Terrorism. Cheltenham (UK), Northampton (MA, USA): E. Elgar, 2007. Further recent books in this field include (in short): D.M. Jones (Ed.), Globalisation and the New Terror (Elgar); I. Rutledge, Addicted to Oil: America's Relentless Drive for Energy (IB Tauris); C. Armson, I.W. Zartman (Eds.), Rethinking the Economics of War (J. Hopkins Univ. Pr.); M. Nest, Dimensions of War and Peace (L. Rienner); R.T. Naylor, Satanic Purses: Money, Myth, and Misinformation in the War on Terror (McGill-Queen's Univ. Pr.); D. Hiro, Blood of the Earth: The Battle for the World's Vanishing Oil Resources (Nation Books); J. Franks, Rethinking the Roots of Terrorism (Palgrave Macmillan); M. Kaldor et al. (Eds.), Oil Wars (Pluto Pr.); A. Siddiqa, Military Inc. (Pluto Pr.); D. Smith, Globalization: The Hidden Agenda (Polity Pr.); G. Soros, The Age of Fallibility: Consequences of the War on Terror (Public Affairs); J. Rees, Imperialism and Resistance (Routledge); A. Williams, Liberalism and War: The Victors and the Vanquished (Routledge); P. Aall et al., Leashing the Dogs of War: Conflict Management in a Divided World (United States Peace Institute Pr.).

This is where the present collection of papers intends to fill a gap in the current literature on arms production, war and terrorism. The volume consists of papers of prominent economic researchers and practitioners from the ranks of different national associations of 'Economists Allied for Arms Reduction – ECAAR' (recently in the US and the UK re-named as 'Economists for Peace and Security – EPS'), in conjunction with heterodox economists of the 'European Association for Evolutionary Political Economy – EAEPE'. Both have established a tradition of annual joint seminars in conjunction with EAEPE's annual conferences, now regularly organised by a new Research Area (RA) within EAEPE on the field. This RA has stated its purpose as follows:

'As power is a category widely dealt with by evolutionary economics, the objective of the RA is more specifically to address defence-related issues in relation with the mode of development of contemporary economies. It has become evident that these issues, long seen as belonging to the history of economic thought or being given minor attention by research in economics, have surfaced as central in the current stage of globalisation. Further discussion and analysis based upon theoretical and empirical research are welcomed on:

- *Political Economy of peace and war. This area of research includes topics such as:*
- *The relations between war and globalisation in the post Cold-war era.*
- *The 'new wars' in many developing and less advanced countries (between 1990 and 2002, almost one third of the world's countries have been plagued with wars or major armed conflicts).*
- *Peace as an international (or global) public good.*
- *Arms industries. This area of research includes topics such as:*
- *The transformations of the arms industry, and of its mode of governance at a macro, and micro level.*
- *The relations between military and commercial technologies in the context of the new security agenda, and of an increase in non-military threats.'*

The present book presents papers of two joint seminars of the type mentioned in Rethymnon (Crete, Greece) in 2004. The collection has been complemented by a selection of papers from the Second International Conference on Defence, Security and Economic Development held at the University of Larissa (Greece) in June 2004. All the papers presented here investigate on

1. what economics has to say today on conflict, war, and terrorism,
2. economic and statistical re-calculations of military spending and arms-production value-added,
3. concentration and financially-led supply-push in the arms industries,
4. a regional case of conflict, military spending and geo-strategic implications in the 'Greater Middle East',
5. civilian alternatives to the mechanism of (counter-)terrorism in conceptional and practical terms.

The book is structured as follows:

In *Part I*, *Michael Intriligator*, UCLA, Milken Institute, and Vice-Chair EPS-US, gives an overview of the positions largely held by 'mainstream' and 'heterodox' *economics* alike *on international armed conflicts, arms races, nuclear war, terrorism, arms proliferation, and international security*. This analysis is concluded by an alternate view of global security, largely developed by Intriligator for many years in the frame of his prominent ECAAR/EPS activities. This proposal is based on a new global security architecture, including existing and new international institutions in the economy, in politics and other areas. It prohibits pre-emption and is particularly distinctive from the illusionary concept of an isolated national security for the USA.

Fanny Coulomb, *Liliane Bensahel*, and *Jacques Fontanel*, University of Grenoble, CESICE, PEPSE, and ECAAR-F, investigate on the conception of *economic war* in economic thought. Economic war is set in relation to many forms of 'State economic conflicts' in a globalised economy, such as sanctions, economic dependence and political vulnerability, and traced out in fields like the increasing links between military and civil industrial production (dual use) and between R&D and intelligence.

In *Part II*, papers provide a more comprehensive, and realistic, picture, as compared to official government reports, of the size and structure of military spending and their statistics, based on more sophisticated economic methods, and of their sectoral, macroeconomic and fiscal significance. *Jurgen Brauer*, Augusta State University, and Vice-Chair EPS-US, uses U.S. National Income and Product Accounts (NIPA) to reconfigure *US military spending*. Taking also into account related interest payment portions on federal debt, the real military expenditure in the US exceeds the official numbers by more than $ 130 billion in 2003.

Working in the same strand, *Gulay Gunluk-Senesen*, Istanbul University, follows up with the value-added of arms production and its relevance for the *sectoral* structure and the national income, in an international comparison. The paper covers production, export and *input-output-structures*. The ten countries under investigation include France, India, Israel, the UK and USA. The paper demonstrates how the *economy* in fact is *permeated* with arms production. It also reveals that *arms production statistics* in themselves seem to be a matter of non-knowledge and national informational discretion – most of the data turn out to be neither compatible within the national accounts nor internationally comparable.

In *Part III*, *John Paul Dunne*, together with his co-authors *Maria Garcia Alonso*, *Paul Levine* and *Ron P. Smith*, University of the West of England, University of Surrey, and Birkbeck College, resp., investigate on the pressures and dynamics of the *restructuring of the international arms industries* after the end of the Cold War. Transitional drops in military spending increased fixed cost pressures and induced a wave of concentration in the arms industries. The paper employs *econometric estimations* to identify some driving forces of this development. The concentration will in fact continue to raise in the future, which makes countries face ever more powerful international arms monopolies that in turn increasingly are able to *dictate public arms procurement* and even military-strategic policies.

Luc Mampaey and *Claude Serfati*, University of Versailles Saint-Quentin-en-Yverlinnes, GRIP and ECAAR-F, resp., build upon these restructurings and take a focus on the role of the *financial markets* in the building of what they call a military-industrial system. They track down the fact that the financial institutions (institutional shareholders) are playing an ever more active role in the mergers and acquisitions in the arms industries. This is not only meant to lock and foreclose the access to Pentagon contracts but also to boost the stock exchange values in the sector-specific *AMEX Defense Index* (DFI) with a combination of high profits and low risks. The paper concludes that the financial markets with this are developing a new war vision, forcing a kind of new permanent war or *war without limits convention*. Against this background, the prospect of more frequent US military interventions appear to become a plausible vision, being additionally fed now from new financial driving forces.

Part IV provides analyses on a local, and *macro-regional, case study*. *Andrew Michael*, Intercollege (Cyprus), draws on the – at first glance only local – *Turkish-Greek* conflict about Cyprus and recapitulates the recent history of the conflict and its continuing tensions. He also refers to the current sociopolitical climate in the surrounding major region. This is where the other two case studies build upon. While *Christos Kollias* and *Susana-Maria Paleologou*, University of Thessaly and University of Ioannina, resp., delve somewhat deeper into the potentials of the Greek-Turkish case by developing a method of *military-tension indexing* and forecasting, *Galip Isen*, Istanbul Bilgi University, embeds the local conflict in the broader geostrategic ambitions, namely the *US Greater Middle Eastern Initiative* – GMEI. In a comparative cultural and religious perspective, the paper concludes, the Western initiative is disappointing by *replicating* the ideals and mentality of the *Cold War* theories and plain *anglocentric modernisation* suppositions which have repeatedly failed earlier and elsewhere because the regional specificities and historical givens had been ignored.

Finally, in *Part V*, the volume undertakes to provide some perspectives on a more peaceful global development. And they do at different levels of specificity. First, *Clark A. Abt,* Abt Associates Inc., Cambridge (Mass.), a pronounced and long-standing counsellor to federal offices in the US, provides his detailed technical and empirical knowledge, not only to analyse mechanisms and ways of a more effective (and more civilian) *protection against biological and nuclear arms and attacks*, but he also puts such detailled technical and engineering solutions in the frame of a more civilian general strategy and vision of security. The paper is convincing with its cutting-edge technical information and economic cost-benefit analysis combined with a larger vision of a more civilian strategy; as compared to the currently official military and pre-emptive, 'national security' policy. Here, the paper takes up the theme of Michael Intriligator's civilian global security blueprint in the first chapter of this book.

The remaining two papers include both a more general and more radical view. *Wolfram Elsner*, University of Bremen, Germany, IISO and Chair ECAAR-D, provides a short paper with theses on a *radical non-interventionist* global order. The paper specifically draws upon knowledge provided by more recent developments in *evolutionary economics* and screens such knowledge (such as historical-time processes, path-dependence, local interactions and cultural proximity) that may support a radical non-interventionist stance. Also, *Lucy L. Webster*, New School University, N.Y., Institute for Global Policy and EPS-US, addresses the causes of *empire and war* in the frame of modern 'heterodox' evolutionary and institutional economics, where *uncertainties*, *cumulative processes* and *path dependencies* provide cornerstones for economic analysis. With her long-standing experience in UN consulting, she develops a vision of decision-making of the lowest possible level, and accompanies it with a staged conception of decision-making at appropriate spatial levels for a more participatory democracy. She also drafts concrete lines of *UN reform* for a better and more effective role of international civilian organisations in a more secure new global peace order. The chapter takes up, elaborates upon and combines with the chapters of Intriligator, Abt and Elsner.

In sum, the present volume presents a coherent selection of chapters with sophisticated economic analyses of the *theoretical*, applied *industrial*, *macroeconomic*, *fiscal policy*, *financial market*, *regional case*, and *alternate policy* dimensions of conflict, war, terrorism, security and peace. The chapters build upon each other, make use of cutting-edge *conventional as well as heterodox economic theories* and largely apply *advanced methodologies*. They jointly centre around the questions of the most crucial recent causes of conflict, war and terrorism and focus on the perspectives of a more peaceful and civilian global order.

Modern economics obviously has a considerable and critical contribution to make to the recent discussions on conflict, war and terrorism and to a more civilian and peacefully organised global security system. This is what the present volume hopefully is able to convey.

PART I:
ECONOMICS
AND CONFLICT, WAR, AND TERRORISM

Chapter 1
ECONOMICS AND THE PROBLEMS OF ARMED CONFLICT, WAR, AND PEACE

Michael D. Intriligator

The purpose of this paper is to review how economics can be used to study armed conflicts and war in the search for peace. Economic reasoning could help to identify possible policies and actions today that could prevent disasters tomorrow. A secondary purpose is to introduce a new concept of security, that of "Global Security."

In the nuclear era the potential implications of arms races and the proliferation of weapons of mass destruction for life and death are staggering. Their political implications in terms of power and influence and their economic implications in terms of resources mobilized for weapons production are of overwhelming importance. In the Post-Cold War era many of the assumptions and conclusions of the earlier period concerning armed conflict must be reconsidered in order to deal with current challenges. Structural changes in the World system since 1989 have included the end of the Cold War and Warsaw Pact; the dissolution of the Soviet Union; the attempted transition of the former socialist states to democracy and a market economy, with only mixed success; the advent of new nuclear weapon states, including Pakistan and North Korea; and the emergence of the United States as the paramount power with a new doctrine for its security, the Bush doctrine of President George W. Bush. An implication of these structural changes is that the problems of armed conflict and war and peace in the current period is different in fundamental ways from the old problems of either the Cold War or the period between its end and the terrorist attacks of September 11, 2001, making it much more significant.

I. Armed Conflicts

I.1. Armed Conflicts as the Scourge of Humanity

The human toll of armed conflict is overwhelming, with tens of millions killed and hundreds of millions in casualties just in the two World Wars in the 20th Century. There are dangers of continual conflict in the 21st Century, including regional conflicts and even the possibility of another global conflict.

At the end of the 19th Century and beginning of the 20th Century there was a belief that armed conflict was a problem of the past, as in the works of Norman Angell and Andrew Carnegie. In that period, however, the world entered a period of the greatest worldwide conflict, including the two World Wars. There is the danger of complacency in believing that international organizations, one or more superpowers, weapons of mass destruction, deterrence, or other mechanisms could avoid major conflicts enveloping a region or even the planet as a whole in yet another world war.

The end of the Cold War and of East-West conflict has led not to a diminution of security problems, as many had expected or hoped for, but rather to their expansion. Indeed, significant problems of conflict exist today. Among the specific dangers are continuing or potential regional international conflicts (e.g. Iraq, Iran, North Korea, Kashmir, Taiwan) and, in addition, internal conflict in failed states in Africa (e.g., Angola, Congo, Cote d'Ivoire, Liberia, Sierra Leone, Somalia, Sudan, Zimbabwe) and Asia (e.g., Indonesia, Myanmar, Philippines, Sri Lanka). In the Middle East and surrounding areas there is continuing unrest and potential conflict stretching in an arc from Morocco to Indonesia. There are further dangers of regional conflicts growing from local issues into a wider conflagration. The danger of conflict could also extend to major nations, including the U.S., the E.U., Russia, and other nuclear weapons states as a result of accidental or inadvertent nuclear war. The further proliferation of nuclear weapons and of other weapons of mass destruction, particularly combined with advanced means for their delivery, enormously intensifies the problems of ensuring global security, as discussed below.

1.2. Conflict Theory

A variety of analytic approaches have been used to study conflict, as discussed in the interpretive guide to the literature on conflict theory in Intriligator (1982), which organizes the literature by eight analytic approaches and eight areas of application. The eight analytic approaches include differential equations, decision theory/control theory, game theory, bargaining theory, uncertainty, stability theory, action-reaction models, and organization theory, while the eight areas of application include arms races, war initiation/war termination/ timing of conflict, military strategy/conduct of war, threats/crises/escalation, qualitative arms race/arms control, alliances, nuclear proliferation, and defense bureaucracy/budgets. Each of these eight analytic approaches could potentially be applied to each of these areas of application, but most work concentrates on a few combinations of analytic approach and area of application, such as the Richardson model of arms races that applies differential equations to the arms race, the application of decision theory/control theory to war initiation/war termination/ timing of conflict, the application of game theory to military strategy/conduct of war, the application of bargaining theory to threats/crises/escalation, the application of stability theory to alliances, the application of action-reaction models to nuclear proliferation, and the application of organization theory to defense bureaucracy/budgets. Thus, the literature tends to neglect many important areas of potential inquiry and many possible alternative methodologies.

1.3. Arms Races

Various approaches have been used to study arms races, including the Richardson model and models based on dynamic optimization. Much of the previous theoretical work on the arms race is in the Richardsonian tradition, which explains the arms race descriptively and mechanically. The Richardson model uses a coupled pair of differential equations to explain the change in levels of weapons in each of two nations as a function of the weapons held by both sides. Later work in this area, by contrast, has used rational choice models to explain the arms race in terms of the behavior of decision makers, making use of the postulates of rationality and maximizing behavior. For example, Brito (1972) used an optimal control approach of optimization in a dynamic setting to explain choices of arms acquisitions over time, while Intriligator (1975) obtained the Richardson model from each of the nations seeking to deter the other. The value of arms acquisitions in such a framework is a consequence of the behavioral decisions of defense decision makers on both sides in seeking either to deter or to attack the other side. For surveys of the arms race literature see Gleditsch and Njølstad (1990) and Sandler and Hartley (1995).

1.4. Regional Arms Races

Unlike the prior East-West arms race of the Cold War, current regional arms races involve lower levels of military technology, arms .imports, and the likelihood that such arms races will lead not to stability via mutual deterrence but rather to the outbreak of conflict. Important examples of the current regional arms races include the buildup of Chinese capabilities as part of its defense modernization and its reaction to the U.S. deployment of a missile defense system, with spillover effects in other nations in East and Southeast Asia; the buildup of weapons on the Korean peninsula, including nuclear weapons in North Korea; buildups of nuclear and conventional capabilities in India and Pakistan; and acquisitions of small arms in many African nations to fight ongoing wars, among others.

The traditional approaches and methods of arms control can be used to study regional arms races, including bilateral, multilateral, and unilateral approaches to limiting, reducing, or eliminating weapons, especially weapons of mass destruction and the means of their delivery.

I.5. *Arms Races and the Outbreak of War*

Some arms races do not but others do lead to the outbreak of war and regime instability. Empirical studies of the outbreak of war suggest that wars are usually consistent with rational decision making on the part of the initiator, that an arms race is less likely to lead to war if the status quo power "loses" the arms race, that conflict between major powers is limited and less likely to lead to war than conflict between a major and a minor power, that major powers and allied minor powers are involved in less hostility than unallied minor powers, and that unallied minor powers do initiate conflicts with major powers but there is no case where an allied minor power initiated a conflict (Bueno de Mesquita, 1981, Siverson and Tennefoss, 1983, Brito and Intriligator, 1995).

I.6. *Accidental or Inadvertent Nuclear War*

Probably the most likely paths to nuclear war are accidental or inadvertent use of nuclear weapons, especially in new nuclear weapons states. A major challenge is that of the possibility of an inadvertent nuclear strike as a result of civil disturbances, chaos, or civil war in nuclear weapons states. The loss of control that would stem from these causes could interfere with the chain of command and could result in accidental or inadvertent use. A policy implication is the value of introducing safeguards against accidental or inadvertent use of nuclear weapons. In the absence of such safeguards the probability of an accidental nuclear war will increase and, as a result, the aggregate probability of war will likely increase. Another policy implication is the importance of agreements ahead of time among the nuclear weapons states on what actions these states might take in various possible contingencies involving the accidental, inadvertent, or intentional use of nuclear weapons.

I.7. *Terrorism*

Terrorism is a nonconventional form of conflict that is of growing importance worldwide, particularly since the September 11, 2001 attacks on the World Trade Center in New York and the Pentagon in Washington, DC and President George W. Bush declaration of a War on Terrorism. Terrorism has many interpretations and definitions, but Enders and Sandler (1995) define it as "the premeditated use, or threat of use, of extra-normal violence or brutality to obtain a political objective through intimidation or fear directed at a large audience... The political objectives of terrorists vary and include the promotion of religious freedoms, economic equality, income redistribution, nationalism, separatism, ideological ends, nihilism, and issue-specific goals." As they note, it has increased in importance and visibility recently as terrorists have taken advantage of advancements in communication, transportation, and technology to intimidate the global community with threats of violence unless political demands are met. Terrorist organizations are numerous and they are increasingly globalized, being able to strike any perceived enemy from safe bases. They have also innovated new approaches to such strikes, as in the September 11 attacks that combined well-established highjacking of airliners with equally well-established suicide bombing, a potent combination that had never been used before. The world may witness other such innovations in the future, such as combining smuggling of goods with weapons of mass destruction, bringing for example, nuclear or biological weapons into a major port on container ships. (See also articles in the journals, Studies in Conflict and Terrorism, Terrorism, and Terrorism and Political Violence.)

I.8. Recent Changes in U.S. Nuclear Weapons Policy

There have been remarkable recent changes in U.S. nuclear weapons policy under the current administration of President George W. Bush that were announced in 2002. They constitute a formal end to the security system and policies of the Cold War and thus represent a discontinuous change in the international security system that calls for discussion, debate, and analysis. They have important implications for potential conflict situations, with the bipolar world of the Cold War having been replaced by a unipolar world with the U.S. as the dominant power or even "hyperpower" in the French terminology. Alliance systems that had existed in the earlier epoch have been replaced by unilateral U.S. preemptive actions as in the Iraq War, with "coalitions of the willing," while arms control has been replaced by unilateral U.S. initiatives.

This section will present these new concepts related to nuclear weapons doctrine and evaluate them. These changes in U.S. nuclear weapons policy were announced in two official documents that were released by the Bush administration in 2002. Both were influenced, in part, by the September 11, 2001 terrorist attacks on the U.S. The first of these official U.S. documents is the Nuclear Posture Review (NPR) that was issued by the U.S. Department of Defense in January 2002. It is a classified document that is mandated by law and produced periodically, the last one having been that of the Clinton administration in 1994. According to the NPR, "A combination of offensive and defensive, and nuclear and non-nuclear capabilities is essential to meet the deterrence requirements of the 21st century." It is a wide-ranging analysis of the requirements for deterrence in the 21st century. It states that it does not provide operational guidance on nuclear targeting or planning. Rather, it states that the Department of Defense continues to plan for a broad range of contingencies and unforeseen threats to the U.S. and its allies in order to deter such attacks in the first place. It does, however, refer to the "…possible use of nuclear weapons in an Arab-Israeli conflict, in a war between China and Taiwan, or in an attack from North Korea on the South." It also refers to the use of nuclear weapons against targets able to withstand non-nuclear attack, in retaliation for attacks by nuclear, biological, or chemical weapons, or "in the event of surprising military developments." It also states that the administration is fashioning a more diverse set of options for deterring the threat of weapons of mass destruction (WMD). Overall, according to the NPR, nuclear weapons play a critical role in the defense capabilities of the United States, its allies and friends and such weapons provide credible military options to deter a wide range of threats, including WMD and large-scale conventional military force. The NPR states that these "nuclear capabilities possess unique properties that give the United States options to hold at risk classes of targets [that are] important strategic and political objectives."

The second of these official U.S. documents is the National Security Strategy of the United States of America (NSS) that was issued by the Office of the National Security Advisor to President Bush in September 2002. It is an unclassified and open public document that is available on the White House web site. According to the NSS, there are plans to ensure that no nation could rival U.S. military strength. The emphasis is on defeating rogue states and terrorists, noting that traditional forms of deterrence will not work against such enemies. It proclaims the doctrine of U.S. preemption, where the U.S. "…cannot let our enemies strike first" and gives arguments for such preemption. For example, it notes that, "For Centuries, international law recognized that nations need not suffer an attack before they can lawfully take action to defend themselves against forces that present an imminent danger of attack." It further states that, "The U.S. has long maintained the option of preemptive actions to counter a sufficient threat to our national security." It should be noted, however, that the U.S. did not preempt in most of the recent wars it has fought, including the two World Wars, Korea, Vietnam, and the Gulf War, while its attempt at preemption in the Bay of Pigs invasion of Cuba was a failure. Far from there being historical precedents, this new policy represents a fundamental shift from the traditional U.S. policy of reaction to one of initiation. It is too early to say whether this policy of preemption in the Iraq War was a success or failure. The NSS notes "To forestall or prevent such hostile acts by our adversaries, the United States will, if necessary act preemptively." Such a policy of preemption is, however, a violation of the UN system that was set up in large part to prevent precisely such preemption, as in Hitler's September 1, 1939 invasion of Poland or Saddam Hussein's August 2, 1990 invasion of Kuwait. The UN Charter forbids a member state from taking military action against another member state unless it has itself been attacked or it has the authorization of the Security Council. The U.S. acted preemptively in the Iraq War, which was consistent with the NSS policy, but a violation of the UN Charter. In terms of international law, the U.S. was as much an outlaw in its attack on Iraq as Saddam Hussein was in his attack on Kuwait. President Bush's West Point Commencement Speech of June 2002 articulates many of the points in the NPR and the NSS. In fact, this speech set the stage for the NSS, which quotes at length from it.

According to the NPR the U.S. reserves the right to use nuclear weapons, thereby possibly breaking the taboo against their use that has existed since 1945. They are treated like other weapons with no sharp distinction from non-nuclear weapons. Nuclear targeting discussions have been a part of U.S. military strategy for some time, but the leak of the NPR provides the first time that an official "hit list" of targets for nuclear weapons has come to light. The NPR lists seven nations as possible targets for U.S. nuclear weapons. First are the two "old" enemies of Russia and China. Second are the three countries listed as members of the "Axis of Evil" in President Bush's 2002 State of the Union speech, namely Iran, Iraq, and North Korea. Third are two countries that are listed by the U.S. as terrorist states: Syria and Libya. Of these seven nations that could be targets of U.S. nuclear weapons, four are non-nuclear weapons states that are parties to the Treaty on the Non-Proliferation of Nuclear Weapons, the NPT, namely Iran, Iraq, Syria, and Libya (North Korea has withdrawn from the NPT). The U.S. along with other nuclear weapons states that are parties to the NPT gave so-called "negative assurances" to non-nuclear weapons states in the NPT, stating that it would not use nuclear weapons against non-nuclear states unless they were allied with nuclear powers. Thus, targeting these four non-nuclear states with nuclear weapons would be a violation of these U.S. negative assurances that were an inducement for these states to join the NPT and that were reiterated at the time of the NPT Review and Extension Conference in 1995. The NPR also calls for lesser reliance on the massive stockpiles of nuclear weapons as a deterrent to attack, with greater reliance on precision-guided weapons to deter attacks. It states that because of improvements in precision-guided weaponry, as demonstrated in the U.S. War in Afghanistan, the U.S. military can now rely more on powerful, highly accurate conventional bombs and missiles that could provide an inducement to start a war.

According to the NPR there is a new triad. The old triad consisted of three different basing modes for nuclear weapons: long-range bombers, land-based missiles, and submarine launched ballistic missiles. By contrast, the NPR refers to a new triad with three component parts of the U.S. strategic system. First are offensive strike weapons, nuclear and non-nuclear, including all three components of the old triad. Second are defenses, both active and passive, including the new national missile defense system. Third is a revitalized defense infrastructure that could "design, develop, manufacture, and certify new warheads in response to new national requirements and maintain readiness to resume underground testing if required."

The Bush administration also obtained agreement from Congress to lift its ban on designing new nuclear warheads, and there are plans to develop two new weapons. One is a low-yield "mini-nuke" weapon that could potentially be used as a weapon in regional conflicts thus possibly changing the role of nuclear weapons from that of deterring war to that of instruments of war. The other is a "bunker buster" that can destroy underground facilities, including missile silos in Russia and elsewhere. Thus, the NPR that calls for indefinite reliance on nuclear weapons with plans to improve the capabilities of the existing arsenal and to revitalize the infrastructure for improving US nuclear forces in the future. It promotes a nuclear strategy of maximum flexibility as opposed to measures for irreversible nuclear disarmament as agreed to at the 2000 NPT Review Conference.

The NSS places major emphasis on preemption and calls for preemption rather than deterrence as the fundamental basis of national security. The Afghanistan and Iraq Wars were the initial cases of such preemption, with the U.S. retaining the right to preempt in order to defend its vital interests. Such a policy of preemption requires massive defense spending, and the U.S. now spends over $500 billion annually on defense, including the Afghanistan and Iraq Wars, which is more than the defense budgets of the rest of the world combined. In addition to its costs, there are significant dangers of preemption. First, it creates antagonism toward the U.S. and possible terrorist attacks. Second, it sends a message to the rest of the world, that they should not attempt to fight the U.S. with conventional weapons, leading to the proliferation of nuclear weapons and other weapons of mass destruction. Third, this policy sets a precedent for other nations to also engage in preemption, including China in Taiwan and India in Pakistan. Fourth, there are dangers stemming from U.S. hubris after its quick defeat of Saddam Hussein's forces in Iraq, despite its problems in winning the peace, with its next step possibly being an invasion of another nation on President Bush's "Axis of Evil" list: Iran and North Korea or possibly others on the NPR nuclear hit list, such as Syria or Libya, or yet others, such as Belarus, or Cuba that were on U.S. Secretary of State Condoleezza Rice's "Outposts of Tyranny" list along with Myanmar and Zimbabwe. These nations will see such a possibility as looming and try to protect themselves, possibly by building nuclear weapons, as has already happened in North Korea or, if that is not possible, other weapons of mass destruction. Military leaders in some of these states drew the lesson from the 1990-91 Gulf War and even more from the 2003 Iraq War that it would be a mistake to fight the U.S. using conventional weapons, calling for their development of weapons of mass destruction, especially nuclear weapons.

There is an alternative to the policies that are enunciated in the NPR and the NSS, namely *global security*, as discussed below. This concept refers to security for the planet as a whole to replace the concept of national security, which is outmoded. National security, which defined up to certain well-defined borders, makes little sense given the globalization that has occurred in recent decades. The goal of global security would be that of protecting the planet as a whole from threats to its vital interests. This approach recognizes the value of global cooperation, in particular, the value of cooperative efforts among the current great powers of the U.S., the E.U., Japan, Russia, China, India, Indonesia, Brazil, Argentina, South Africa, and others. It recognizes the need to create a new global system comparable to the creation of a new world system after World War II, in the period from 1945 to 1949, one that would encompass not only security but also economics, politics, and other issue areas. This new global system would treat problems of security, both military and non-military, through strengthening existing international institutions or creating new global institutions. These new institutions of global governance could be built, in part, on the UN system and its components. They would involve supranational decision-making and authority, with enforcement capabilities, transparency, and accountability and with global perspectives and responses. Participation in the global decision making process would be through cooperation. There would be a prohibition against preemption by any one nation, no matter how powerful, in favor of collective action through the UN. Such a system of global security should be preferred to the current system of the U.S. as a hegemonic global power.

II. Arms Proliferation

II.1. *The Nature of Arms Proliferation*

Arms proliferation refers to the possibility of nations acquiring nuclear weapons, other weapons of mass destruction, and delivery systems (See Davis and Frankel, 1993). Thus, proliferation refers to the spread of weapons of mass destruction - nuclear, chemical, biological/bacterio-logical, and radiological weapons - and also sophisticated missile and aircraft capabilities for the delivery of such weapons. The problem of nuclear proliferation is, of course, an old one, going back to the first atomic bomb explosions in 1945, which led to speculation as to when other nations would develop such capabilities, the so-called "nth country problem." The new problem of nuclear proliferation in the post-Cold War world, however, is different in several respects from the old problem, however, making it much more significant.

The result of the proliferation of weapons of mass destruction and the means for their delivery and of increased arms sales, particularly to nations in unstable regions, would likely be the creation of enormous instabilities. Nuclear weapons have not only perceived military or security value to nations acquiring them, but they are also seen as valuable in diplomatic, political, and economic terms. Thus, there are many incentives for nuclear proliferation, with relatively few disincentives.

The example of North Korea shows that the nonproliferation regime, including the NPT and the various institutions set up to limit access to nuclear weapons production needs considerable tightening. Specific initiatives would include challenge inspections, full-scope safeguards, stricter limits on dual-use technologies that could have military use, active criminalization of the supply of sensitive technologies, closer surveillance of arms imports, strict monitoring of the production and inventories of fissile material, and the return of spent fuel rods.

These newer aspects of nuclear proliferation imply both a new set of challenges in the proliferation of nuclear weapons and greater instability at the regional and global levels. The result is a major challenge to global security.

II.2. *Implications of the End of the Cold War for Proliferation*

The Cold War and the bipolar order had imposed stability and predictability in international affairs but it is now over. Now the situation is more unstable and unpredictable, suggesting the possibility of new threats to security and less predictability of allies and international organizations and thus possibly making acquisition of independent nuclear capabilities more attractive. One aspect of the end of the bipolar order is that states in the developing world have become increasingly marginalized, ignored by the major nations. During the Cold War both East and West courted the nations of Africa, Asia, and Latin America, but now they are largely ignored. There are only a few ways in which they can have the attention of the world: one is by economic importance, especially ownership of oil reserves or other strategic commodities; another is geostrategic significance; and yet another is via the possession of nuclear weapons. Some nations may conclude that the only way to be taken seriously by the world community is via the acquisition of nuclear weapons, which can be used both as a lever for regional or international recognition and as a bargaining chip for political, economic, and other goals. Yet another aspect of the end of the bipolar order is the presence of several regional arms races without the influence of the former superpowers.

II.3. *Proliferation as a Major Threat to International Security*

A major challenge to global security for the future will be that of proliferation, including the spread of both nuclear and chemical weapons and sophisticated missile and aircraft capabilities for the delivery of these weapons of mass destruction. While there have been some positive developments on the nonproliferation front in recent years, particularly in South Africa, the coming decades may witness the further spread of such weapons. This spread of these weapons could be followed by threats to use such weapons or even the actual use of these weapons, particularly in regions of instability. Countries in these regions are increasingly making or obtaining via international trade advanced conventional weapons, chemical weapons, advanced military aircraft, missiles, and even components and technologies that could lead to the development of nuclear weapons. In addition, there is the advent of dual-purpose technologies and, perhaps of most importance is the possible diversion of Russian fissile material and nuclear experts to nations seeking nuclear weapons.

The result of the proliferation of weapons of mass destruction and the means for their delivery and of increased arms sales, particularly to nations in unstable regions, would likely be the creation of enormous instabilities. An important aspect of the instabilities that could result from these developments is the attempt of nations to become regional or even global powers via nuclear proliferation. As already noted, some national leaders may perceive that the only way for a nation to be taken seriously on the world scene is via the acquisition of nuclear weapons. Such weapons have not only perceived military or security value to nations acquiring them, but they are also seen as valuable in diplomatic, political, and economic terms. Thus, there are many incentives for nuclear proliferation, with relatively few disincentives. In fact, many of the disincentives can be reduced or avoided altogether if nations follow the Israeli model of covert development of nuclear weapons, with no test, no announcement, and a stated policy of ambiguity or denial. Nations following the course of covert development can have most of the benefits of nuclear weapons with few of the costs.

Once a nation has nuclear weapons, there is an incentive for their regional antagonists to develop their own, leading to chains of proliferation. The result of these chains of proliferation is that the proliferating nation may be less secure in the proliferated region than if the region had no such weapons. Thus, while the short-term effects of developing nuclear weapons may be seen as positive from the perspective of the nation developing them, the long-term effects may, in fact, be negative. Similarly, from a global perspective, while it may appear to be in the interest of a single nation to develop nuclear weapons capability, from a worldwide standpoint the effects are generally to increase instability and thus to impact negatively on global security.

II.4. *Demand Factors in Nuclear Proliferation*

A useful way to analyze nuclear proliferation is to consider both the demand for and supply of nuclear weapons. Among demand factors in seeking nuclear weapons are their possible use in war, as in the U.S. use of these weapons against Japan in 1945, or to deter an opponent (as in the case of the U.S. and the Soviet Union in the Cold War). Other demand factors are their use as a weapon of last resort if survival is threatened (as in the case of Israel) or for use in regional conflicts either for direct use or to deter outsiders (as in the case of India and Pakistan). Yet another demand factor is for prestige (as may apply to the U.K. and France).

The nuclear capabilities of a perceived enemy or a regional rival can lead to possible *chains of nuclear proliferation* with negative long-term effects. The main chain historically proceeds from the U.S. fear of Nazi Germany that led it to its own development of the atomic bomb, but then leading the Soviet Union to develop these weapons. The chain continues with the development of these weapons by China and then ultimately to India and Pakistan, perhaps continuing with Iran. There are also side influences on the United Kingdom and France and separate chains involving other nations, such as in the Middle East and South America.

The end of the bipolar order of the Cold War has made nuclear weapons acquisition more attractive as a way of guaranteeing a nation's security. As already noted, there is a perception in many nations that the only way to be taken seriously on the world scene is via the acquisition of nuclear weapons, with nations having these weapons commanding respect and with others largely marginalized apart from those with economic strength or oil or other strategic resources.

The escalation of terrorism by states or subnational groups has begun to include nuclear and other weapons of mass destruction, such as the Aum Shinrikiyo attack on the Tokyo subway using sarin gas, a chemical weapon.

II.5. *Supply Factors in Nuclear Proliferation*

Traditional approaches to nonproliferation limit supply and access to technology via secrecy and export controls, but now this is inadequate, given the lower cost of acquiring nuclear weapons.

The supply of fissile material, including highly enriched uranium and plutonium, is the key to proliferation, not weapons design, handling capability, delivery vehicles, etc. A source of fissile material is that leaking from the former Soviet Union and from other former Warsaw Pact nations – the problem of so-called "loose nukes." (See Campbell, Carter, Miller, and Zraket, 1991 and Wedar, Intriligator, and Vares, Eds, 1992). A move to a worldwide plutonium economy, with greater reliance on plutonium in the production of energy in nuclear power plants, especially in breeder reactors, and with greater movements of plutonium in international commerce could provide this supply. Major examples include the continued development of nuclear power in France, Japan, and Russia and the enormous shipments of plutonium from Europe to Japan to be used in a breeder reactor. Plutonium can be used in the manufacture of nuclear weapons, so its greater use nationally and greater movements internationally could lead to the acquisition of a key ingredient in nuclear weapons development.

One important source of supply is technology transfers and sales of sensitive materials and equipment particularly via exports to nations in the developing world by a small number of nations, the five permanent members of the UN Security Council. These international arms and technology sales differ in many respects from previous such sales. They involve more sophisticated weapons, means of delivery, and technologies and fewer restrictions on the use of these weapons and the technology. Arms exporters today are largely motivated not by military or diplomatic considerations, as in the past, but rather largely by commercial aspects of these sales. Their goal is to earn foreign exchange and to keep military production units in operation in the absence of domestic sales. Furthermore, there are enormous economic pressures not only on Russia and the United States but also on the United Kingdom, France, China, and other nations to export weapons and technology and to sell weapons to the developing world, rather than closing down or converting military production lines and destroying existing military stocks. These nations will have to reach some agreements on reducing arms exports and also exports of sensitive technologies and dual-use products, possibly establishing a new regime limiting exports either worldwide or to regions of concern, such as the Middle East.

The potential brain drain of nuclear experts, including scientists, engineers, and technical workers, particularly those from the former Soviet Union is another source of supply by providing technical assistance to nations trying to build nuclear weapons. Nations of the developing world could pay such experts many times their current salaries. There may also be ideological or religious motivations for nuclear experts from the central Asian and Transcaucasus republics of the former Soviet Union to help neighboring nations, such as Iran, in the production of nuclear weapons. It must be met by providing appropriate opportunities for these experts in new scientific projects, funded by consortia of governments and by public and private institutions. A similar program should be established for experts from all nuclear weapons states, who might be encouraged to work collaboratively on new nonmilitary scientific projects, including energy and environmental research.

II.6. Managing Nuclear Proliferation

The most effective approaches today are those that influence demand by incentives and disincentives, suggesting the value of a strategy of managing proliferation, focusing on influencing demand by incentives and disincentives. This approach would represent a shift to a strategy of managing proliferation rather than preventing it, focusing on the most dangerous cases with policies tailored to specific circumstances of the nation and the region, including:
- nuclear guarantees to allies not acquiring nuclear weapons;
- tightening of both the Nuclear Nonproliferation Treaty (NPT) and the missile;
- Technology Control Regime (MTCR);
- economic rewards and punishments;
- sanctions;
- diplomacy.

II.7. Overt vs. Covert Proliferation

Overt proliferation involves secret development, test, and announcement of capabilities, as in the U.S. model of 1945, followed by the USSR in 1949 and the U.K. in 1952, representing three new nuclear nations in the first decade, 1945-1955. This was followed by France in 1962 and China in 1964, representing two new nuclear nations in the second decade, 1955-1965, and India in 1974, representing one new nuclear nation in the third decade, 1965-1975. None followed these until the May 1998 nuclear tests in India and Pakistan, adding Pakistan as an overt nuclear nation.

Covert proliferation involves secret development, no test, and no announcement of capabilities, with a policy of ambiguity and denial as in the Israeli model of the 1970's and up to the present, as it has never officially admitted to having nuclear weapons. This Israeli model was followed by India, which in effect switched from an overt to a covert approach following its one test in 1974, labeled a "peaceful" nuclear explosion, then switching back in 1998 to an overt one. South Africa and Pakistan also followed this model, the former eventually destroying its nuclear weapons and the latter switching to an overt approach in May 1998. Others may have also followed it, with some eventually dropping their nuclear program, such as Canada and Sweden and perhaps South Korea and Taiwan. Such covert development suggests the value of intelligence and inducements to comply with the non-proliferation regime. In such "opaque" proliferation the nation developing nuclear weapons never admits to their existence but usually does give some hints to suggest that it has such weapons (See Frankel, Ed., 1990). By developing weapons covertly nations can retain many of the supposed advantages of nuclear weapons states, including having a weapon of last resort, deterring regional rivals, achieving some degree of hegemony in a region, and enhancing international status and prestige. At the same time they can avoid incurring certain of the costs of overt proliferation, including antagonizing allies, losing technical assistance, suffering international opprobrium, and perhaps even attracting a surgical strike on its nuclear facilities. When taking account the possibility of covert proliferation, there are some new potential proliferators that must be added to the traditional list of nations that might be developing nuclear weapons.

The issue of covert nuclear proliferation should be dealt with directly by recognizing its existence and by using new technologies for intelligence gathering to reveal the capabilities of nations using this route to nuclear weapons.

II.8. Potentially Stabilizing Aspects of Nuclear Proliferation

Most previous work on proliferation has assumed, explicitly or implicitly, that additional nuclear powers would be destabilizing in the sense of increasing the probability of war. However, the political scientist Kenneth N. Waltz in Waltz (1981) and Sagan and Waltz (2003) concluded that more nations with nuclear weapons would reduce the chance of conflict. Intriligator and Brito (1981) and Brito and Intriligator (1983) analyzed the consequences of additional nuclear weapons states on crisis stability and concluded that nuclear proliferation may have different qualitative effects on the probability of nuclear war depending on the number of existing nuclear nations and the level of weapons held by the various countries involved. Intriligator and Brito found that, in certain circumstances, but not universally, in contrast to Waltz, having an additional nuclear power in the system may reduce rather than increase the probability of deliberate nuclear war. This effect occurs when the restraining influence of the additional nuclear weapon state on the prior states with nuclear weapons offsets the destabilizing influences of there being an additional state able to start a nuclear war and an additional potential initiator of an accidental or inadvertent nuclear war, which are also destabilizing. Historical examples include the acquisition of nuclear weapons by the U.K. and France that further restrained the Soviet Union. Gallois (1961) argued that French acquisition of nuclear weapons would raise the stakes of a potential conflict and thereby make nations more cautious and thus reduce the chance of nuclear war. Another example might be India and Pakistan where, by raising the stakes the nations are less likely to resort to confrontation or war, with their nuclear weapons acquisition leading to a situation of mutual deterrence.

However, this whole line of research is open to question since Brito and Intriligator (1996) have shown that qualitative predictions about the change in the probability that individual nations will initiate a nuclear war as the number of nuclear powers increases are not sufficient to make predictions about the change in the aggregate probability of a nuclear war.

The overall implication for policy is that one must look at each situation and evaluate it. Not all proliferation situations are the same, with some more destabilizing than others and with some even possibly promoting stability.

II.9. Policy Issues Related to Proliferation

The examples of Iraq apparently not having a nuclear weapons program and North Korea having one, with the latter having developed a small number of these weapons suggest the need for new policies related to proliferation.

A fundamental new policy would be a tightened nonproliferation regime, including strengthening the NPT and IAEA, allowing for challenge inspections and full-scope safeguards, stricter limits on dual-use technologies, closer surveillance of arms imports, and closer cooperation in limiting exports of equipment and technology. All nuclear weapons states, whether overt or covert, should be given inducements to comply with the restrictions of the nonproliferation regime. In addition, it is necessary to tighten the nonproliferation regime, including not only the NPT but also the IAEA, the suppliers club, and the supply of material for nuclear power and research reactors. Specific initiatives would include challenge inspections, full-scope safeguards, stricter limits on dual-use technologies that could have military use, active criminalization of the supply of sensitive technologies, closer surveillance of arms imports, and return of spent fuel rods. It would also be important to provide alternatives to nuclear scientists and engineers from the former Soviet Union, and safeguards relating to highly enriched uranium and plutonium, limiting their production, transport, and storage by a fissile material control regime. The Chemical Weapons Convention prohibits the production, transport, or storage of chemical weapons. This treaty might be the basis for a similar ban on the production, transport, or storage of plutonium. In fact, banning the transport and storage of plutonium is probably more urgent than banning the transport and storage of chemical weapons. It is also necessary to counter the move to a worldwide plutonium economy via collaborative international agreements, reached on the basis of both nonproliferation and environmental concerns. The renunciation of breeder reactor technology and of massive international shipments of plutonium must be done on a worldwide basis.

The importance of recognizing the dangers of accidental or inadvertent nuclear war that tends to be underestimated, calls for improved intelligence and command, control, communications, and information. There is also a need for contingency planning and for international cooperation in the sharing of information and dealing with various possible contingencies. The issue of accidental or inadvertent nuclear war must be treated via sharing of technical information as to how to control nuclear weapons (e.g., Permissive Action Links); information exchange; and agreements among all states with such weapons, building on the Soviet - U.S. agreements in this area. Of particular importance would be agreements ahead of time among the nuclear weapons states on what actions they would take in various possible contingencies involving the accidental, inadvertent, or intentional use of nuclear weapons.

Another important policy initiative would be that of finalizing and putting into place the Comprehensive Test Ban Treaty (CTBT), with testing replaced by simulation studies and greater reliance on existing databases.

The India-Pakistan May 1998 tests were valuable in focusing greater global attention on the issue of nuclear proliferation, but a mistake in focusing attention on South Asia as it just represented a shift from covert to overt status for both nations. More serious threats lie elsewhere, especially North Korea, Iran, Syria and Algeria.

Overall, the threat to global security represented by nuclear proliferation must be met by a set of policies, adopted on a global basis, that would either reduce the extent of proliferation or reduce its negative impacts. These policies must be based on a new form of international order that would restore stability and predictability in international affairs. As one possibility, a new concert of major nations, possibly through the United Nations and with the leadership of the United States, might be able to provide guarantees to nations facing military and other threats to their security or to help them establish regional cooperative security arrangements with the participation of other nations and international organizations so as to defuse their possible interest in nuclear weapons development. Finally, world leaders and international organizations must be reminded that nuclear proliferation is a major challenge to global security. In particular, all current nuclear weapons states must set an example by collective action, in extending and strengthening not only the NPT but also the Missile Technology Control Regime (MTCR); limiting or eliminating nuclear testing; taking the initiative on a new treaty on chemical weapons; and reaching agreements on reducing arms and technology exports, possibly establishing a new regime limiting weapons such exports worldwide or in regions of concern, such as the Middle East. In fact, the traditional approaches and methods of arms control can be used in the area of nonproliferation as a further approach to global security. These include bilateral, multilateral, and unilateral approaches to limiting, reducing, or eliminating nuclear weapons and other weapons of mass destruction and the means of their delivery. These newer approaches to and policies for nonproliferation, addressing both the traditional and the newer developments in the area of nuclear proliferation, could prevent proliferation or mitigate its effects and thus could play a significant role in ensuring global stability.

II.10. The Most Dangerous Cases of Nuclear Proliferation

North Korea is extremely dangerous and now apparently does have a few nuclear weapons with plans to make even more. It is in a desperate economic situation, including famine. It is isolated from the rest of the world and as a result, their leaders tend to believe their own propaganda, especially that concerning the U.S., South Korea, and Japan. It has both nuclear capabilities and ambitions. Being surrounded by nuclear nations it perceives the need for its own nuclear weapons that would be the equalizer of the much larger military capabilities of the U.S. and the much larger economic capabilities of South Korea. An added incentive is its people's belief in independence and self-reliance. It has delivery systems in its missiles. It resumed work on its nuclear program partly as a result of the U.S. reneging on the 1994 Agreed Framework to provide heavy fuel oil and light water reactors in return for it freezing its nuclear program.

Iran resumed the nuclear weapons that had been started under the Shah but was discontinued after the 1979 revolution. It has grievances against the U.S. and Israel and there are the pressures of religious dogma and fundamentalism in a theocratic state. It sees nuclear weapon as giving it status in the Islamic world as well as a means to protect itself from its enemies. It is in the process of obtaining some of the needed technology and equipment from Russia, although Russia claims that the transfer of technology and equipment is no different than what the U.S. has provided too many nations worldwide. It will require strong disincentives to once again stop its nuclear weapons program.

Russia is very dangerous, with thousands of nuclear warheads and with some types, especially tactical nuclear weapons (torpedoes, land mines, etc.) not adequately safeguarded, with a potential for accidental or inadvertent use. It has enormous stockpiles of fissile material and chemical weapons. It has nuclear scientists and engineers who have not been paid and have access to nuclear material and facilities.

Other Soviet successor states, including Ukraine, Belarus, and Kazakhstan, are also potentially dangerous. They had large arsenals of nuclear weapons that they returned to Russia, but they have technical expertise in designing, building, storing, deploying, and maintaining nuclear weapons. They also have nuclear scientists and engineers who have not been paid and have access to nuclear material and facilities. Some also have extremist leaders and economies in critical condition, with a potential for political disruption.

II.11. Overall Conclusion with Respect to Nuclear Proliferation

The challenge now is to create a new system of international security that reflects current world realities and treats various threats, including, specifically, the proliferation of nuclear weapons. Nonproliferation policies thus must play a major role in any new system of international security.

Overall, the conclusion of this analysis is the importance of managing proliferation, focusing on the most dangerous cases and reducing the demand for nuclear weapons by raising the costs of proliferation in these cases.

III. A New Concept of Security: "Global Security"

III.1. The Need for a New Global Order to Replace the Earlier Bipolar Order

The earlier bipolar order, with two "superpowers" in the United States and the Soviet Union, had imposed stability and predictability in international affairs from 1947 to 1992. Some sort of international order that would restore stability and predictability in international affairs must replace this old bipolar order of the Cold War. This "New Global Order," using the terminology of the past U.S. President George H. W. Bush, must be "new" in reflecting current realities; must be "Global" in applying to the whole planet, rather than a particular region or nation; and must involve "order" rather than disorder. The challenge is to create a new system of international security that reflects current world realities and treats various threats, including arms races and the proliferation of nuclear weapons. Arms control and nonproliferation policies thus must play a major role in any new system of international security.

Now the situation is more unstable and unpredictable, suggesting the possibility of new threats to security and less predictability of allies and international organizations. One aspect of the end of the bipolar order is the presence of several regional arms races without the influence of the former "superpowers." Yet another aspect of the end of the bipolar order is that states in the developing world have become increasingly marginalized, ignored by the major nations. During the Cold War both East and West sometimes courted the nations of Africa, Asia, and Latin America, but now they are largely ignored. Some nations may conclude that the only way to be taken seriously by the world community is via the acquisition of nuclear weapons, which can be used both as a lever for regional or international recognition and as a bargaining chip for political, economic, and other goals.

III.2. Defining "Security" and "Global Security"

A necessary step in the formulation of a new system of international security is that of defining the concept of "security" itself. There are, in fact, several aspects of a definition of "security" that must be taken into account in order for the concept to be relevant to the current world system.

First, in the light of global interdependence, it is necessary to treat security from an international and, ideally, from a global perspective, rather than from a national perspective. Thus, in terms of scope, the traditional concept of "national security," must be replaced by the newer concept of "*global security*," defined here as *the absence of threats to the vital interests of the planet*. (See Intriligator, 1991, 1994 and Gould and Sutton, 2002) The world is so connected and integrated that it is impossible to confine security to arbitrarily defined national frontiers. Furthermore, such security is gained not at the expense of another state but rather in conjunction with the security of other related states. Using the language of economics, security is a type of public good, with non-rival and non-excludable benefits, where more security for other states does not diminish any one state's security. In earlier periods, national security was frequently given as an example of a public good, a type of good for which one person's consumption of more national security does not diminish the national security of another person. Currently, however, this type of interpretation can be given at not just the national level of individual people but also at the international level of individual nations, with global security an international public good.

Second, just as security must be looked at from a broader global perspective, rather than merely a national perspective, in terms of content and substance, security must extend well beyond its traditional military dimension. Global security must treat, as part of its legitimate concerns, the interrelated military, political, economic, environmental, health, and other dimensions of security. Even within the narrower and traditional definition of security, involving the prevention of military threats to the vital interests of a sovereign nation or group of allied nations, there are newer challenges to global security. These newer challenges stem from military instability, including border and other regional conflicts, internal ethnic conflicts and civil wars, terrorism, and potential conflict or war situations. Of particular concern is the possibility of insurrection, the breakdown of order, and civil war in nuclear weapons states, which could lead to nuclear threats, the use of nuclear weapons, and even accidental or intentional nuclear war.

Third, the major focus of security concerns over the last fifty years has been Europe. Now, however, it is necessary to treat not just the security problems of Europe but also those of other regions, particularly regions of actual or potential conflict in the developing world and also the nonmilitary security problems of the world as a whole. A major area for global security concern is the Middle East and surrounding areas in view of its geostrategic location, its oil resources, the weapons in the region, and the several fundamental conflicts and antagonisms of the region. Europe remains, however, a major area for global security concern in view of the presence of major nuclear power states, the potential problems stemming from the presence of nuclear weapons in the successor states to the Soviet Union, and potential problems of nuclear proliferation in several nations in Europe.

Fourth, in terms of mechanisms to achieve the goal of global security, an increasingly important mechanism to achieve this goal is that of international cooperation, understood here to mean coordinated action among two or more nations so as to achieve a common goal. Such cooperation provides a major mechanism for dealing with global problems and achieving common goals, including those of global security. Wider international cooperation can treat global problems, including not only military threats but also nuclear proliferation and other threats to global security. Indeed, international cooperation could represent a new paradigm for global security, replacing earlier approaches to national and international security.

Fifth, in order to achieve the goal of global security there must be a rethinking of the instruments that could be used to solve the collective action problem. In particular, global security must reconsider the role of regional and international institutions as possible instruments to provide the public good of global security. The United Nations has emerged in the recent past as an important body for settling regional conflicts and for countering aggression, the role that was originally intended for it, particularly for the Security Council. Existing and new regional and international institutions could play important roles in addressing both military and nonmilitary threats to global security.

Sixth, the concept of global security must take account of the change in the distribution of power that has occurred in the international system. The era of "superpowers" is over, and the international system is returning to something resembling its earlier configuration, when it was dominated by several major powers, including the United States, Russia, United Kingdom, France, Germany, Japan, and China. In terms of military capabilities and geostrategic significance, however, it is necessary to add to these traditional major powers several other nations, including Ukraine, Kazakhstan, India, Pakistan, Taiwan, South Korea, North Korea, Indonesia, Brazil, Argentina, Israel, Iraq, Iran, Egypt, and South Africa.

Seventh, it is necessary to formulate new theories and analytic frameworks for global security to replace traditional theories such as containment, balance of power, deterrence, and hegemonic stability. These new theories will have to take explicit account of global interdependence and of the bilateral, trilateral, and other relations, particularly cooperative relations that exist or could exist among the great powers. An important aspect of these new theories should be the treatment of international cooperation as a mechanism for achieving global security, using the techniques of game theory, simulation, and other analytic approaches. Another aspect of these new theories will focus on the interaction between domestic politics and global security, building on the empirical observation that liberal democracies are not likely to engage in war with other liberal democracies and thus suggesting the value of this form of government for global security.

These different aspects of the definition of global security point to the need to reconceptualize the entire concept of international security and the mechanisms and institutions required to achieve it.

III.3. The Search for A New Concept of Global Order

One possibility is a unipolar world dominated by United States, which would serve as the policeman of the world. A historical analogy might be Pax Britannica when the United Kingdom dominated the world. This "Pax Americana" appears to be the plan adopted by President George W. Bush in the document prepared by his National Security Advisor Condeleeza Rice, *The National Security Strategy of the United States of America* and that he adopted in September 2002. Reinforcing this strategic document is the Pentagon's, *Nuclear Posture Review,* produced by the U.S. Department of Defense in January 2002. That calls for the use of nuclear weapons in various contingencies and against various possible states, including Russia, China, Iran, Iraq (before the Iraq War), North Korea, Syria and Libya.

An alternate and perhaps better possibility is a new concert of major nations, possibly through the United Nations and with the leadership of the United States. The nations involved might include the present Permanent Five members of the UN Security Council plus Germany, Japan, and perhaps others. This new concert might be able to provide security guarantees to nations facing military and other threats to their security or to help them establish regional cooperative security arrangements with the participation of other nations and international organizations so as to defuse their possible interest in nuclear weapons development. It would restore stability and predictability in international affairs.

References

Avenhaus, Rudolf, Victor Kremenyuk, and Gunnar Sjöstedt, Eds, Containing the Atom, Lanham: Lexington Books, 2002.

Betts, Richard K. Ed, Conflict after the Cold War: Arguments on Causes of War and Peace, 2nd ed., New York: Longman, 2002.

Boulding, Kenneth E., Conflict and Defense; a General Theory, New York, Harper, 1962.

Boulding, Kenneth E., Stable Peace, Austin: University of Texas Press, 1978.

Brito, Dagobert L., "A Dynamic Model of an Armaments Race," International Economic Review, 13: 359-375.

Brito, Dagobert L. and Michael D. Intriligator, "Arms Races and Proliferation," in Keith Hartley and Todd Sandler, Eds, Handbook of Defense Economics, Amsterdam: North-Holland Publishing Co., 1995.

Brito, Dagobert L. and Michael D. Intriligator, "Conflict, War, and Distribution," American Political Science Review, 79, 1985, 943-957.

Brito, Dagobert L. and Michael D. Intriligator, "Proliferation and the Probability of War: A Cardinality Theorem," Journal of Conflict Resolution, 40(1), March 1996, 204-212.

Brito, Dagobert L., Michael D. Intriligator and Adele E. Wick, Eds, Strategies for Managing Nuclear Proliferation -- Economic and Political Issues, Lexington: Lexington Books, 1983.

Bueno de Mesquita, Bruce, The War Trap, New Haven: Yale University Press, 1981.

Bueno de Mesquita, Bruce, and David Lalman, War and Reason: Domestic and International Imperatives, New Haven: Yale University Press, 1992.

Carlsnaes, Walter, Thomas Risse and Beth A. Simmons, Editors, Handbook of International Relations, London: SAGE, 2002.

Campbell, Kurt, Ashton Carter, Steven Miller, and Charles Zraket, Soviet Nuclear Fission: Control of the Nuclear Arsenal in a Disintegrating Soviet Union, CSIA Studies in International Security, No. 1, Cambridge: Center for Science and International Affairs, Harvard University, November, 1991.

Carment, David and Albrecht Schnabel, Eds, Conflict Prevention: Path to Peace or Grand Illusion? Tokyo, New York: United Nations University Press, 2003.

Cirincione, Joseph, with Jon B. Wolfsthal and Miriam Rajkumar, Deadly Arsenals: Tracking Weapons of Mass Destruction, Washington, D.C.: Carnegie Endowment for International Peace, 2002.

Cirincione, Joseph, Ed, Repairing the Regime: Preventing the Spread of Weapons of Mass Destruction, New York: Routledge, 2000.

Davis, Zachary S. and Benjamin Frankel, Eds, The Proliferation Puzzle, London: Frank Cass.

Enders, Walter and Todd Sandler, "Terrorism: Theory and Applications," in Keith Hartley and Todd Sandler, Eds, Handbook of Defense Economics, Amsterdam: North-Holland Publishing Co., 1995.

Frankel, Benjamin, Ed, Opaque Nuclear Proliferation: Methodological and Policy Implications, London: Frank Cass, 1990.

Gaddis, John Lewis, "A Grand Strategy of Transformation," Foreign Policy 133 (2003): 50-57.

Gallois, Pierre, The Balance of Terror: Strategy for the Nuclear Age. Translated from the French by Richard Howard. Boston, Houghton Mifflin, 1961.

Geller, Daniel S. and J. David Singer, Nations at War: A Scientific Study of International Conflict, Cambridge Studies in International Relations: 58. Cambridge: Cambridge University Press, 1998.

Gleditsch, Nils-Petter and Olav Njølstad, Eds, Arms Races: Technological and Political Dynamics, Oslo: International Peace Research Institute; Newbury Park: Sage Publications, 1990.

Gould, Robert M. and Patrice Sutton, "Global Security: Beyond Gated Communities and Bunker Vision," Social Justice 29.3 (2002).

Guoliang, Gu, "Redefine Cooperative Security, Not Preemption," The Washington Quarterly 26.2 (2003).

Hartley, Keith and Todd Sandler, Editors, Handbook of Defense Economics, Amsterdam: Elsevier, 1995.

Heisbourg, Francois, "A Work in Progress: The Bush Doctrine and Its Consequences," The Washington Quarterly 26.2 (2003).

Hirshleifer, Jack, The Dark Side of the Force: Economic Foundations of Conflict Theory, Cambridge, New York: Cambridge University Press, 2001.

Hirshleifer, Jack, "Theorizing about Conflict," in Keith Hartley and Todd Sandler, Eds, Handbook of Defense Economics, Amsterdam: Elsevier, 1995.

Hoffman, Stanley, "The High and the Mighty: Bush's National Security Strategy and the New American Hubris," The American Prospect 13.24 (2003).

Intriligator, Michael D., "Defining 'Global Security'," Disarmament, 14 (October 1991), 59-72.

Intriligator, Michael D., "Global Security After the End of the Cold War," Presidential Address, Peace Science Society (International), Conflict Management and Peace Science, 13(2) (1994), 1-11.

Intriligator, Michael D., "On the Nature and Scope of Defence Economics," Defence Economics, 1 (1990), 3-11.

Intriligator, Michael D., "Prospects for Arms Control: Bilateral, Unilateral, and Multilateral," in Jürgen Brauer and Manas Chatterji, Eds, Economic Issues of Disarmament, New York: New York University Press, 1992.

Intriligator, Michael D., "Research on Conflict Theory: Analytic Approaches and Areas of Application," Journal of Conflict Resolution, 26 (2) (June 1982), 307-327.

Intriligator, Michael D., "Strategic Considerations in the Richardson Model of Arms Races," Journal of Political Economy, 83 (1975), 339-353.

Intriligator, Michael D., "From Conflict to Cooperation in the Study of International Security," in Michael D. Intriligator and Urs Luterbacher, Eds, Cooperative Models in International Relations Research, Boston: Kluwer Academic Publishers, 1994.

Intriligator, Michael D., and Dagobert L. Brito, "A Possible Future for the Arms Race," in Nils Petter Gleditsch and Olov Njolstad, Eds, Arms Races: Technological and Political Dynamics (London: Sage Publications, 1990).

Intriligator, Michael D., and Dagobert L. Brito, "Can Arms Races Lead to the Outbreak of War?" Journal of Conflict Resolution, 28 (1) (March 1984), 63-84.

Intriligator, Michael D., and Dagobert L. Brito, "Nuclear Proliferation and the Probability of Nuclear War," Public Choice, 37: 247-260, 1981.

Intriligator, Michael D., and Dagobert L. Brito, "Accidental Nuclear War: A Significant Issue for Arms Control," in Derek Paul, Michael D. Intriligator, and Paul Smoker, Eds, Accidental Nuclear War (Toronto: Science for Peace, 1990).

Intriligator, Michael D., and Dagobert L. Brito, "Minimizing the Risks for Accidental Nuclear War: An Agenda for Action," in Häkan Wiberg, Ib Damgaard Peterson, and Paul Smoker, Eds. Inadvertent Nuclear War: The Implications of the Changing Global Order (Oxford: Pergamon Press, 1992).

Isard, Walter and Charles H. Anderton, "Arms Race Models: A Survey and Synthesis," Conflict Management and Peace Science, 8 (1985), 27-98.

MccGwire, Michael, "Shifting the Paradigm (Western Ideology of the Cold War)," International Affairs 78.1 (2002).

Midlarsky, Manus I., Ed, Handbook of War Studies, Boston: Unwin Hyman, 1989.

Midlarsky, Manus I., Ed, Handbook of War Studies II, Ann Arbor: University of Michigan Press, 2000.

"Nuclear Weapons in the Former Soviet Union," entire issue of Arms Control Today, 22, no. 1 (January-February 1992).

O'Hanlon, Michael E., "The New National Security Strategy and Preemption," Brookings Institution (2002).

Reiss, Mitchell, Bridled Ambition: Why Countries Constrain their Nuclear Capabilities, Washington, D.C., Woodrow Wilson Center Press; Baltimore, Md.: Distributed by the Johns Hopkins University Press, 1995.

Reiss, Mitchell, Without the Bomb: the Politics of Nuclear Nonproliferation, New York: Columbia University Press, 1988.

Reiss, Mitchell and Robert Litwak, Eds, Nuclear Proliferation after the Cold War, Washington, D.C. Woodrow Wilson Center Press: Distributed by Johns Hopkins University Press, 1994.

Sagan, Scott Douglas and Kenneth N. Waltz, The Spread of Nuclear weapons: a Debate Renewed, 2nd ed., New York: W.W. Norton, 2003.

Sandler, Todd and Keith Hartley, The Economics of Defense, Cambridge: Cambridge University Press, 1995.

Schelling, Thomas C, Arms and Influence, New Haven, Yale University Press, 1966.

Schelling, Thomas C, The Strategy of Conflict, Cambridge: Harvard University Press, 1960.

Schelling, Thomas C. and Morton H. Halperin, with the assistance of Donald G. Brennan, Strategy and Arms Control, New York, Twentieth Century Fund, 1961.

Schneider, Gerald, Katherine Barbieri, and Nils Petter Gleditsch, Eds, Globalization and Armed Conflict, Lanham, Md.: Rowman & Littlefield, 2003.

Siverson, Randy and M. Tennefoss, "Power, Alliances, and International Conflict, 1815-1965" American Political Science Review, 77, 1983, 1057-1069.

Sokolski, Henry D., Best of Intentions: America's Campaign against Strategic Weapons Proliferation, Westport, Conn.: Praeger, 2001.

U.S. Department of Defense, Nuclear Posture Review, The Pentagon, January 2002.

U.S. Office of the National Security Advisor, The National Security Policy of the United States of America, The White House, September, 2002.

Waltz, Kenneth N., The Spread of Nuclear Weapons: More May be Better, London: International Institute for Strategic Studies, Adelphi Papers, No. 171, 1981.

Wedar, Carin Atterling, Michael D. Intriligator, and Peeter Vares, Eds, Implications of the Dissolution of the Soviet Union for Accidental/Inadvertent Use of Weapons of Mass Destruction, Tallinn: Estonian Academy of Sciences, 1992.

Chapter 2
THE CONCEPTS OF ECONOMIC WAR
AND ECONOMIC CONFLICTS
IN A GLOBAL MARKET ECONOMY

Fanny Coulomb, Liliane Bensahel, Jacques Fontanel

The concept of economic war raises two main questions, that of the function devolved to the economy in the political choices and that of the opportunity of economic interventionism. Mercantilists have always asserted the primacy of politics (the power of the Prince) on economics, contrary to the liberal thought[1]. The evocation in some political discourses of the necessity of a "Europe power" in front of United States and emerging countries may ensue from this perspective. On the other hand, the pure liberalism cannot admit the existence of an economic permanent war, as it would mean admitting both the violent nature of the market and the necessity of a State offensive action.

The current international economic relations seem nevertheless more than ever conflicting. The economic weapon (boycott, embargos, etc.), widely employed during the Cold war, is still used today, but with other forms and other objectives. Besides, numerous resources previously devolved to the military field, for example in espionage, has been since 1991 allocated to geoeconomic objectives, notably in the United States. Several works published at the end of 1980s have moreover announced the battle to come between the industrial major powers (and mainly between the poles of the Triad, United States, Europe, Japan), notably that of Thurow[2] in United States or Harbulot[3] in France. The current popularity of the concept of economic war stems maybe partially from the search for new antagonisms since the fall of USSR. So, the famous anonymous report on the "undesirable" peace, first published in United States in 1967[4], showed that the existence of a foreign enemy and the permanence of a state of war or of war preparation were necessary for the cohesion of the American society.

The economic globalization process therefore seems to aggravate economic tensions among nations. The dominion of industrial nations on the

---
[1] Coulomb F. (2004), *Economic theories of peace and war*, Routledge, London and New York, pp. 13-24.
[2] Thurow L. (1992), *Head to head: The coming economic battle among Japan, Europe, and America*,Wm. Morrow & Co., New York.
[3] Harbulot C. (1992), *La machine de guerre économique: Etats-Unis, Japon, Europe*, Economica, Paris.
[4] Lewin L.C. (1996 [1967]), *Report from Iron Mountain On the Possibility and Desirability of Peace*, Free Press, New York. Cf. Fontanel J., Coulomb F. (2005), *Galbraith, economist of the peace*, article to be published.

world economy (70 % of foreign trade flows and 80 % of the foreign direct investment flows on average since the beginning of 1990s) seems today jeopardized by some particularly offensive emerging countries, such as China, India, South Korea, Mexico or Brazil. Now any modification of the balance of power represents a factor of potential conflict. Today, the protectionism remains high at the world level: if the customs duties on the goods are on average inferior to 5 %, they remain significant on some products, even if it is especially the non-tariff protectionism which blocks the entry on the markets of industrial nations today. The failure of the World Trade Organisation at Cancun on the agricultural issue is one of the numerous conflicts on State subsidies and aids. Besides, the "trade wars" between major powers have not decrease since the beginning of 1990s, on the contrary, as shown by the high number of cases submitted to the Dispute Settlement Body (within the World Trade Organization), since its creation in 1995.

Other elements are revealing of the multiplicity of the economic conflicts. The disclosure of the existence of a system of world communications interception, organized by the United States and some allies (the Echelon system) and of its use for the benefit of big national firms during the 1990s, has much contributed to strengthen the thesis of a not declared, secret but true economic war. Other operations may also be evoked, as a use of systematically undervalued national currencies by some countries to favor their exports, and other measures of "unfair competition". The wave of international mergers and acquisitions in the 1990s within the Triad, the threats of relocation, the use of information (and disinformation) campaigns to achieve economic objectives, as in the case of the GMO (genetically modified organisms), are so many facts which may be analyzed in terms of "trade war". However, the use of this concept to characterize competitive confrontation on markets, even supported by the public power, is not necessarily justified on the theoretical plan.

The concept of economic war, widely evoked since the end of 1980s, has indeed always remained vague, both on its contents and on its analytical foundations. In a previous meaning, its field of application was limited to the use of the economic weapon and to the international economic sanctions. In a wider sense, it is often used to describe the interstate confrontation in international economic relations.

This concept however raises several essential issues: by giving up comprehending international economic relations in terms of power, do not some countries risk to be quickly overtaken on the commercial and technological plan, for the benefit of more offensive countries? Do the chances of a country in the "economic war" come from its historic inheritance and from its culture, or from the State action, or other factors? But at first, is there an economic war?

Having discussed the opportunity of the use of the concept of economic war, we shall try to put in evidence the various current possibilities of using economy for power objectives.

I. From the Economic Weapon to Trade Conflicts: the Economic War, a Misused Concept

The concept of economic war, which was originally precise, has been progressively broadened and transformed into a polysemic expression. For the strategists, it covers a very precise sense: it is about the use of economic means for military, political or strategic objectives, in a situation of war or of political tensions. On the other hand, the utilization of this notion to characterize the economic confrontation on markets may be questioned. The issue is indeed to know what allows then to distinguish a so-called economic war from "normal" competition in a market economy.

I.1. *The Economic Weapon in the Service of the Foreign Policy*

The first meaning of the "economic war" is that of the use of economic weapons during a military conflict. Some past examples of blockade have revealed the importance of this weapon during a war. The Napoleon's continental blockade against England aimed at the ruin and bankruptcy of the British economy. Actually, it has generated grave economic problems both in England and in the other European countries. But it has also led France to a policy of ceaseless conquests, to achieve the solidity of the blockade in all continental Europe, until the military rout. Its political and economic cost was thus very high for France. Also, during the First World War, the Allies have undertook to block the maritime trade of the central powers, in particular Germany, to break their supply in raw materials and in energy necessary for the maintenance of their force. This strategy proved to be both worthwhile and very expensive, because it has provoked an excessive submarine war from Germany, which could have been disastrous for the Allies.

Beyond the military field, the concept of economic war can be also applied to the interstate strategies of coercion by economic means in peacetime. So, the international economic sanctions represent measures of economic war, because it is a question of imposing to the opponent some damages until it is urged to modify its policy, or so that opponent groups are encouraged to take the power. The country initiating these retaliatory measures is ready to accept a decrease of their own economic prosperity, what is a necessary condition for the use of the "war" term. In this context, the "game" is, at least in the short run, doubly negative, a priori more negative for the target than for the aggressor, even if it is difficult to foresee the final result.

The principle of international economic sanctions as a substitute for armed conflicts has aroused many hopes at the beginning of the XXth century. The League of Nations, created in 1920, so aspired to allow a pacific regulation of conflicts thanks to these measures. But this institution has discredited itself in the 1930s, because of its lacks of reaction during the Japanese invasion of Manchuria in 1931 and that of Ethiopia by Mussolinian Italy in 1935. It will not recover from these grave failures. The principle of the international economic sanctions had nevertheless many supporters, among which John Maynard Keynes, who in 1937 declared himself convinced of the efficiency of such measures[5].

The use of international economic sanctions has been frequent after World War II. But after more than half a century of use, the efficiency of the economic weapon may be questioned. Often, they have not been sufficient to meet their political, strategic and\or economic purposes assigned by the sender country. Besides they often turned out expensive for the latter. So, the COCOM, set up by the United States and their allies in 1949 and lifted in 1994, which controlled the export of strategic products (containing ultra-modern technologies, not exclusively military) towards USSR, showed itself expensive for American and European companies, and of benefit to countries which did not respect these rules. Also, the American embargo against Cuba ended in a nationalization of the American interests on the island and in a development of politico-economic relations between Cuba and Soviet Union. In 1991, the economic sanctions taken against Iraq did not prevent the first Gulf war. Other international initiatives have showed to be only partial success, as the actions against South Africa or North Rhodesia, even if it had taken the international community at least two decades to reach an agreement on penalties against the Apartheid countries. And the American policy of broad economic sanctions against Iran, permanent since the 1979 revolution, has not reached its objectives. Now the United States supports the European initiative toward Iran of economic incentives in exchange for curbing its nuclear program.

The regimes subjected to economic sanctions have often managed to find other sources of supply with third countries, through trade diversion. A

---

[5] Coulomb F. (2004), *op.cit.*, p. 160.

study of R. Caruso[6] using a gravity equation to estimate the bilateral trade between U.S. and 49 target countries shows a larger negative impact of extensive and comprehensive sanctions than limited and moderate ones. These ones induce a slight positive effect on other G-7 countries aggregate bilateral trade, because of a 'sanction-busting'. The unilateral extensive sanctions induce a negative 'network effect', as other countries will also disrupt their trade with the target country.

But the experience has shown that the target country may also reorganize its own productive structures. So, South Africa, confronted from 1970 with the sanctions of OPEC countries has developed a prosperous petrochemical industry from coal which guaranteed its energy self-sufficiency. Also, in 1976, the embargo of the United Nations on weapons has led to the implementation of a South African arms industry which quickly became important at the world level. According to F. de Klerk, the economic sanctions against South Africa would nevertheless have cost 1,5 of GDP a year to the country during the 1970s and 1980s[7]. But even in cases international economic sanctions have succeeded to durably weaken the target economy, their political efficiency was questionable. As it had already been the case with the Castro regime, Saddam Hussein's power after 1991 was strengthened by the measures considered as inequitable by a population united, voluntarily or not, around its leader.

The use of the economic weapon does not limit itself to the implementation of blockade or embargo. It may also be restrictions of imports, freezing of assets or suspension of aids. Moreover, the economic assistance can also part of a strategy of economic war. So, the supply of aid, the guarantees of investment or the preferential trade agreements can be used for political, strategic or economic purposes, as shown by D. Baldwin, who then speaks about "positive sanctions"[8]. Washington economic aid is clearly based on the American economic and strategic interests. Today, its food aid is mainly made of GMO, the production and outlets of which the national producers hope to develop.

I.2. The Use of the Concept of Economic War in Peacetime

The success of a "widened" notion of economic war in industrial nations during these last years is partially explained by the relative ideological emptiness left by the disappearance of the Soviet enemy. At the beginning of

---

[6] Caruso R. (2003), "The impact of international economic sanctions on trade: an empirical analysis", *Peace Economics, Peace Science and Public Policy*, 9 (2), 1-34.
[7] De Klerk F. (2004), in *Géoéconomie*, n° spécial « Sanctions économiques. Quelle efficacité politique ? Quelles conséquences humaines », n°30, été, p 46/47.
[8] Baldwin D. A. (1985), *Economic Statecraft*, Princeton, Princeton University Press.

the 1990s, in the euphoria resulting from the worldwide spreading of the market economy model and of the idea of « the end of the history », many analysts have put forward the hypothesis of a definitive pacification of international economic relations, at least between major powers. This idea was not new. Since the XIXth century, numerous liberal economists have spread the thesis of cosmopolitanism, inherited from the Physiocrats, by evoking the pacification of international economic relations and the decrease of military conflicts thanks to increasing trade interdependences[9]. The theory of A. Smith, systematized by J.B. Say, explained at the end of the XVIIIth century the loss resulting from mercantilism and colonialism, and the superiority of a model of development based on increasing trade relations with prosperous nearby countries. In this context, the notion of economic war is not pertinent, as the interest of each country is to reach always larger foreign markets, and thus to let nearby economies thrive within the framework of a general decrease of trade restrictions. The theory of Ricardo's comparative advantages indeed explains how the international trade can create supplementary wealth for all partners, with regard to a situation of autarky. The analysis does not deal with issues of power, though Ricardo states that the international trade development, which is a priori favourable to all countries, can nevertheless be more advantageous for some than for the others. In a recent article, P.A. Samuelson[10] has shown that the gains coming from free trade globalization are not always shared by all exchange partners. A technological change leading to productivity gains in one country may benefit this country alone, while "permanently hurting the other country by reducing the gains from trade that are possible between the two countries". This negative effect is not a 'short-run adjustment cost' but rather a 'long-run Schumpeterian cost'. However, Samuelson does not advocate protectionism, as "Tariffs are the breeder of economic arteriosclerosis."[11]

The liberal optimism inherited from the XIXth century has given birth to a current of pacifist liberal economists, particularly in France, notably with Bastiat or Chevalier, who anticipated at the beginning of the XXth century the disappearance of international conflicts, due to a military and tariff disarmament[12]. However the globalization process of that time, which had aroused so many hopes of world peace, has been interrupted by World War

---

[9] Coulomb F. (2004), *Economic theories of peace and war*, Routledge, London and New York, Part 1 Chapter 2.
[10] Samuelson P.A. (2004), "Where Ricardo and Mill Rebut and Confirm Arguments of Mainstream Economists Supporting Globalization", *Journal of Economic Perspectives*, 18 (3),135-146.
[11] op.cit., p. 143.
[12] Coulomb F. , Fontanel J. (2003), "War, peace and economics", in Galbraith J.K. (ed.), *Economics of peace and security*, EOLSS (Encyclopedia of Life Support System), www.eolss.net.

I, which had been foreseen by F. Engels. Contrary to the liberalism, the Marxist theory had developed, sometimes implicitly, the idea of an economic war between major powers. Karl Marx himself had explained that the international trade was a transposition of the class struggle on the international scene[13]. The theorists of imperialism of the end of the XIXe-begining of the XXth century have underlined the link between economic and military conflicts, in a time when the struggle against the decline of the profit rate seemed to develop on an international scale. It is the Russian economist N. Bukharin who evoked this subject the most explicitly (he uses moreover the expression of « economic war ») in his work of 1915, *"Imperialism and world economy"*[14]. He describes a new stage of capitalism development, that of the " State capitalism », characterized by an increasing integration of economies on international markets, with the development of financial capital and the internationalization of production. The State involvement in the defence of national interests on the foreign scene explains the increase in the number of international conflicts, with at first "economic wars", that may degenerate into military conflicts. Bukharin so admitted that the State played a determining role on international economic structures, therefore challenging the pure economic determinism. But the changes of the international economy after 1945 have not confirmed the forecasts of the theorists of imperialism, who (in particular Lenin) announced the disappearance of capitalism following the exacerbation of economic and political tensions between imperialist major powers. The existence of international institutions of regulation or the several agreements between large dominant firms are some of the characteristics tending to weaken the interpretation of current international economic relations in terms of economic war.

However, the seeming triumph of the liberal model at the beginning of the 1990s did not annihilate for all that the alternative theories[15]. First, the liberal position that trade interdependence reduces conflict's likelihood has not been satisfyingly confirmed by statistical studies: in a recent article, Keshk, Pollins and Reuveny[16] show that the use of an adequate simultaneous equation model of trade does not validate the liberal claim that trade reduces conflict. Moreover, some "realist" economists have underlined the maintaining of interventionism and of practices opposite to liberalism, including interfirms relations. The widened concept of economic war, which spread es-

---

[13] Coulomb F. (2004),*op.cit.*, p. 121.
[14] Boukharine N. (1969 [1915]), *L'économie mondiale et l'impérialisme*, Editions Anthropos, Paris.
[15] Coulomb F. (2003), « Pour une nouvelle conceptualisation de la guerre économique », in Daguzan J.F. and Lorot P. (eds), *Guerre et économie*, Ellipses, Paris, 73-87.
[16] Keshk O., Pollins B.M., Reuveny R. (2004), "Trade still follows the flag: the primacy of politics in a simultaneous model of interdependence and armed conflict", *The Journal of Politics*, 66 (4), 1155-1179.

pecially from the second half of the 1980s, has then been used to give sense to apparently neutral international economic relations. Some economists have then accredited the idea according to which economic conflicts should replace military ones. Many works on the economic war have indeed been published at the beginning of the 1990s, from Gilpin[17] to Thurow[18] or Luttwak[19]. The concept of geoeconomics, used by le latter, now designates the new instruments and the objectives of a State willing to increase the national economic power on the international scene. At the end of 1980, Luttwak then proposed a reaction of the American government to stop the economic decline, through an unprecedented trade and technological offensive.

The idea of an active support of governments for the national economic development has repeatedly been corroborated. Several examples may be mentioned, as the measures of the Japanese government to maintain the Yen systematically underestimated during the 1970s, the implication in the Airbus-Boeing duel of their respective States (through direct loans or indirect aid), the use of the " big ears " of the NSA for economic purposes, the aggressive takeover bids of the 1980s or the increasing use of disinformation campaigns to compromise a rival firms. For some analysts, these cases confirm the reality of an economic war between the big industrial nations, with the combined and complex action of governments and companies. K. Zeng[20] has explained in a recent study that the trade wars are more likely among democratic developed countries, as these ones have similar patterns of comparative advantage, what exacerbate the competition. On the contrary, trade retaliation against developing countries face resistance from U.S. sectors that benefit from trade with them, because of complementary trade structures between developed countries and developing ones.

The link between the industrial potential of a country and its capacity to influence the standards of the international system and to widen its sphere of influence, notably through policies of commercial and technical aid, may also be underlined[21]. Moreover, some political decisions can be considered

---

[17] Gilpin R. (1987), *The political economy of international relations*, Princeton University Press, Princeton.
[18] Thurow L. (1992), *Head to head: The coming economic battle among Japan, Europe, and America*,Wm. Morrow & Co., New York.
[19] Luttwak E.N. (1993), *The endangered American dream*, Simon & Schuster, New York.
[20] Zeng K. (2004), *Trade threats, trade wars: bargaining, retaliation, and American coercive diplomacy*, Ann Arbor, University of Michigan Press.
[21] Borrus M., Zysman J. (1992), "Industrial competitiveness and American national security", in W. Sandholtz et al. (1992), *The highest stakes - The economic foundations of the next security system*, Oxford University Press, New York, Oxford, pp 7-52.

as operations of economic war. So, the acceleration of the arms race with USSR by Ronald Reagan at the beginning of the 1980s, with the Strategic Defence Initiative project, has drived USSR to increase its military, what finished exhausting its economy, so preparing the conditions of its collapse[22]. Besides, the recent terrorist attacks have revealed the vulnerability of industrialized economies, notably because of the economic and financial concentration in some zones or of the necessity of preserving the confidence in the stability of the world financial system.

For all that, the theoretical foundations of the broad conception of "economic war" remain vague. They have sometimes been linked with "neo-mercantilism" and with the "neorealist" current in international relations. This neo-mercantilist logic leads to widen the analysis of the national security to the economic sphere. However, the notion of economic war becomes less pertinent while broadening.

I.3. A Confusion Between Economic War and Competition

The current economic discourse distinguishes between trade disputes and trade wars. A trade dispute is a disagreement between two or more countries about the legitimacy of some national measures supporting trade. It may be settled by the WTO dispute settlement mechanism. Trade war describes a situation where two or several State use strategies of tariffs and non-tariff barriers against each other, in a process of trade retaliation. The concept of economic war is less frequent, but has a broader sense, as it includes not only the use of trade policy, but also the one of industrial policy, of diplomatic influence or of economic intelligence through public means. The analysis of international relations in terms of economic war may seem appealing, in the context of an aggravated economic competition, sometimes with the support of the States. However several major arguments lead to criticize the use of this concept.

- At first, an economic war supposes a "zero or negative sum game", with for the aggressor the acceptance of losses to weaken or annihilate the opponent. Now, the contemporary economic reality is quite different. The economic collapse of a region may create problems in the whole world economy, as shown during some financial crises. None of their competitor countries is pleased with the excessive debts of the United States, which represents a threat for all economies. Also, a stagnation of the American economy is not wished by

---

[22] Fontanel, J. (2004), *Guerres et conflits économiques*, Fragments de Cours, UPMF, Grenoble pp.29-31.

the European countries, as it would limit important their own development.
- Then, the current evolution of international economic relations does not confirm the thesis of an increasing economic competition tbetween major powers, leading to numerous tensions and conflicts. On the contrary, the development of international mergers & acquisitions during the 1990s has strengthened the movement of industrial concentration at the world level[23]. Many strong value-added industries now have a structure of international oligopoly, like the car industry, telecommunications or the large-scale distribution. This trend does not necessarily lead to an increased competition between "giant firms"; on the contrary, these may conclude agreements, therefore distorting competition. States are then obliged to lead a competition policy to dismantle non-competitive agreements, cartels and illicit collusions of companies, which may go against the consumer's interest.
- Today, 40 % of the international trade is an intrafirm trade, "captive", the price and modalities of which are decided by the parent company, out of the market competition[24]. The scenario of an always more exacerbated competition between rival firms should then be reconsidered, even if the use of a military vocabulary to characterize firms strategies is widely spread today.
- Concerning the States, it is difficult to develop a general discourse of their involvement in an " economic war ", situations being much varied. If the United States seem offensive on the economic scene since the 1990s, Japan has on the contrary given up many of the interventionist characteristics linked to its successful past model export development. As for the European Union, it seems more worried of deepening the economic liberalization than to promote a policy of power[25]. The criticism of the European policy from specialists of " economic intelligence " and\or partisans of Europe's power have multiplied in scientific reviews and various reports; all regret the lack of weakness of European responses to the American

---

[23] OCDE (2001), *Le nouveau visage de la mondialisation industrielle*, Paris.
[24] Guannel B., Mabile S., Plateau C. (2002), « Les échanges internationaux au sein des groupes », *Le 4 pages du SESSI*, n° 167, novembre.
[25] Cf. Cohen E. (2004), « Etats-Unis / Europe. Entre partenariat et compétition économique », *Questions Internationales* n°9, La Documentation Française.

trade and technological offensive[26]. It seems difficult today to defend the idea that the European Union is really involved in an offensive strategy of economic war. The weakness of some national systems of economic intelligence in Europe (in particular in France), the lack of "think tanks" and well as of a real European strategic thought and of political unity, do not allow to speak about economic war. Europe seems actually little concerned (or worse, disarmed) by the deliberated policy of power based on cultural, religious and economic values, led by the United States.

Today, the broadened conception of economic war therefore seems not operational. It would be preferable to refer to "States economic conflicts in a globalized market economy".

II. The Economy in the Service of States Power

The "extended" use of the concept of economic war, though unfair, allows at least to underline the power struggles in the world economy and the involvement of States for the benefit of the national power, in a " néomercantilist " perspective. But it is not sure that all the major powers are involved in an open " economic war " with their main competitors. To make the war, it is necessary to be two. The current international relations are characterized by the American hegemonic will; to limit this one, the other potential powers use the state diplomacy, within the framework of a peaceful coexistence.

II.1. *Economic Dependence and Political Vulnerability*

J. Schumpeter[27] considered that economic dependence was the only possible case allowing the use of the expression of economic war. According to him, the economic war corresponded to a specific international situation, characterized by the limitation of supply sources resulting from the monopoly on a particular product by a single country. Judging this case very improbable, he had then rejected the concept of economic war to characterize the interstate competition on the world market.

Beyond the simple quarrel of vocabulary, it may be noticed that the study of the questions of economic dependence and vulnerability have only rarely been dealt by economists. These problems are nevertheless central for

---

[26] See for example Baumard P. (2004), « Les stratégies de puissance technologique des nations: de la maîtrise des actifs critiques à la stratégie de dominance », in Ecole de Guerre Economique, *La France a-t-elle une stratégie de puissance économique?*, Editions Lavauzelle, Paris.
[27] Schumpeter J.A. (1950 [1942]), *Capitalism, socialism and democracy*, New York, Harper.

the international balance of power. A.O. Hirschman published in 1945 a pioneer analysis in this field, entitled *"National power and the structure of foreign trade"*[28] which regrettably aroused only few subsequent developments. Considering that the various countries lead a "power-minded policy" and that the laissez-faire policy was an exception, he tried to analyze the vulnerability of national economies to the use of the economic weapon (like quotae, trade and capital investments controls and the other instruments of economic war) by one or several countries, as well as the possibilities of using foreign trade as an instrument of political pressure. Measuring (by an index of trade concentration) the dependence of a country towards foreign countries, and therefore, its vulnerability, he showed that States exert their influence to modify trade flows for their benefit. The analysis of Hirschman may be compared to the one of F. List, who was opposed to an international competition between economies at uneven levels of development.

A recent article[29] of Askari, Forrer and Hachem deals precisely with the vulnerability to economic sanctions, defined as susceptibility to economic loss resulting from an economic sanction. The case of U.S. sanctions is especially studied; the authors use simple equations to measure the potential vulnerability to sanctions, not only of merchandise trade but also of services trade, transfer payments (including workers' remittances and foreign aid), capital investments (foreign direct investment and portfolio investment) and other foreign assets. Unsurprisingly, the authors conclude that "the bigger a country's economy is, the more integrated it is in the global economy, and the more diverse it is, the less vulnerable it is to sanctions. However, the results for Syria go against this evident conclusion because Syria had very little economic activity with the U.S. that could be sanctioned."[30]

The real meaning of the economic war appears here: the economic power or vulnerability has a direct influence on the level of national security. But rather than of a war, one should speak about a situation of unegalitarian relative power.

Thus, the problem of economic dependence did not necessarily ease since 1945. To give only one example, 89% of the exports of Mexico are made towards the United States today. This may question the unbalanced economic relations between both countries. But economists do not agree on the issue of the economic impact of a high export concentration ratio. A

---

[28] Hirschman A.O. (1980 [1945]), *National power and the structure of foreign trade*, University of California Press, Berkeley.
[29] Askari H., Forrer J., Yang J. and Hachem T. (2005), "Measuring vulnerability to U.S. foreign economic sanctions", *Business Economics*, April, 41-55.
[30] Op.cit., p. 54.

study of the UNCTAD[31] shows an apparent relation between a high export concentration ratio and a weaker economic development in some less developed countries, compared with other developing countries. Besides, some economic studies on small countries have tended to show that the more open an economy, the higher its income volatiliby, like Rodrik[32] and Easterly and Kraay[33]. Such conclusions have been contested by a recent study of M. Jansen[34], which shows the impact of a high level of export concentration on the income volatility of less developed countries. The author concludes, though this hypothesis is not tested, that the lesser openness of LDC's markets may explain a higher vulnerability to income volatility than in small economies also characterized with a high rate of export concentration. Beyond this debate, the data shows a parallel structure of export concentration and income volatility of different groups of countries.

II.2. *The Interweaving of the Interests of the Military Sector and the Civil Sector in the Advanced Capitalist Societies*

The link between the civilian and military sectors is an essential aspect of the "economic war", in the field of social organization, of technological development and of the use of military means for economic purposes.

During the 1980s, the Japanese and German economies were generally considered as the most suitable to the international economic competition ones. However, the crisis undergone by these two countries during the 1990s has led to moderate this optimism. The reforms of their model seem to have confirmed the victory of the Anglo-saxon capitalism on the Rhenish one. And yet the idea of the superiority of the Rhenish model was not new, and it was essentially based on the specific link between the military sector and the civilian one within societies. In his publication of 1915, *Imperial Germany and the industrial revolution*[35], T. Veblen underlined the tendency of "modern" capitalist societies (Anglo-saxon capitalism) to become more and more peaceful, as " commercial interests " predominate against "dynastic interests". On the other hand, the dynastic societies (like Japan or Germany) remain marked by specific mental customs inherited from feudal era: military

---

[31] UNCTAD (2004), *Trade and development benchmarks: a work in progress*, Eleventh session, note by the UNCTAD Secretariat, 13-18 June, Sao Paulo, p. 6.
[32] Rodrik D. (1997), *Has Globalization Gone too Far?*, Washington DC: Institute for International Economics.
[33] Easterly W. , Kraay A. (2000), « Small States, Small Problems? Income, Growth and Volatility in Small States », *World Development* 28,11:2013-2027.
[34] Jansen M. [34] (2004), *Income volatility in small and developing economies: export concentration matters*, World Trade Organization, Geneva.
[35] Veblen T. (1964 [1915]), *Imperial Germany and the industrial revolution*, Augustus M. Kelley, New York.

conflicts and mercantilist policies are essential for the survival of these systems. However, the dynastic model of society should normally disappear and be replaced by that of modern one, but this theory is not determinist. In the early1980s, several analyses have taken up this distinction between two types of capitalism, and have underlined the superiority of the Rheinish capitalism in the field of economic war, compared with the Anglo-saxon one. These analyses generally developed the idea of a decline of the Anglo-saxon capitalist model (and thus of the American economy). Thus, J.K. Galbraith[36] links his concept of technostructure with the importance of the military sector in the American economy; L. Thurow[37] discusses the distinction between two types of capitalism, with regard to the balance of power; R. Väyrynen[38] analyzes the role of the military sector in the process of industrialization and draws it conclusions as for the respective performances of the studied savings. He shows that the countries which had at first a net perception of the stakes of economic war and which society remains marked by the military organization, have an advantage in the current international economic competition. However, the evolutions of the American economy during the 1990s tended to contradict this diagnosis.

And nevertheless, the specific link between the military sector and the civilian sectors may have based the renewed success of the American industry. The economic impact of military research& development is widely discussed today. In Europe, as in the United States, the armament firms now realize an important part of their turnover in the civilian sector, since the cuts of defence budgets. This facilitates transfers from military to civilian sectors, in technologies, products or human resources. The question of the impact of R&D on the rise of industrial productivity remains polemical today[39]. Indeed, some technologies at first focusing on the military sector, as computers or satellite communications, seem to have played an important role in the American growth during the 1990s and to have given the country the control of numerous ultramodern technologies[40]. Certainly, econometric analyses have been little numerous to show a link between the growth of the American industrial productivity and the development of these new technologies. It seems however that, if it is true that in the short-term, pat-

---

[36] Galbraith J.K. (1969 [1967]), *The new industrial state*, Penguin Books, Harmondsworth.
[37] Thurow L. (1992), op.cit.
[38] Vayrynen R. (1992), *Military industrialization and economic development - Theory and historical case studies*, Genève, UNEDIR, Aldershot, Dartmouth.
[39] Coulomb F., Fontanel J. (2005), « An economic interpretation of French military expenditures », article, to be published in *Defence and Peace Economics, fall 2005*.
[40] Alesina, A., Giavazzi, F. (2004), 'Inégalité de l'Europe en matière d'investissement de défense', *Project Syndicate*, http://www.project-syndicate.org/article_print_text?mid=842&lang=4.

ents ensuing from the military R&D are limited, most of the modern technologies have nonetheless been at first developed in the military sector. Besides, the increasing use of intelligences for economic objectives can have an impact on the level of military expenditures, notably in the United States where the structures of economic intelligence are particularly important.

Beyond the statistical debate, this issue represents an essential stake for the understanding of the national economic dynamics, in particular for industrial nations, which dedicate an important part of their public R&D to the military sector. France spent in 2003 about 2 billion euros on the military R&D against 3 billion euro for the United Kingdom. But globally in Europe the ratio military R&D expenditures / public R&D expenditures (24,2 % for France) is very lower than that of the United States, where it reaches 54,4 %[41]. As the military sector remains out of the world trade organisation negotiations, the use of military expenditures in purposes of " industrial policy" may be an explanatory factor of their level in the united states. In France also, the industrial policy seems always more concentrated on defence. so, a ministerial report of 2002[42] showed that one third of the companies financed through some defense programs were also financed by some large traditional technological programs. Furthermore, the military sector perceives a part of the civilian budget of R&D (1,9 billion euro in 2003) [43]. But today France remains below Anglo-saxon countries in military R&D, following the example of the other European countries.

Expenditures of Military Research, Except Nuclear, in Billion Euros.

	1999	2000	2001	2002	2003
France	2.15	2.03	2.11	1.85	1.99
United Kingdom	3.51	3.81	3.91	3.35	2.95
Germany	1.19	1.22	1.15	0.85	1.08

Source: French National Assembly, Loi de Finances 2004, tome IV.

A report of the French Defence Observatory in 2002 had used the concept of " technological disarmament " in Europe, beyond a simple delay with regard to the United States. If the European military expenditures represented then 40 % of those the United States, the ratio was only 25 % for the R&D expenditures and 12 % for the R&T ones. This report underlined the strong

---

[41] Perrier J.J. (2003), 'Que pèse le militaire dans la recherche française ?', *Revue du Vivant* n°1, www.vivantinfo.com/numero1/recherche_militaireimp.html. Chiffres de l'OCDE 2003, base MSTI.
[42] Ministère de la Jeunesse, de l'Education et de la Recherche, DEPRD, résultats 2000, estimations 2001 et objectifs socioéconomiques du BCRD 2002.
[43] Rapport au Sénat n°117 sur la loi de programmation militaire 2003-2008.

support of the American government in favour of the national firms on R&D, notably in the aerospace. In front of this policy, there is no European policy of power.

Another aspect of the relation between the civilian and military sectors is that of the use of military means for economic purposes. The policies of « economic intelligence », led by some firms or some states, seem central today to gain markets. It is in reaction to the offensive Japanese policy of economic information that the United States have worked out a doctrine of economic security. In November, 1993, the State secretary Warren Christopher so considered, in a paragraph titled "Economic Security", that *"security in the post-cold war era will depend as much on strong economies as on strong arsenals. This administration understands that America's strength at home and its strength abroad are interlocking and mutually reinforcing. That is why President Clinton and I have placed economic policy at the heart of our foreign policy."*[44]

One of the first consequences was the National Information Security Program, to prevent the risks linked with the circulation of strategic information for the American firms. But the concept of "economic security" must be also understood as an offensive instrument. So, some adjustments of the American legislation now allow the theft, the seizure and the transfer of confidential information by information agencies, opening the way to the use of a policy of interception, influence and manipulation. The role of the program "Echelon", revealed in Europe in 1997, is essential. The NSA (National Security Agency) used repeatedly this system for the benefit of American firms. European companies as Airbus or Thomson CSF have indeed been subject to economic espionage, according to the first European report on this subject[45]. The American economic intelligence system has besides been strengthened by the creation of the *Advocacy Center*, which allows the use by national companies of all public means (including information agencies), to help them with regard to foreign competition[46]. They are inserted into a vaster set of private information agencies, many were of which have been created by former CIA members. More widely, the studies on the American policy of influence underline the action of several actors with imbricated interests, as pension funds, non-governmental organisations, *think-tanks*,

---

[44] "The strategic priorities of American foreign policy" - Secretary of State, Warren Christopher speech – transcript; US Department of State dispatch </p/articles/mi_m1584>, nov 22, 1993.
[45] Commission temporaire sur le système d'interception ECHELON (2001), *Projet de rapport sur l'existence d'un système d'interception mondial des communications privées et économiques (système d'interception ECHELON)*, Rapporteur Gerhard Schmid, Parlement Européen, Bruxelles.
[46] Carayon B. (2003), *Compétitivité économique et cohésion sociale*, La Documentation Française, Paris, pp. 121-129.

higher education diplomas (type MBA) or the attraction of foreign students[47].

In contrast with the American model of "economic power", some European countries are far behind, and notably France. Certainly, a French system of communication interception, nicknamed "Frenchelon", managed by the DGSE, is used for industrial espionage. But apart from that, the French resources of economic intelligence seem very few. Two reports[48] on this issue, published in 1994 and 2004, stigmatized France's backwardness on economic intelligence, and more widely, on economic security's stakes. In France, the "ordonnance" of 1959 still limits the scope of this concept to economic or industrial espionage against enemy powers. Several cases have however alerted some leaders on the necessity of protecting some key firms, essential for the long-term growth and national security. The takeover by American capital of the French firm Gemplus, the inventor of the smart card, has made the French legislation evolve towards a better protection of to strengthen the protection of strategic firms against foreign control[49].

II.3. What Future for Strategic Trade Policies?

The idea of a States implication in the economic competition is quite widespread today. However, the evolution of economic structures can decrease the interest for this type of policy. So, Japan has suffered a grave economic crisis during 1990s, in spite of its advance in economic intelligence and in the role of the government in the promotion of the economic interests abroad. For some economists, these policies exercise only a limited effect, and the relative ineffectiveness or the illegality of numerous instruments of the "geoeconomics" may justify their critic or their abandonment. So, if the new theory of the international trade showed the interest of the public policy in case of imperfect markets, barriers to entry or positive externalities, in the practice, the difficulty targeting the good industries and the possible costs linked to the " strategic commercial policy " come to moderate the optimism for this type of solution.

P. Krugman[50] has indeed criticized the "strategic commercial policy" presented by J.A. Brender and B. Spencer: certainly, the public support to specific industries (through subsidies or tax allowances) is theoretically

---

[47] Pichot-Duclos J. Général (2004), *Les guerres secrètes de la mondialisation*, Editions Lavauzelle, Paris.
[48] Martre H. (1993), *Intelligence économique et stratégie des entreprises*, Commissariat Général du Plan, Paris. Carayon B. (2003), *Compétitivité économique et cohésion sociale*, La Documentation Française, Paris.
[49] Carayon B. (2003), op.cit., p. 42.
[50] Krugman P.R. (Ed.) (1986). *Strategic" Trade Policy and the New International Economics*, MIT Press, Cambridge.

beneficial, as it allows the state-owned firms to enter "imperfect" markets with strong entry barriers (as it was the case for Airbus in the 1980s); moreover, this policy also favors the development of industries liable to generate « positive externalities », as high technology ones. However, according to Krugman, it is difficult to target the adequate industries for public support. Besides, the risk of reprisals or of similar measures on behalf of a rival country limits the advantage of these measures (because of the "prisoner dilemma"). So, in practice, the cost of industrial or of strategic commercial policies may be superior to its advantages. A recent study of J. DeCourcy[51] based on a strategic trade policy model between two countries shows that it is jointly optimal for both governments to allow their firms to participate in the same cooperative R&D, and that allowing cooperation in R&D can be superior to the use of R&D subsidies.

Besides, the existence of lobbies, which incite the government to set up protective measures of some industries, leads to question the efficiency of protectionist policies. They may be contrary to the general interest; as an example, the American system of *Foreign Sales Corporations (FSC)*, which supports the exports of some American multinationals thanks to a system of tax allowances, gives rise to the dissatisfaction of numerous manufacturers in the United States which do not benefit from this system. Indeed, retaliatory measures of the European Union (which were authorized by the WTO in 2004) has provoked a loss of their export markets. The case of the FSC is therefore a subject of discord in the United States.

According to R.B. Freeman[52], the importance of trade in economic growth is exaggerated by political leaders, either by the ones who advocate for trade treaties and open markets and by their opponents, to reinforce their arguments. Trade wars are therefore put forward in the political debate, "to attract the attention of the public".

So, the interventionism may provoke "perverse effects", which may cast doubt on the efficiency of the offensive economic strategies led by some States. Moreover, all countries do not necessarily choose a policy of power. As stated below, the European policy does not match the criteria of an interventionist "geoeconomic policy". Besides, the regionalization of the world economy does not inevitably reinforce the economic war. The questioning about the nature of economic agreements, the number of which have doubled during the 1990s, according to the figures of the WTO, still

---

[51] DeCourcy J. (2005), "Cooperative R&D and strategic trade policy", *Canadian Journal of Economics*, 38 (2). 546-573.
[52] Freeman R.B. (2004), "Trade wars: the exaggerated impact of trade in economic debate", *The World Economy*, 27 (1), 1-23.

remains today. Do they show a reorganization of the world economy between protectionist blocks or on the contrary an accelerated liberalization within regional borders, towards a greater globalization? These agreements seem to have difficulty to go beyond the stage of the free trade area (according to the WTO, free trade areas represent more than 70 % of the existing trade agreements)[53] and to adopt joint institutions. The European Union, which is the most advanced regional agreement in the world, has undertaken accelerated reforms of liberalization and privatization, but there have been no changes concerning the "policy of power", in particular the industrial policy, demanded by economists in favour of interventionism. 40% of the current regional trade agreements reported to the WTO are interregional agreements[54], that is between country belonging to different regional zones, as the APEC (Asian-Pacific Economic Cooperation), which gather about twenty countries. The scenario of a regionalization-liberalization thus seems more credible today than that of a reorganization of the world economy in big conflicting regional blocks, leading a relentless economic war.

Conclusion

The extensive use of the concept of economic war is not necessarily judicious. Certainly, there are important conflicts between States and between firms, as well as public or private strategies (sometimes unfair) in favour of the economic power. But to speak about an economic war is excessive, while it is only an aggravated economic competition.

It is indeed advisable to distinguish the "economic war" from the "State conflicts in a global market economy". In the first case, the costs are beared by both opponents, who are ready to sacrifice a part of their prosperity to reach their objectives. In the second case, the game outcome may be positive ; the question is not to weaken the opponent, but rather to eventually improve the power, the independence and the prosperity of the Nation. In this game, the State gives new cards to the national competitors. It is not an economic war, but a rather a game with " loaded dices", what explains that international organizations are often in conflict with States and are sometimes asked to modify the rules of international trade by the major powers when they do not defend their interests.

---

[53] www.wto.org/english/tratop_e/region_e/sem_nov03_e/boonekamp_paper_e.doc.
[54] www.wto.org/french/tratop_f/region_f/region_f.htm.

PART II:
MILITARY SPENDING AND ARMS EXPORTS – THE MACROECONOMIC AND SECTORAL PICTURES

Chapter 3
UNITED STATES MILITARY EXPENDITURE

Jurgen Brauer

This paper reviews United States military expenditure for the past few decades. The major message is that use of federal budget-based military expenditure data should be avoided. The economically relevant data to use are those recorded in the U.S. National Income and Product Accounts (NIPA). For 2003, the difference between Department of Defense budget-based and NIPA U.S. military expenditure amounts to well over $100 billion dollar. Even the NIPA data are incomplete as they fail to allocate a proportion of interest-payments on the federal debt to the national defense account.

I. Measuring United States Military Expenditure

United States military expenditure is not large and rapidly growing; instead, it is *larger* and rapidly growing – larger that is than reported in the news media, and larger than the public appears to have in mind. The numbers the news media report come off the federal budget decision-making process, that is out of administration requests for, congressional debate on, appropriation of, and spending authorization for funds for the national defense function of the U.S. government. For government officials, either in the executive or legislative branch, it makes sense to look at budget requests and to debate, appropriate, and authorize funds for the national defense budget line item. But economists and the public-at-large have (or should have) a different objective. We need to look at overall military-related expenditure, regardless of whether this is budgeted in the national defense line item or budgeted elsewhere.

To provide the reader with an inkling of the order of magnitude of that difference, think, for 2003, of roughly $400 billion national defense budgeted outlays versus $500 billion national defense outlays as recorded in U.S. National Income and Product Accounts (NIPA, for short). That is, the United States spent about 25 percent more on national defense – when looked at through economists' eyes – than the numbers one hears bandied about in the news media. And even the NIPA numbers are incomplete, as the accounting framework does not allocate a proportion of interest payments on the accumulated federal debt back to the military sector of the economy. In 2003, for example, that would add at least another $35 billion of federal spending that should properly be counted as military-related expenditure so that, for 2003, we approach $520-530 billion in national defense outlays as opposed to the $400 billion or so in budgeted national defense outlays – a difference on the order of 33 percent.

In what follows, I provide some detail on where the media and the public ordinarily obtain the numbers and on where economists look for more appropriate numbers. I also take a look at a break-down of the numbers in terms of spending on personnel, procurement, operations, and other areas.

Prominent sources for countries' military expenditure include the North Atlantic Treaty Organization (NATO), the Stockholm International Peace Research Institute (SIPRI), and the United States Department of State's Bureau of Verification and Compliance (US BVC).[1] For NATO countries,

> *"... military expenditures are from NATO publications and are based on the NATO definition. In this definition, (a) civilian-type expenditures of the defense ministry are excluded and military-type expenditures of other ministries are included; (b) grant military assistance is included in the expenditures of the donor country; and (c) purchases of military equipment for credit are included at the time the debt is incurred, not at the time of payment."*[2]

NATO figures are available from various issues of *NATO Review*. The U.S. BVC uses NATO figures for its own publication, *World Military Expenditures and Arms Transfers*. Likewise, the Stockholm International Peace Research Institute (SIPRI) uses NATO figures to report U.S. military expenditure.[3] In a word, three of the world's best known comparative sources on countries' military expenditure use the same figures for United States military expenditure. This is good news. The bad news is that these figures do not match what the United States itself reports about its own military expenditure.

---

[1] Formerly known as the U.S. Arms Control and Disarmament Agency, ACDA.
[2] Cited from p. 194 of WMEAT (1999/2000).
[3] The NATO *Review*, the U.S. BVC, and the SIPRI data all are easily accessible online. SIPRI's military expenditure definition is: "Where possible, SIPRI military expenditure include all current and capital expenditure on: the armed forces, including peace keeping forces; defense ministries and other government agencies engaged in defense projects; paramilitary forces when judged to be trained, equipped and available for military operations; and military space activities. Such expenditures should include: all expenditures on current personnel; military and civil retirement pensions of military personnel; social services for personnel and their families; operations and maintenance; procurement; military research and development; military construction; military aid (in the military expenditures of the donor country). Excluded military related expenditures are: civil defense; current expenditure for previous military activities; veterans benefits; demobilization; conversion of arms production facilities; and destruction of weapons." This is taken from www.sipri.org [accessed 9 May 2004].

In the U.S. there are two primary sources on military expenditure data. One source is the United States Budget or, more precisely, the so-called *Historical Tables*, a document supplementary to the annual fiscal year budget request by the administration to Congress. This is issued annually to Congress by the Office of Management and Budget (OMB) from within the President's office. The *Historical Tables* capture for prior fiscal years not the budget requests, nor the appropriations, but the actual outlays. The other source is information contained in the aforementioned National Income and Product Accounts (NIPA), produced by the Bureau of Economic Analysis (BEA) in the Department of Commerce.

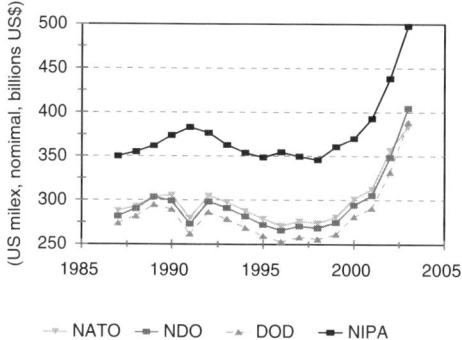

Figure 1: U.S. Military Expenditure, 1987-2003.

NATO: according to NATO/SIPRI/BVC definition; NDO: national defense outlays according to the Historical Tables; DoD: Department of Defense according to the Historical Tables; NIPA: the National Income and Product Account measures. All in nominal billions of U.S. dollars. NATO 2003 is an estimate.

OMB's *Historical Tables* distinguish between two budget line items. Line item 051 includes all Department of Defense (DoD) outlays. In contrast, line item 050 includes all "national defense outlays" (NDO).[4] Since the latter include military expenditure in agencies other than the DoD – for instance, military-nuclear activities budgeted within the Department of Energy – the numbers for line item 050 are larger than the DoD numbers in line item 051, but still are generally slightly below NATO figures (see figure 1).

The differences between the NATO and the NDO measure are insubstantial. For 1996, for instance, NATO reports U.S. military expenditure of

---

[4] The easiest way to access time series for these numbers is via the statistical appendix to the annually issued *Economic Report of the President* (available online).

$271 billion (nominal), whereas the *Historical Tables* report $266 billion for NDO (and $253 for DoD outlays). The truly amazing difference occurs with respect to the NIPA data. For 1996 this amounted to $355 billion (nominal), a difference of $84 billion over the NATO numbers.

I.1. The Historical Tables

Let us take a closer look at the budget-based data. Under the heading of "Outlays by Function and Subfunction," table 3.2 of the *Historical Tables* shows budget line "050 – National defense." Importantly, the *Historical Tables* provide detail on the subfunctions included within national defense outlays. For recent fiscal years they include (with numbers in billions of nominal dollars):

	2001	2002	2003
051 Department of Defense - Military			
Military personnel	73,977	86,799	106,744
Operation and maintenance	111,964	130,005	151,408
Procurement	54,986	62,515	67,926
Research, development, test, evaluation	40,455	44,389	53,098
Military construction	4,977	5,052	5,851
Family housing	3,516	3,736	3,784
Other	1,085	-545	-1,492
051 Subtotal, Department of Defense - Military	290,960	331,951	387,319
053 Atomic energy defense activities	12,931	14,795	16,029[5]
054 Defense-related activities	1,609	1,809	1,572
050 Total, National defense	305,500	348,555	404,920.

According to NATO, military aid to other countries should be included. Doing so yields

152 International security assistance	6,560	7,907	8,619
for a total of	312,060	356,462	413,539.

For 2001 and 2002, these numbers are almost identical to those reported by NATO.[6] The differences amount to about $6 billion. Since some of these outlays include legacy items – for instance occupational illness and radiation exposure compensation funds for employees at military-nuclear sites – it is unclear why the NATO definition would restrict military expenditure mainly

---

[5] Figures for atomic-energy defense activities include operations as well as environmental management (remediation, restoration) at military-nuclear sites.

[6] With a time-lag, they will eventually be reported by SIPRI and BVC as well. NATO numbers themselves lag behind the data revision in the U.S., hence the difference between the $414 billion reported for 2003 in the *Historical Tables* and the NATO estimate of $384 billion. In a word, the reporting sequence is from the budget data to NATO to SIPRI and BVC. Revisions in the budget data will eventually show up with a one or two year time lag in the other data sources.

to *current* outlays and not include all of the *legacy* cost of past military activities. Adding veterans benefits and services would result in

700 Total, Veterans benefits and services	45,039	50,984	57,018
for a total of	357,099	407,446	470,557.

Even with the addition of international security assistance and veterans' benefits and services, the accounting is incomplete. For example, for budget FY2004, an "Iraq relief and reconstruction fund" and "operating expenses of the coalition provisional authority" are placed, at $7.006 billion, in line item "151 – International development, humanitarian assistance." So is a program called "Andean counter-drug offensive" – at $966 million. A "special defense acquisition program" of $3 million is placed under "155 – International financial programs." The same line item contains $759 million for the U.S. Export-Import Bank, whose web site reveals substantial support for the Iraq war. There are other millions and billions tucked away in other budget function line items. For instance, "armed forces retirement homes" is budgeted under "600 – Income security" at $66 million for FY2004. "DoD Medicare eligible retiree health care fund," at $5.171 billion, and $571 million for "biodefense counterdefense acquisition," both for FY2004, are put in line item "550 – Health." Likewise, "Naval petroleum reserve operations" are budgeted, at $18 million, under "270 – Energy." And one would think that a portion of the $22.291 billion budgeted for FY2004 for "250 – General science, space, and technology" will result in military applications. Thus, the $470 billion computed above for FY2003 understate total United States military, defense, and security outlays by several billion dollars.

If one therefore takes a different tack and moves from the *functional* budget line items in the *Historical Tables* to the *agency* budget line items, one finds the following numbers (in billions; for FY2003 there are slight differences in the numbers for Defense, Military 051 but not for National Defense, 050):

	2001	2002	2003
Defense, Military	291,015	331,951	388,870
Veterans affairs	45,050	50,884	56,887
Other defense-civil programs	34,164	35,157	39,883
Total defense outlays by agency	370,229	417,992	485,640
versus functional line items 050, 152, 700	357,099	407,446	470,557.

The "other defense-civil programs" line probably includes nuclear weaponry, international security assistance, and other defense and security-related programs and agencies, so that the total of $486 billion for FY2003 comes close to the functional accounting ($470 billion) if the additional items hinted at were included. For practical purposes, then, using the *agency* outlays as given in the *Historical Tables* is a workable approximation to the United States' total federal military, defense, and security outlays, or military expenditure for short.[7] Indeed, subtracting out the Veterans Affairs line yields the numbers NATO reports to within a few million dollars.

As argued above, military expenditure should include all legacy costs. Thus, if NATO includes several billions of dollars in "environmental management" at military-nuclear sites – surely a legacy cost – why not include Veterans Affairs? On this argument one must also include a prorated portion of the national debt and, hence, a portion of the federal government's annual net interest payment on the debt. If, for simplicity, one calculates the proportion of "total defense outlays by agency" of all federal government outlays and allocates a corresponding portion of federal net interest payments back to the military sector, one gets the following (in billions of nominal dollars):

	2001	2002	2003
Defense, Military	291.0	332.0	388.9
National defense outlays by agency	370.2	418.0	485.6
Total federal government outlays	1,863.8	2,011.0	2,157.6
Total federal net interest outlays	206.2	171.0	153.1
Allocated interest to national defense	41.0	35.5	34.5
Total national defense outlays	411.2	453.5	520.1

For FY2003, the outlays by the defense department of $389 billion understate the thus calculated total national defense outlays of $520 billion by about thirty-three percent. Clearly, for FY2003 the largest components of the $131 billion difference stem from the inclusion of the Veteran's Affairs budget of $57 billion and the allocated portion of net interest payments, at $34.5 billion.

That legacy payments due to prior-year military effort should not be disregarded in accounting for the country's military expenditure is made clear by an alternative way of thinking about budgeting. Economically, fully funded current-year military activity should include provision for future

---

[7] One cannot simply add up the *agency* items – defense, veteran affairs, other defense-civil programs, homeland security, international assistance, and so on. The reason is that only the budgetary break-down by *function* will show what proportion for instance of the Department of Energy budget should be allocated to national defense outlays. Within-agency military-related items appear to have been captured in the "other" line.

costs the current activity entails. This might be called "full-cost budgeting." Future Veteran's Affairs and net interest expenses incurred on account of current military activity would thus become part of a fully costed, budgeted, and funded current activity.

II. Adjusted Total U.S. Military Expenditure

Military expenditure figures adjusted for "full-cost budgeting" can be computed back to 1962. Figure 2 shows the comparison between DoD outlays and the calculated total U.S. military expenditure in real dollars (base year 2000). I applied the chain-type price index for federal national defense outlays (*Economic Report of the President 2004*, table B-7, p. 295, where the deflator for the year 2003 is taken from the average for the first three reported quarters). It is important to use the military-specific deflator because inflation within the defense sector has been much higher than inflation in the non-defense sector. For instance, between 2000 and the third quarter of 2003, prices generally went up by 5.87 percent but for federal national defense items prices went up by 7.66 percent.

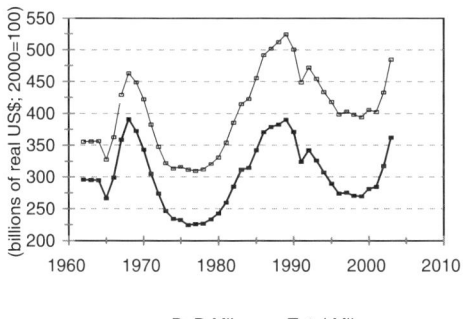

Figure 2: U.S. Department of Defense vs. Total Military Expenditure, Real Dollars (base year – 2000).

In figure 2 one sees the familiar post-Vietnam U.S. military expenditure reduction in the 1970s, the Carter/Reagan build-up of the late 1970s and the 1980s, the post-cold war reduction of the 1990s, and the post-9/11 build-up of the early 2000s. One also sees that the end of the post-cold war peace dividend already occurred in 1996 when DoD and total military expenditure leveled off at about $275 and $400 billion, respectively (in inflation-adjusted dollars). Nonetheless, since GDP grew throughout this period, military expenditure as a percentage of GDP continued to fall (see figure 4 later on).

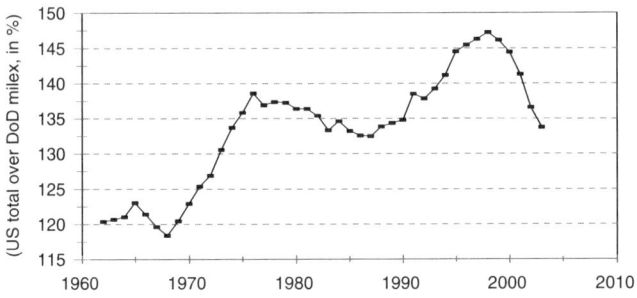

Figure 3: U.S. Total Military Expenditure vs. DoD Outlays.

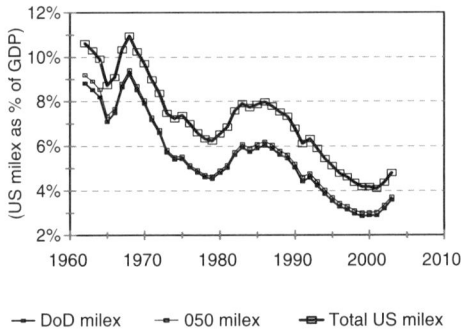

Figure 4: U.S. Total Military Expenditure as a Percentage of GDP.

DoD milex is budget line item 051; 050 milex is the larger "national defense outlays" or NDO line item; total U.S. milex is as computed in this chapter.

Figure 3 shows the understatement of DoD outlays to total U.S. military expenditure in percentage terms. The understatement of DoD outlays has grown worse over time, from between 20 to 25 percent in the 1960s to between 35 to 45 percent since the mid-1970s. In 1962, the gap between DoD and total military expenditure was on the order of $60 billion dollar in inflation-adjusted terms. By 2003 this gap has grown to just over $122 billion, also in inflation-adjusted terms.

The understatement of DoD versus total military expenditure results of course in a corresponding understatement of such spending with respect to U.S. GDP (figure 4). For FY2003, for example, the DoD outlays amount to 3.6 percent of GDP but total military expenditure amounts to 4.8 percent of GDP, 1/3 higher.

III. U.S. National Income and Products Accounts (NIPA)

There is no intent here to artificially inflate total U.S. military expenditure. In fact, another United States federal government agency reports national defense numbers almost as large as mine. The Bureau of Economic Analysis in the Department of Commerce produces the United States National Income and Product Accounts (NIPA). For calendar (not fiscal) year 2003, NIPA reports total national defense outlays of $497.7 billion, which breaks down into $437.2 billion for consumption outlays and the remainder for gross investment in structures and equipment ($60.5 billion). This does not include an allocated portion of federal net interest payments (BEA, 1988, p. 4). If these were allocated and included, NIPA's number for total U.S. military expenditure would be $497.7 plus $34.5 billion, i.e., $532.2 billion, about $12 billion larger than my estimate.

As regards official U.S. government data, the NIPA numbers are the most comprehensive and conceptually complete (except for the interest payment allocation). They are therefore the preferred data to use in economic analysis and should be the preferred data to use in the national and international debate.

The NIPA numbers on national defense outlays are extraordinarily detailed and, to my knowledge, have not yet been "harvested" by academic researchers. I provide a descriptive look here. All data can be accessed and downloaded in ready-made spreadsheets from the BEA's web site. Detailed quarterly and annual figures on National Defense Consumption Expenditure and Gross Investment are available as from the first quarter of 1972 (I/1972). Even though this excludes most of the Vietnam-era years, over thirty years of quarterly data might permit researchers to test for example the degree to which national defense outlays may have been used as a tool in fiscal stabilization policy. (The complete list of defense-relevant line items in the NIPA tables is shown in appendix table 1.) The following figures and discussion provide some examples of what is available. Where needed, items are inflation-adjusted and indexed to the base year 2000.

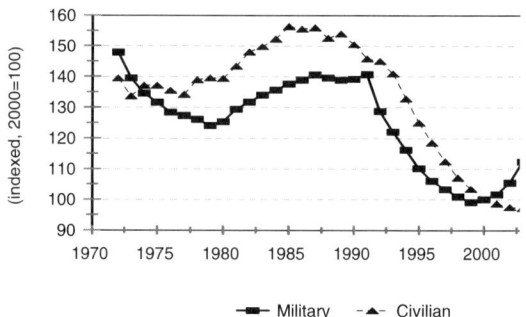

Figure 5: Total Compensation, Military vs Civilian DoD Employees, Real dollars (indexed to 2000 = 100).

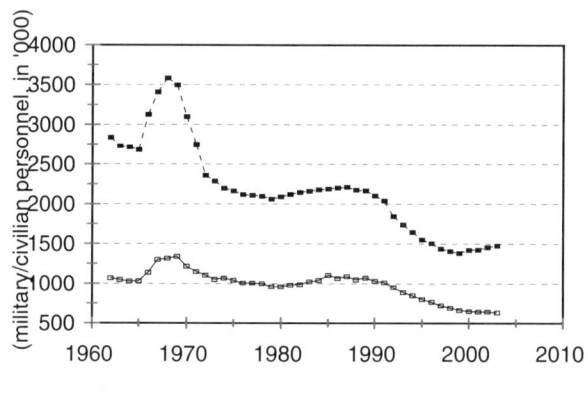

Figure 6: U.S. Military and Civilian DoD Personnel, in Thousands.

Figure 5 shows that during the Carter/Reagan cold-war build-up and, again, during the post-9/11 period the total wage bill for military employees increased. For civilian defense employees an increase in the total wage bill for the post-9/11 years has not yet occurred. For the post-Vietnam and post-cold war years, compensation for both categories of employees fell drastically.

This of course reflects changes in the underlying numbers of military and civilian personnel (figure 6, for DoD only).[8]

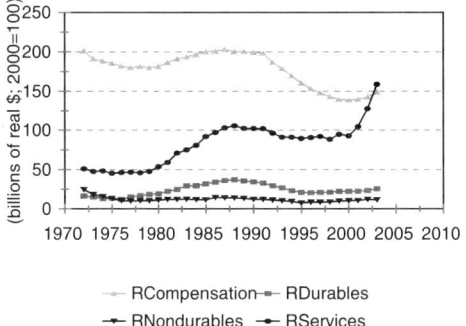

Figure 7: **Major Components of Real Defense Consumption (Billions of Dollars; 2000 = 100).**

Figure 12, placed in the appendix because of the size of the figure, consists of six bar charts, the price indices – indexed to 2000 – for gross investment in six types of military equipment, namely aircraft, missiles, ships, vehicles, electronic equipment and software, and other equipment. To ease comparison, all charts are drawn to the same scale. Price index reductions are especially evident in missiles and electronics since the early 1980s. The aircraft price index stabilized in the 1990s, perhaps because of the inclusion of electronic components. In contrast, the indices for ships, vehicles, and other equipment have risen steadily, but all three of these indices flattened out during the low-inflation period of the late 1990s.

Figure 7 shows changes in the composition of inflation-adjusted national defense outlays from 1972 to 2003. The top line reflects spending on the overall defense-related wage bill (but not including compensation covered under the "services" rubric). Oscillating between $150 and $200 billion per year, the dollar figure dropped somewhat post-Vietnam, rose during the Carter/Reagan build–up, fell post-cold war, and has risen again since 9/11.

---

[8] The use of "civilian contractors," e.g., the services of private military companies, is captured under the "services" rubric. For example, "personnel services" increased from $22.9 billion in 2000 to $51.1 billion in 2003 (nominal dollars). See figure 7.

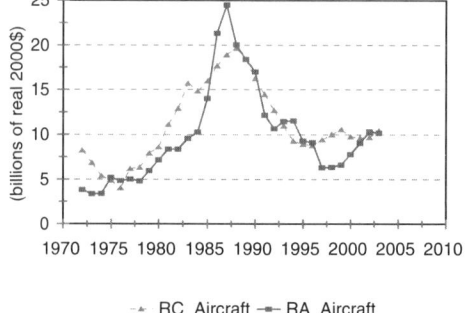

Figure 8: Consumption (RC) and Gross Investment (RA) in Aircraft, Real Dollars (base year = 2000).

The line in the middle of the graph denotes real spending on service items. According to the NIPA tables, this includes research and development, installations support, weapons support, personnel support, transportation of material, and travel of persons. The "services" item also includes expenditure on "civilian contractors" or private military or military-service companies. Consumption of hardware – durable and non-durable – is shown in the bottom two lines, also in billions of inflation- adjusted dollars. This reflects use and depreciation of previously acquired hardware.

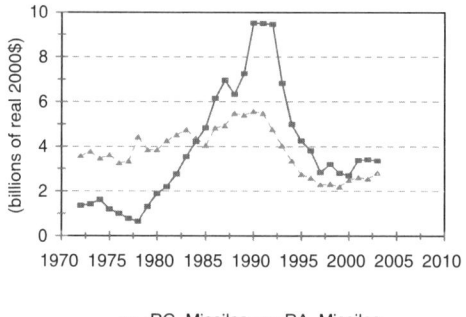

Figure 9: Consumption (RC) and Gross Investment (RA) in Missiles, Real Dollars (base year=2000).

Figure 9 shows consumption and gross investment (acquisition) for missiles, also in real terms. As for aircraft, there is a remarkable acquisitions drive during the Carter and Reagan terms. In both cases – aircraft and missiles – the figures reveal unusual plateau-patterns around 1991 and 2001-2003, i.e, around the Persian Gulf war, and the Afghanistan and Iraq wars.

It is useful to compare consumption of hardware with acquisition (gross investment) of hardware. This is done in figures 8 to 11 for directly comparable items, namely aircraft, missiles, ships, and vehicles. For example, figure 8 shows, in inflation-adjusted billions of dollars, consumption of and gross investment in military aircraft. Consumption appears to lead gross investment. Consumption grows in the Carter and Reagan administrations, with a particularly pronounced acquisitions drive in Mr. Reagan's two terms of office.

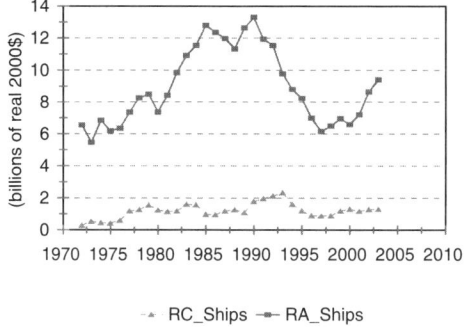

Figure 10: Consumption (RC) and Gross Investment (RA) in Ships, Real Dollars (base year = 2000).

The data displayed in figure 10, for ships, clash with preconceptions. As before, there is a notable acquisitions boom during the Carter and Reagan administrations, a post-cold war draw-down thereafter, and a renewed increase as from the mid-1990s. But it has been widely reported that the United States Navy has decommissioned a very large number of vessels since the Reagan dream of building a 600-ship Navy just failed to be realized. It would appear that the decommissioning has not (yet) led to a corresponding depreciation and write-off and is thus not reflected in the consumption data.

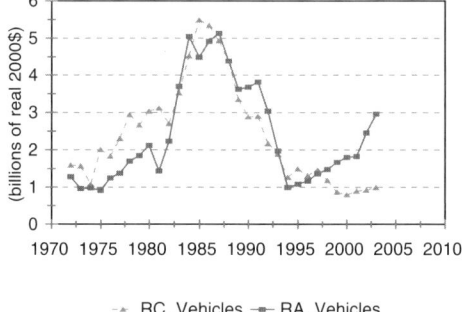

Figure 11: Consumption (RC) and Gross Investment (RA) in Vehicles, Real Dollars (base year = 2000).

Finally, figure 11 shows the consumption and gross investment data for military vehicles. These, too, show a build-up during the Carter and Reagan years, the post-cold war reductions, and the renewed build-up since the mid-1990s. As for aircraft, vehicle consumption and gross investment are patterned reasonably close to each other, except for a sustained ten-year acquisition boom starting in 1995. In sum, considerable, and considerably detailed, information is available on total United States military expenditure, but it does not appear that this has yet been exploited in the academic literature for developing and testing hypotheses about expenditure patterns and the impact of this spending on the U.S. and other economies. One question of particular importance is the degree to which these data can help to disentangle the role of private military companies and civilian contractors in U.S. military operations.

IV. The Cost of U.S. Military Expenditure

IV.1. The Inflationary Cost

Beyond the *Historical Tables* and NIPA numbers, there are costs other than federal government budgeted costs. For example, it is generally acknowledged that U.S. wars are inflationary. This may be tolerable in times of low capacity utilization but since the average U.S. war lasts longer than the average U.S. recessionary period in or during which wars have occurred, wars ultimately stimulate aggregate demand beyond what is needed to return the economy to its long-run growth potential. Wars would thereby be expected to contribute to inflation (erosion of purchasing power) via demand-side pressure (so long as they are deficit-financed, which they usually are).[9, 10]

IV.2. Other Costs

Periods of conflict and war also tend to result in reductions in non-defense government spending (federal, state, and local) as well as in reductions of private consumption of durable and nondurable items (e.g., Gold, 1997). Furthermore, the Afghan and Iraq wars in particular rely to an unprecedented degree on U.S. reservists that are pulled out of their normal, civilian-life occupations. Their employers need to cope, often by having to offer overtime pay to their remaining employees. (The posts that reservists leave are not necessarily filled by employing a second person since reservists usually have a right of return to the position they left, and employers do not want to be stuck with paying for two positions once a reservist returns.) Other costs of U.S. conflicts include for instance the massive structural adjustment in the transportation and tourism industry post-9/11, the effect of political uncertainty on businesses' gross private domestic investment, and even such nuisance costs as increased airport screening and wait times. In addition, a respectable argument can be made that the current conflicts in Afghanistan, Iraq, and the Middle East are at least partially responsible for higher energy costs. Furthermore, a plausible argument can be made that other global commodity and financial markets are perturbed by uncertainty in war, and uncertainty always increases costs as people engage in defensive and risk-avoidance behavior they would not otherwise undertake. These costs are difficult to quantify.

IV.3. The Benefits

Economists do not dispute that some degree of security, defense, or military expenditure is warranted to provide a country's citizens (as employees and investors) with credible assurance that makes them willing to invest in their own economy and thereby to contribute to the development of the quality and quantity of the labor and capital stock (human and physical capital) and to long-run economic growth potential.

---

[9] If wars are tax-financed, current consumption would decline and the demand-stimulus might be zero or, at any rate, small.

[10] As is well-known, a large part of the U.S. federal government budget deficit is in fact financed via its current-account deficit (a current-account deficit is a capital-account surplus). Thus, the current U.S. wars in Afghanistan and Iraq are, in some measure, financed by countries with whom the U.S. carries a large trade deficit, China and Japan in particular.

The difficulty lies in deciding when "too much" military expenditure results in diminishing or even negative returns. Even prior to 11 September 2001 economists argued that U.S. military expenditure had reached the point of diminishing returns with adverse effects on the economy.

Conclusion

The main finding of this chapter is that news media and the public-at-large pay unwarranted attention to U.S. Department of Defense budget numbers. At about $390 billion, for FY2003, these understate the total U.S. military expenditure of $520 by about $130 billion.

References

[BEA] US Department of Commerce. Bureau of Economic Analysis. *Government Transactions*. Methodology Paper Series MP-5. Washington, DC: Government Printing Office. November 1988. Available online at: http://www.bea.gov/bea/ARTICLES/NATIONAL/NIPA/Methpap/methpap5.pdf [accessed 10 May 2004].

Gold, David. 1997. "Opportunity Costs of Military Expenditures: Evidence from the United States," pp. 109-124 in J. Brauer and W. Gissy (eds.) *Economics of Conflict and Peace*. Brookfield, VT: Avebury.

[WMEAT] US Department of State, Bureau of Verification and Compliance. 2000. *World Military Expenditures and Arms Transfers, 1999/2000*. Washington, DC.

Appendix

Table 1: National Defense Consumption Expenditures and Gross Investment Itemization.

1 National defense consumption expenditures and gross investment
2 Consumption expenditures \1\
3 Gross output of general government
4 Value added
5 Compensation of general government employees
6 Military
7 Civilian
8 Consumption of general government fixed capital \2\
9 Intermediate goods and services purchased \3\
10 Durable goods
11 Aircraft

12 Missiles
13 Ships
14 Vehicles
15 Electronics
16 Other durable goods
17 Nondurable goods
18 Petroleum products
19 Ammunition
20 Other nondurable goods
21 Services
22 Research and development
23 Installation support
24 Weapons support
25 Personnel support
26 Transportation of material
27 Travel of persons
28 Less: Own-account investment \4\
29 Sales to other sectors
30 Gross investment \5\
31 Structures
32 Equipment and software
33 Aircraft
34 Missiles
35 Ships
36 Vehicles
37 Electronics and software
38 Other equipment

Source: National Income and Product Accounts, Bureau of Economic Analysis, US Dept of Commerce (online).

Notes:

1. National defense consumption expenditures are defense services produced by government that are valued at their cost of production. Excludes government sales to other sectors and government own-account investment (construction and software).
2. Consumption of fixed capital, or depreciation, is included in government gross output as a partial measure of the services of general government fixed assets; the use of depreciation assumes a zero net return on these assets.
3. Includes general government intermediate inputs for goods and services sold to other sectors and for own-account investment.
4. Own-account investment is measured in current dollars by compensation of general government employees and related expenditures for goods and services and is classified as investment in structures and in software.
5. Gross government investment consists of general government and government enterprise expenditures.

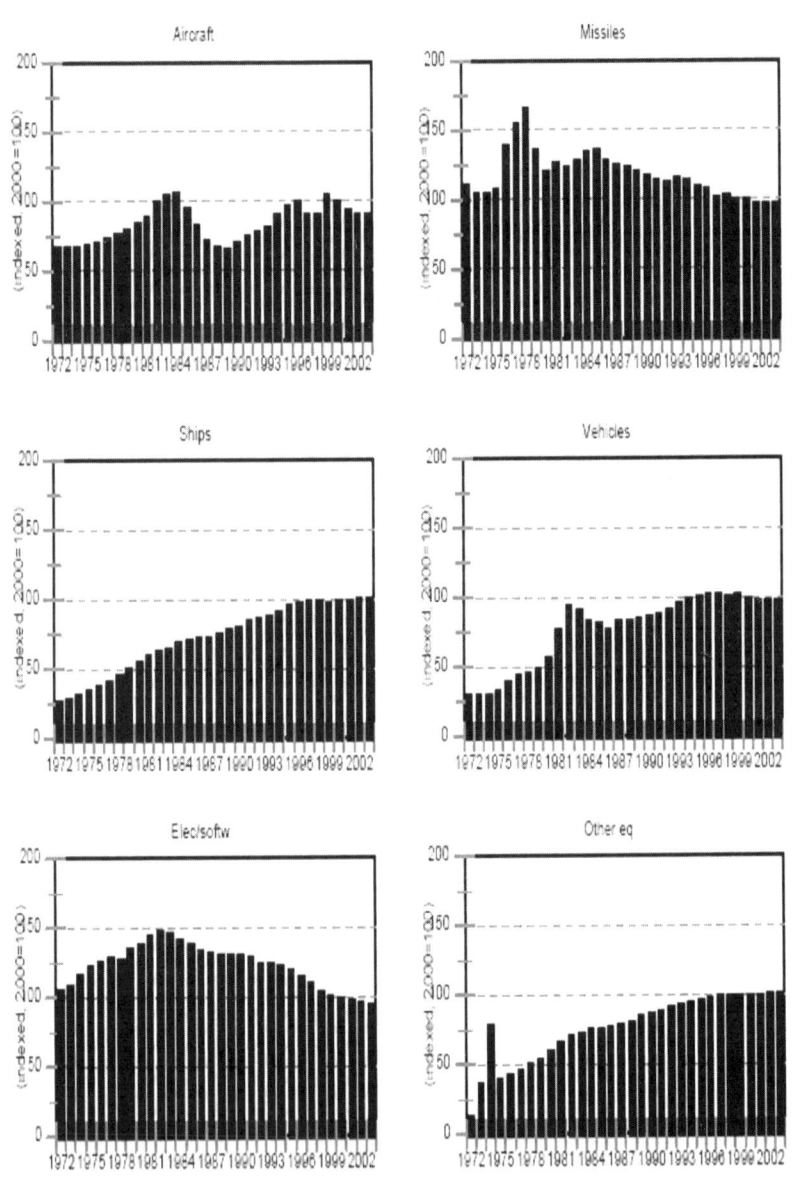

Figure 12: Prices, Indices, Gross Investment in Military Equipment (indexed 2000 = 100).

Chapter 4
ACCOUNTING FOR ARMS
IN INPUT-OUTPUT AND NATIONAL INCOME ACCOUNTS

Gulay Gunluk-Senesen

Introduction

Input-output (I-O) models exploring impacts of arms production on the economy are rather rare in the literature. Complexity of related production and industry classification problems emerge as main restricting factors. This paper discusses conceptual, measurement and Input-Output modeling issues of arms in the context of national income accounting, which provides a consistent data framework for the whole economy.

Arms production is an economic activity. Its current stance in the overall production structure, as well as changes in its relative position in time for any national economy is a research issue of interest. Reconciliation of this aspect with the international dimension improves assessment e.g. of competitiveness and specialisation. In either scope, a consistent and comparable data framework is a prerequisite.

The Input-Output (I-O) model provides insight to the structure of production consistent with national accounts. Despite its generally adopted static version, dynamic version is also available with the inclusion of capital accounts. Furthermore, computable general equilibrium models incorporate this production structure with behavioural macro-econometric equations. In either framework, focus can be on a specific production sector or a group of sectors. However, research in English on defence along these lines is almost nil.[11] The very few exceptions are Leontief (1980), Leontief and Duchin (1983), Duchin (1983), Dunne (1985) and Balakrishnan and Devi (1996), Hoffman et al (1996), and Turner (2004). The approach in Leontief and Duchin (1983) is unique in this area due to its context: the role of military sectors is explored and projections are made for the world economy, based on a world I-O model. The very recent work of Turner (2004) estimates employment effects of government purchases and exports of defence goods for UK with I-O data but the modelling sequence is not explicitly stated.

The role of defence related industries in the overall production system and hence in the economy is an interesting but challenging research area.

---

[11] See papers published in *Economic Systems Research* (by Routledge for the International Input-Output Association) and *Defence and Peace Economics* (Carfax).

The challenge basically lies in the definition of industries involved. The recognition of the issue goes back to Ayres (1983) and Brauer (1991). Recently, Birdi et al. (2000:602-603) discuss data problems associated with government defence related purchases from domestic producers on the basis of I-O sectors for South Africa. They identify 12 of 45 manufacturing industries as *potential* (emphasize added) providers of weaponry. For example, other chemical products sector is a critical supplier of the explosive materials used in ammunition and other weaponry production. Similarly, military equipment covers lethal weapons as well as dual use equipment. Hence the production sectors involved are of a wide range. Perhaps the best available instructive documentation on defence suppliers is Dowdall et al. (2000), a country case study for the UK.

The long recognized and analyzed concepts and definitions regarding defence related industries notwithstanding, in this paper the focus is on a subset of the broad category, i.e. "Destructive weapons" as defined in the United Nations (UN) 1993 *System of National Accounts* (SNA) in UN (1993). The next section presents the I-O modelling framework and national income formation with special reference to weapons. Section 3 analyses the definitions for weapons production and exports in the UN and EUROSTAT guidelines in a comparative perspective. I-O data tables for various countries are compared in section 4 on the basis of their classification of industries. The final section provides an assessment of findings and challenges for future research.

I. Arms in National Income and Input-Output Accounting: Conceptual Framework

The spill over impacts of arms production on the rest of the production structure, especially via its backward linkages, has been an almost fully established fact for long. (e.g. see Ayres, 1983; Deger and Sen, 1983). However, measuring the extent of these impacts has been quite problematic. Analogous to the research question: "What are the actual costs of arms transfers (i.e. arms imports)?" in Brzoska (2004), a question like "What are the economic benefits of arms production and sales?" is at least as challenging. The set of answers involves potential impacts with respect to production sectors, factors and resources, therefore has a broader coverage than GDP growth. The starting point then could be national income accounting, since a strict condition of consistency between production and expenditure activities is imposed at the start. Namely, for any industry i ($i = 1,2,........n$; $j = 1, 1,2,.......n$)

Domestic Output $_i = \Sigma_j^n$ Intermediate Deliveries$_{i,j}$ + Final Deliveries$_i$ (1)
Recall that
Σ_i^n Final Deliveries$_i$ = GDP. (2)
And the contribution of any industry i to overall GDP is:
GDP$_i$ = C$_i$ + I$_i$ + G$_i$ + Exports$_i$ − Imports$_i$. (3)
Within this framework, (1) corresponds to
x = Ax + y (4)
which is the basic Input-Output model. Here x is the column vector for n sectoral outputs, y is the column vector for n sectoral final demands, A is the fixed (in the short run) technology coefficients for intermediate (intersectoral) inputs.

"The impact of a change in the final demand of a specific sector on the rest of the economy" is found in the basic Input-Output model by
x = (I-A)$^{-1}$ y = Ry. (5)

Since $r_{ij} = \Delta X_i / \Delta Y_j$, for any specific sector j, r_{ij} shows the "potential output change in the ith sector as a result of direct and indirect intermediate input demand, induced by one unit change in the final demand of sector j." Then, $\Sigma_i r_{ij}$ gives the *total backward linkage* of j, i.e. "potential output change in the whole economy, due to a one unit change in the final demand of sector j." It is obvious that the sector i (and/or j) could well be the arms producing industry so that its economic impacts could be studied in the same way as one would study agriculture or textiles.

The extensions of the I-O model are manifold: e.g. employment, imports, energy, pricing aspect of final demand impacts is commonly incorporated (see Gunluk-Senesen, 1998; Dietzenbacher and Gunluk-Senesen, 2003; Gunluk-Senesen and Senesen, 2001; Miller and Blair, 1985). An alternative framework would incorporate the interaction of the group of arms production related industries with the rest of the economy: Define

industry group 1: arms related industries: weapons/arms and ammunition
industry group 2: other industries in the economy.

Then (4) would be redefined as

$$\begin{bmatrix} x1 \\ x2 \end{bmatrix} = \begin{bmatrix} A11 & A12 \\ A21 & A22 \end{bmatrix} \bullet \begin{bmatrix} x1 \\ x2 \end{bmatrix} + \begin{bmatrix} y1 \\ y2 \end{bmatrix}$$ (6)

and R in (5) would be redefined accordingly
R = I + (R1 - I) + (R2 - I) R1 + (R3 - I) R2 R1. (7)
Here, R1 incorporates direct impacts of the group's final demand change on the same industry group, R2 involves cross impacts on the other group and

finally R3 incorporates indirect impacts on the same group (see Gunluk-Senesen and Senesen (1990) for details).

The solutions for a single arms industry or a group of arms producing industries in the models (4) and (6) require explicit definitions of related activities. The basic source for international guidelines for national income accounting is UN (1993). Items 6.167-172 and 10.65-68 of the UN (1993) (pp. 145-6, 227 and 306) state that only for military purpose weapons are intermediate goods and not investment goods: "Destructive weapons such as missiles, rockets, bombs, etc. cannot be treated as fixed assets because they are not in fact used repeatedly or continuously in production. Although durable, they are single use goods. Moreover, the actual use of such weapons in combat to destroy lives and property cannot be construed as production of goods or services. By extension, vehicles and equipment, whose function is to release such weapons should also not be treated as fixed assets. All expenditures on equipment for the military have by default to be treated as intermediate consumption". However recent work on the revisions of the 1993 SNA have evolved towards treating military systems as fixed assets on the grounds of their durability, because "military weapon systems are used continuously in the production of defence services, even if their peacetime use is simply to provide deterrence." (Moulton, 2003). In February 2004 the advisory expert group (AEG) on national accounts meetings approved this revision with the justification that "the production accounts measure economic activity and not well being."[12] The revisions in progress will obviously have implications for our accounting framework. In case it is put into practice in the future, the switch, *per se*, from a "value laden" position to a "realistic" or "neutral" position towards arms, would also be worthwhile for assessment.

Focusing on the components of final demand, we can deduct that arms are not private consumption goods.[13] They can be regarded as part of investment goods. The purchasers of arms from the producers are restricted to government and rest of the world. Therefore, government current and investment expenditures and exports are the final demand categories where arms would be accounted for in final demand.

It then follows that arms production contributes to GDP via investment, government consumption and exports and the I-O model is appropriate in finding out the relative significance of this sector in the economy. In our as-

---

[12] http://unstats.un.org/unsd/cr/nationalaccount/aeg/decision of the aeg classification of military.doc.
[13] Take bombs for example. They are intermediate in the UN (1993), but bombs are finished goods ready for final use, traditionally for military purpose, so they are not to be purchased by private consumers.

sessment of the data framework, we will leave out the two components of the final demand: investment and government expenditure, as the former for arms is not yet fully established and the latter is self-defined, though not without measurement problems (e.g. see Brauer, 2004; Gunluk-Senesen, 2001). A comparative survey on the definition of weapons as a productive activity and as an export activity in international practice follows next.

II. Weapons in National Income and Input-Output Accounts: Practice

Our starting point is the international classification of arms, since it provides guidelines for the construction of national data bases like national income statistics and input-output tables which are by default, in coherence with national income accounts. For this purpose, we compare the UN and EUROSTAT classifications for weapon production and exports.

II.1. Production

The United Nations Statistics Division (UNSD) classification

The 3.1 version of the *International Standard Industrial Classification (ISIC) of All Economic Activities* explicitly classifies weapons and ammunition under code D-Manufacturing. Under division no. 29: Manufacture of machinery and equipment, not classified elsewhere (nce), i.e. code 292 involves the Manufacture of special purpose machinery and hence class 2927 is Manufacture of weapons and ammunition. This classification corresponds to sub-sectors under codes 33299, 33641, 33699 and 811 in the *North American Industry Classification System* (NAICS) (US) 2002.

A more detailed classification is presented in Table 1 (see appendix). Note that the industry includes non-military, civilian purpose weapons as well. A surprising fact is that despite this classification, UNSD does not collect production data on this item.

EUROSTAT Classification for Weapons and Ammunition, NACE, Rev.1.1

The 1.1 version of the *General Industrial Classification of Economic Activities in the European Communities (NACE)* explicitly classifies Weapons and Ammunition under code D- Manufactured Products. Under code DK (no.29: Machinery and Equipment (nce), code 29.6 is the Weapons and Ammunition sector. A more detailed classification is in Table 2 (see appendix).

Mawdsley and Quille (2003:26) point out that "National armaments policies, comprising defence procurement policy, defence industrial policy (including exports) and defence related research policy still vary considerably within the EU-15" and that "...defence products are exempted by treaty from the Single Market...." This implies that there would not be comparable production data available for the European Union.

On the other hand, under the *Structural Business Statistics* (SBS) framework, EUROSTAT collects data from business enterprises registered with respect to their main activity. Weapons and ammunition (DK 29.6) sector is one of these activities. Reservations for under-recording and confidentiality notwithstanding, there are only one set of available data, as presented in Table 3 (see appendix).

Here, the only item related to the contribution of weapons to GDP is the value added item. Country composition of this item is available neither for 2000 nor for more recent years. Besides, this set of survey information has weak links to the national income aggregates. We will discuss exports related information in Table 3 in the next sub-section. It is obvious from tables 1-3 that there is not a coherent international coverage for weapons as an economic activity.

II.2. Exports

Analysis of arms exports in the defence economics literature has dominantly relied on data for arms transfers provided by SIPRI and USACDA (USBVC). Despite disparities in the information, both of these sources register international arms transfers in the broader security context, as is well known.[14] They are not covered in this paper, because their coverage is broader than the economic one would involve. Similarly, due to its focus on security not economics, the *UN Register of Conventional Arms*, like SIPRI and ACDA, also is not in strict compliance with exports in connection to production accounts.

The early work of Smith et al. (1985) outlines problems of arms exports data faced by economists. The problems associated with data on arms trade are outlined in detail in Sandler and Hartley (1995), as well as in Brzoska (2004). It seems there has been little improvement in the last two decades in the data usable for purely economic aspects of arms trade.[15] In fact, strict

---

[14] For an analysis of the volume versus value aspects of these transfers see Levine, et al. (1998). The focus therein is however on imports.

[15] E.g. interviews with experts in State Institute of Statistics and Foreign Trade Undersecretariat of Turkey reveal that transactions related to weapons fall outside their domain, therefore related are data not compiled.

adherence to UN (1993) definition implies that arms exports should be among "exported intermediate goods" like e.g. fabric yarns. However, in practice their exporting procedures are quite different from those of yarns. Governments strictly regulate exports of weapons. Therefore, they are perhaps the best documented items in foreign trade, in terms of content, volume and value. The information is not disclosed in general. It should also be noted that the terminology is not identical in production and trade accounts: "weapons" is replaced by "arms" in export classification.

The United Nations Statistics Division (UNSD) Classification

There are no guidelines for arms exports in the 1993 SNA. The *Standard International Trade Classification* (SITC) Rev. 4 of the UN includes a classification for weapons and ammunition, with code 891, under the heading: arms and ammunition. The UNSD database on this category is available for time series and countries. It is immediately clear that the UN classifications for production (Table 1) and international trade Table 4 (see appendix for both) are not comparable in coverage.

EUROSTAT Classification (CN 2006)

Discussions in progress on the EU Code of Conduct on Arms Exports apparently focus on categories and recipients, not explicitly linked to production. (e.g. see www.isis-europe.org and www.fco.gov.uk*).* We also note that trade of "military goods" are classified among specific movements subject to confidentiality in the *EC Statistics on the Trading of Goods. The Combined Nomenclature* (CN) for external trade for 2006 classifies arms and ammunition under code 93, for which a simplified list is presented in Table 5 (see appendix). Data with regard to this item and its components is not available.

Referring to Table 3, note that monetary values for exports and imports (extra and/or intra EU) are not available in this data set compiled from business units. Trade shares of arms and ammunition appear to be in significant in machinery production and overall manufacturing. However it is interesting to see that arms and ammunition exported to non-EU countries have a high trade surplus share in the overall trade volume. Trade surpluses in weapons and ammunition are observed for Italy, Germany, France, Belgium, Sweden and UK (Sura, 2003). Recall that these interpretations are limited to survey data, which would only partly be related to overall exports and imports in the GDP sense.

As Table 2 is not comparable to Table 5, it is not possible to analyze the role of the WA sector in the EU economy, for example, with available data bases of the EUROSTAT. Besides, Table 4 is not coherent with Table 5 either, leading to the assessment that for both production and trade, international classifications differ even in broad terms. Presence of a classification of weapons and ammunition hence does not automatically lead to availability of corresponding data. Even the rather standard format of input-output tables is not without problems regarding the economic role of the weapons/arms and ammunition sector.

II.3. Reflections On Data: I-O Tables

The basic guidelines for Input-Output tables are given in UN (1993). *European System of Accounts* 1995 is a further documentation to establish the standards for European statistics. NACE-CLIO provides the version used for the compilation of I-O tables for Europe. In the Annex of the NACE, Rev.1.1 (in effect from 1 January 2003), production activities are classified for 99 sectors (*Official Journal of the European Communities*, 10.1.2002). However as Table 6 reveals, I-O tables for EU countries do not reflect a harmonious classification in terms of the number of sectors. Furthermore, regrouping of the above discussed classifications of industries into input-output classifications (CLIO) for industries does not explicitly include weapons and ammunition for most of the countries. This item is generally classified under "other/special purpose machinery and equipment". Also note that the SBS data and I-O data are not linked, and SBS does not provide information on intermediate transactions and external trade in the national accounting sense.

Table 6 (see appendix) also includes summary information for non-EU countries, which were collected on the basis of ease of access. For some countries, detailed industrial classification, so that WA could be traced was available, however no such information exists for Denmark, Israel, Japan, South Korea and Thailand. On the other hand, I-O tables for France, South Africa, UK and USA explicitly include arms related industries. These data would enable the calibration of the simpler varieties of the I-O models summarized in section II, hence the study of the economic role of arms production for the whole economy in a consistent framework. One such exercise is presented for UK in the Appendix.

The US input-output data sets stand out as the most detailed information sources on production. Even back in early 1980s, a 496-sector input-output table (for 1972) was available. Leontief & Duchin (1983:14) note that "this table includes eight sectors which "produce goods exclusively for military use: new military construction, repair and maintenance of military facilities, missiles, tanks, small arms, two categories of ammunition and other ordnance. It does not, however, distinguish the input structures for three important categories of military hardware-aircraft, ships and communications equipment-from the input structures of their civilian counterparts." With 6 sub-sectors for arms production, present USA I-O data is the most suitable one for solutions with the two-block I-O model, among those listed in Table 6.[16] Still, a cross-check with national income aggregates would be necessary, as the UK exercise below shows.

Concluding Remarks

Production of arms, as an economic activity, involves purchasing of intermediate inputs from the domestic production sectors as well as from abroad and employing factors of production. Its revenues come from sales of secondary products to domestic production sectors, and sales of final products to mainly government and to foreign buyers under government regulation. This particular production activity itself might also be under close surveillance. Still, wages, profits, taxes etc. paid out of the value added created, are also economic aspects of this activity. Although conceptually possible, as would be for any other economic activity e.g. textile production, this consistent framework is not usually reflected on comparable data.

International guidelines of UN and EU for classification of data for arms production and trade are not in harmony with each other on one hand, and within themselves, on the other. Data on economic activities, without exception bear problems due to the diversity between ISIC (for production) and SITC (for trade) classification systems. However, it is much more likely to attain cohesion with a moderate aggregation for e.g. textiles than arms.

The lack of harmony between data and the disguised nature of information on arms production and trade, both at national and international levels, pose serious challenges to research on "the economic value of arms". Under these circumstances overestimation and underestimation are equally likely. Furthermore, as Martin et al. (1999:779) note for UK "arms exports is an emotional topic". One "cold" alternative, also in line with the revisions in UN SNA, then would be to reduce the scope of unknowns regarding arms, so that it becomes a correctly measured economic activity. Research on its

---

[16] Note however that matrix operations with these large data sets are relatively cumbersome. Furthermore, US data conform to North American Industry Classification System (NAICS), hence they are not directly comparable to EU and UN classifications for sectors.

positive/negative implications for "economic well being", an aspect despised by the revisions in UN SNA, would then stand on a solid and strong base.

References

Ayres, R. (1983) 'Arms production as a form of import-substituting industrialization: the Turkish case', *World Development*, 11(9): 813-823.

Balakrishnan, V. and Devi, S. U. (1996) 'Impact of defence expenditure in input-output framework', *in Studies in Indian Economy*, edited by R.K. Koti et al., Bombay: Himalaya Publishing House: 147-158.

Birdi, A., Dunne, J. P. and Saal D. S. (2000) 'The impact of arms production on the South African manufacturing industry', *Defence and Peace Economics*, 11: 597-613.

Brauer, J. (1991) 'Arms production in developing nations: the relation to industrial structure, industrial diversification and human capital formation', *Defence and Peace Economics*, 2: 165-175.

Brauer, J. (2004) "United States Military Expenditure", Paper presented at the 2nd *International Conference on Defence, Security and Development*, Larissa, Greece, 18-20 June 2004.

Brzoska, M. (2004) 'The economics of arms imports after the end of the cold war', *Defence and Peace Economics*, 15(2): 111-123.

Chalmers, M., Davies, N.V., Hartley, K. and Wilkinson, C. (2002) 'The economic costs and benefits of UK defence exports, *Fiscal Studies*, 23(2): 343-367.

Deger, S. and Sen, S. (1983) 'Military expenditure, spin-off and economic development', *Journal of Development Economics*, 13: 67-83.

Dietzenbacher, E. and Gunluk-Senesen, G. (2003) 'Demand-pull and cost-push effects on labor income in Turkey, 1973-90', *Environment and Planning A*, 35(10): 1785-1807.

Dowdall, P., Braddon, D. and Hartley, K. (2000) *The Value of the Defence Industry to the UK Economy (VODE-Defence Industry Supply Chain Literature and Research Review*, DTI, UK.

Duchin, F. (1983) 'Economic consequences of military spending', *Journal of Economic Issues* (pre-1986), XVII/2, June: 543-553.

Dunne, J. P. (1985) 'Using input-output models to assess the employment effects of military expenditure: A comparative assessment', paper presented at the *IIASA 6th Input Output Task Force Meeting*, Warsaw, Poland, December.

Dunne, J. P. and Perlo-Freeman, S. (2004) *Lock, Stock and Barrel*, OXFAM, 202918.

Gunluk-Senesen, G. (1998) 'An input-output analysis of employment structure in Turkey: 1973-1990', *Economic Research Forum Working Paper,* WP 9809, Cairo, Egypt.

Gunluk-Senesen, G. (2001) 'Measuring the extent of defence expenditures: the Turkish case with Turkish data', *Defence and Peace Economics*, 12(1): 27-41.

Gunluk-Senesen, G. and Senesen, U. (1990) 'An analysis of the Turkish transportation sector in the context of a two-group industry model', *Transportation Research*, 24 B (4): 299-313.

Gunluk-Senesen, G. and Senesen, U. (2001) 'Reconsidering import dependency in Turkey: the break-down of sectoral demands with respect to suppliers', *Economic Systems Research*, 13(4): 417-428.

Hoffman, S., Robinson, S. and Subramanian, S. (1996) 'The role of defense cuts in the Californian recession: Computable general equilibrium models and interstate factor mobility', *Journal of Regional Science*, 34(4):571-595.

Johansson, U. (2006) 'Manufacture of machinery and equipment in Europe', *Statistics in Focus*, Industry, Trade and Services, 10/2006, EC. *http//epp.eurostat.cec.eu.*

Leontief, W.W. (1980) 'The world economy in the year 2000', *Scientific American*, September: 207-231.

Leontief, W. and Duchin, F. (1983) *Military Spending: Facts and Figures, Worldwide Implications and Future Outlook*, USA: OUP.

Levine, P., Mouzakis, F. and Smith, R. (1998) 'Prices and quantities in the arms trade', *Defence and Peace Economics*, 9: 223-236.

Martin, S. (1999) 'The Subsidy Savings from Reducing UK Arms Exports', *Journal of Economic Studies*, 26(1): 15-37.

Martin, S., Hartley, K. and Stafford, B. (1999) 'The Economic Impacts of Restricting UK Arms Exports', *International Journal of Social Economics*, 26(6):779-802.

Mawdsley, J. and Quille, G. (2003) *The EU security strategy: a new framework for ESDP and equipping the EU rapid reaction force* (*www. isis-europe.org*).

Miller R.E. and Blair, P.D. (1985) *Input-Output Analysis: Foundations and Extensions*, USA: Prentice-Hall.

Moulton, B. R. (2003) 'Canberra II Group's Recommendations to Treat Military Weapon Systems as Fixed Assets, Canberra II Group on Non-Financial Assets', 17 December 2003.

*http://unstats.un.org/unsd/crnationalaccount/aeg/*backgroundmilitary.*doc*.

Sandler, T. and Hartley, K. (1995) *The Economics of Defense*, Great Britain: CUP, ch.10.

Smith, R., Humm, A., Fontanel, J. (1985) 'The economics of exporting arms', *Journal of Peace Research*, 2(3): 239-247.

Sura, W. (2003) 'Machinery and equipment industries in the EU', *Statistics in Focus*,Theme 4-18/2003, EC.

http//ec.europa.eu/enterprise/mechan_equipment/eurostaten.pdf).

Turner, A. J. W. (2004) 'Estimated UK employment dependent on Ministry of Defence expenditure and defence exports', *Defence and Peace Economics*, 15(4): 331-342.

UN (1993) *System of National Accounts 1993*, ST/ESA/STAT/SER.F/2/Rev.4, United Nations: USA.

Acknowledgements

Thanks are due to M. Atthanassiou, , J. Beutel, P. Dowdall, F. Duchin, S. Bar-Eliezer, R. Janscn, K. Chareonwongsak, C. Loo, J. O. Paek, N. Rainer, A. Rivkin, P. Ritzmann, J. M. Rueda-Cantuche, I. Van Reenen, N. Sakurai, S. Zografakis who provided background material/I-O data. Special thanks are due to W. Sura for patient guidance for the European Union data bases.

Appendix

I-O MODEL FINDINGS WITH THE 1995 UK DATA

In this appendix, we first outline the position of the Weapons and Ammunition sector within the national income accounting framework for UK. The data source is the *1995 UK Analytical Input-Output Tables*, of the Office for National Statistics, UK. Secondly, we present findings with the I-O model and discuss their plausibility in the light of alternative data and recent research on defense/arms/WA exports of UK, a unique case in the literature so far.

I. BASIC ACCOUNTING:

Currency: £ mn. Year: 1995, i = 67: Weapons and Ammunition (WA)

Note: There are minor rounding errors in the original data.

Domestic Output $_{67}$ = Σ_j^n Intermediate Sales $_{67,j}$ + Final Sales $_{67}$
1432 = 793 + 639

793 = (WA$_{67}$ + PubAd$_{67}$ + other$_{67}$) = (220 + 523 + 50)

639 = (C$_{67}$ + I$_{67}$ + ΔStcks$_{67}$ + G$_{67}$ + Expts$_{67}$) = (5 + 1 − 115 + 0 + 749)

Domestic Output $_{67}$ = Σ_i^n Intermediate Purchases$_{i,67}$ + Gross Value Added $_{67}$
1432 = 657 + 775

657 = (WA$_{67}$ + other$_{67}$) = (220 + 437)

775 = (wage$_{67}$ + Π_{67} + net tax$_{67}$ + M$_{67}$ + adjustment$_{67}$)
= (364 + 117 + 15 + 306 − 26).

II. I-O MODEL SOLUTIONS FOR UK WITH EQUATIONS (4) AND (6)

$n_1 = 1$ (WA, no.67)
$n_2 = 137$ (rest of the economy) $n = n_1 + n_2 = 138$

Own direct impact multiplier: $r1_{67,67} = 1/(1-a_{67,67}) = 1/(1-0.153) = 1.181522$

Backward linkage of WA on WA: $r_{67,67} = 1.181897$

WA's Internal propagation ratio: $r1_{67,67} / r_{67,67} = 0.99968$
(combined cross and own indirect effects)

Total Backward Linkage of WA: $\Sigma_i\, r_{i,67} = 1.825701$.

The WA accounts for the 0.06 % of the total output in the UK economy. With a one-unit change in its Final Demand inducing 1.8257 units of output expansion in the economy, the WA is the 46th sector among the 138 sectors ranked in descending order with respect to backward multipliers. The backward linkage of the WA is above the overall average.

65 % of this expansion by WA exports etc. is generated on WA itself and the remaining 35 % is generated on other industries, mainly on wholesale distribution, metal forging and pressing, and banking and finance. These sectors are also leading in WA's purchases of intermediate inputs.

Note that Government WA purchases are made by Public Administration, included among the 138 industries in the I-O tables. Therefore Exports (749) is the major final demand component for the WA sector in UK. Exports to non-EU countries (642) are very important compared to exports to EU (107). WA exports to non-EU constitute almost 45 % of the sector's total output and 1.05 % of total goods exports to non-EU. Besides, UK WA has a trade surplus ($EX_{67} - M_{67}$: 749 − 306 = 443).

I-O data show that the share of WA exports in total goods exports of UK is 0.5 %. However, Martin et al. (1999) estimate the share of UK defense exports as 3.1 % in total goods exports in 1995. UK arms exports in 1995 amount to $ 1.2 bn in UNSD-COMTRADE database. Problems regarding coverage of arms/defense related industries again emerge as the main source of controversies in data. But the export aspect intensifies the problems of an economic assessment. As consistency with national income accounting is not complied with in practice, I-O model solutions should be interpreted with reservations. This aspect is also significant for other modelling exercises.

Research on UK arms exports (e.g. see Chalmers et al. 2002; Dunne and Perlo-Freeman, 2004, Martin, 1999; Martin et al. 1999), unfold technical and measurement aspects along with the political and business ones. Although there is yet not such comprehensive and comparable research on arms/defence exports for other countries, we would expect by insight that the challenges posed by the UK case prevails universally.

Table 1: **United Nations Statistics Division classification for Weapons and Ammunition, ISIC, Rev.3.1**

Class: 2927   Manufacture of Weapons and Ammunition

tanks and other fighting vehicles
heavy weapons (artillery, mobile guns, rocket launchers; torpedo tubes, machine guns)
small arms (revolvers, shotguns, light machine guns)
air or gas guns and pistols
war ammunition
military ballistic and guided missiles
Also hunting, sporting or protective firearms and ammunition
explosive devices such as bombs, mines, torpedoes.

Source: *http//unstats.un.org/unsd/cr/registry/.*

Note: *UNSD ISIC Draft Rev.4 allocates these items under 2520, 3030 and 3040 codes (http//unstats.un.org/statcom/doc06/ISIC-Rev4.pdf).*

Table 2: EUROSTAT Classification for Weapons and Ammunition, NACE, Rev.1.1.

Class 29.60.1 Weapons and Ammunition and parts thereof (pt)

> Motorized tanks and other armoured fighting vehicles and pt
> Military weapons, other than revolvers, pistols, swords and the like
> Revolvers, pistols, other firearms and similar devices, other arms
> Bombs, missiles and similar munitions of war, cartridges, other ammunition and projectiles and parts thereof
> Parts of military weapons and other arms.

Class 29.60.9 Installation, maintenance and repair services of weapons and weapons systems

Source: *http//europa.int/comm/eurostat/ramon/cgi/.*

Note: *NACE Draft Rev.2 classifies these items under 25.40, 30.30, 30.40, 33.11. (http://forum.europa.eu.int/irc/dsis/nacecpacon/info/data/en/index.htm#.).*

Table 3: Weapons and Ammunition (WA) Industry (29.6) in the EU*.

		Weapons and Ammunition (29.6)	WA % share in Machinery (DK)	WA % share in Manufacturing (D)
Employment	2000	52 400	1.7	0.2
	2002	70 000	2.0	0.2
Value Added	2000	bn € 2.9	1.9	0.2
	2002	bn € 3.2	1.9	0.2
Exports non-EU 2001			0.7	0.1

Imports (2001)		0.0	0.0
Exports-Imports as % of exports+imports (non-EU) (2001)	43.2		

* excludes Denmark, Luxemburg, Netherlands.

Source: Johansson (2006), Sura (2003).

Table 4: UNSD Classification for Arms and Ammunition, SITC, Rev.4

Commodity: 891 Trade of Arms and Ammunition

    armoured fighting vehicles and arms of war
    Bombs, grenades, torpedoes, mines, missiles and the like, parts thereof
    Parts and accessories of weapons.

    Also: non-military arms.

Source: *http://unstats.un.org/unsd/trade/SITCrev4.pdf.*

Table 5: CN 2006 classification for Arms and Ammunition (External Trade).

93   *Arms and ammunition; parts and accessories thereof*

    Military weapons, incl. sub-machine guns
    Revolvers and pistols
    Firearms and similar devices which operate by the firing of an explosive charge, e.g. sporting shotguns and rifles, muzzle-loading firearms,
    Spring, air or gas guns and pistols, truncheons and other non-firearms
    Parts and accessories for weapons and the like of heading 9301 to 9304, n.e.s.
    Bombs, grenades, torpedoes, mines, missiles, cartridges and other ammunition and projectiles and parts thereof, incl. buckshot, shot and cartridge wads, n.e.s.
    Swords, cutlasses, bayonets, lances and similar arms and parts thereof and scabbards and sheaths.

Source: http://ec.europa.eu/comm/eurostat/ramon/nomenclatures/.

Table 6: Weapons Production in Input-Output Tables for Selected Countries

Country	Data Year	Weapons Producing Sector(s)	Total # of Sectors	Data Source
DENMARK	2002	n.a.	130	SD
FRANCE	1996	Materiels d'armament (#26) Produits de la construction navale (#32) Produits de la construction aeronautique (#33)	98	INSEE
GREECE	1996	(weapons and ammunition and parts thereof included in 'special purpose machinery)	122	NSNSSG
INDIA	1983-84	(arms and armaments included in 'other machinery')	60	CSO
ISRAEL	1995	n.a.	65	CBS
JAPAN	2000	n.a.	104	SSD-MIAC
KOREA, REP.	2000	n.a	75	NSO
SOUTH AFRICA	2000	Weapons and ammunition (#107)	153	SSA
SPAIN	2000	(weapons and ammunition and parts thereof included in 'special purpose machinery).	118	NIS
SWEDEN	2000	(weapons and ammunition and parts thereof included in 'special purpose machinery).	57	SCB
THAILAND	2000	n.a	180	NSO
TURKEY	1998	(weapons and ammunition and parts thereof included in 'special purpose machinery)	97	TUIK
UK	1995	Weapons and Ammunition (# 67)	138	ONS
USA	1997	Ordnance and accessories (#332A) Ammunition(bombs, grenades, torped.) (#33299A) Small arms (rifles, machine guns (#332994) Other mil. weapons, mortars (#332995) Military armoured vehicles and tanks, parts (#336992) Guided missile and space vehicle (#336414)	498	BEA

PART III:
THE EVOLUTION
OF THE INTERNATIONAL ARMS INDUSTRIES
AND THE INCREASING ROLE
OF THE FINANCIAL MARKETS

Chapter 5
THE EVOLUTION OF THE INTERNATIONAL ARMS INDUSTRY

J. Paul Dunne, Maria Garcia Alonso, Paul Levine, Ron P. Smith

The end of the Cold War led to a large drop in military expenditures and the demand for arms. This paper examines how the firms that produced those arms responded and how the Western defence industry evolved. The arms industry is somewhat unusual in that its customers, governments, can shape the structure of supply by their procurement policies and regularly use those policies to try to create the type of Defence Industrial Base that will best provide them with the type of arms they think that they will need in the future. Government defence industrial policy thus sets a perimeter within which arms firms can set their corporate strategy. It is a loose perimeter in that firms can lobby to change policy and they can go off and find other governments to sell to (subject to arms export control policies, another part of the perimeter); but it is a perimeter, a constraint on corporate strategies. Thus in making their strategic choices, companies were making judgements about what governments would accept, or could be made to accept by the methods of persuasion arms firms usually employ.

Below we examine the policy context; review the options available to companies; consider various ways of explaining changes in concentration; measure the change in concentration in the industry; discuss some econometric issues and present some econometric evidence on the growth of arms sales by firms. The empirical analysis is largely based on the annual estimates SIPRI makes of the 100 largest arms producing companies. The final section has some concluding comments.

I.   Policy Context

World military expenditures and arms exports peaked in the middle 1980s, fell gradually at first with improving East-West relations, then fell rapidly with the disintegration of the Soviet Union. BVC (2000), previously ACDA, estimates that world military expenditure fell at about 6% per annum in real terms over the decade 1987-1997, -7.3% a year in the developed world and -0.9% a year in the developing world. The most dramatic fall was in the former Soviet Union. The arms trade dropped by a half between the 1987 all time high of $81.5 billion and the 1994 trough of $42.2 bn (in 1997 prices), rising to $54.6bn in 1997. The Asian crisis of 1997 subsequently hit arms sales, since this was an area where demand had been strong. Procurement of weapons also fell sharply. SIPRI (2000) estimate that arms production (domestic demand plus exports minus imports) in 1997 was 56% of its 1987 level in the US, 77% in France and 90% in the UK.

Production for the military is not homogeneous. It consists of a whole range of products, from small arms to large complicated weapon systems as well as material that is not directly military. Here we will emphasise major weapons systems. These have particular characteristics that have over the years have led to particular corporate structures. They involve high fixed R&D costs financed by the governments and fairly short production runs with steep learning curves. Production is concentrated in relatively few states, in contrast to small arms production, which is relatively standard and widely dispersed (Dunne, 1995). In addition, many of the components that go into the major weapons systems are commercial 'off-the-shelf' (COTS) products, produced by manufacturers would not see themselves as part of the arms industry. Indeed, the use of standard commercial components is an increasing feature of the industry.

The high fixed R&D costs and the steep learning curves, with costs falling sharply with each further unit produced, mean that major weapons producers can gain economies of scale and that their minimum efficient scale is large relative to the size of the market. This means that, on the one hand, governments have been concerned that the drop in demand following the Cold War would drive firms below their minimum efficient scale, but. On the other hand competition helps keep down prices and to stimulates innovation by firms. This tension between the benefits of scale and the benefits of competition has been the central defence industrial policy dilemma for the last 40 years. A discussion of the structure at the end of the Cold War can be found in Smith (1990).

The end of the Cold War produced not just a quantitative change in the amount of weapons required, but a qualitative change in the type of weapons required. During the Cold War planning was straightforward, it was fairly clear where, how, and with whom war would be fought if it came. After the Cold War there is much less certainty, though it became apparent that the Cold War weapons that made up the bulk of the NATO inventory are unlikely to be what is required. Given the long leads times and the commitments made by government bodies, research teams and companies, there are still pressures to continue to produce these weapons systems and to find roles for them. There has, however, been a clear and important qualitative change in the nature of technology. There were two aspects to this. First, investments in military technology paid off and some, though not all, smart precision-guided weapons actually met the promises that had long been made for them. The power of these, mainly US, technologies was demonstrated in the Gulf. Second, the relative positions of military and civilian technology were reversed. From the end of World War II to the 1980s, military technology had tended to be in advance of civilian technology, but by the 1990s in many areas, particularly electronics, military technology lagged the civilian sector. This was largely because the long lead times involved in military procurement meant that much of the technology was obsolete before the system came into service. Eurofighter, a 1980s design, is not even in service yet. Whereas in the past the spin-off of military technology to the civilian sector was the focus of concern and an important argument for the value of military production, now the focus is more on spinning-in civilian technology to the military. Many areas of technology which were once the preserve of the military and security services, such as cryptography, are now dominated by commercial applications. Fitting civilian technology into military applications can be difficult as the UK found in developing a new tactical radio for the army. Fortunately, when in action UK troops can supplement the heavy 1970s radios issued to them, with their personal mobile phones.

Traditionally, because the state, which had strong national preferences, was the customer, major countries largely relied on their domestic defence industries. Unlike most manufacturing industries, which went multinational, the arms industry remained national. Smaller countries which could not afford the large fixed costs imported major weapons systems. With the fall in demand, the ability of even the major countries to maintain a domestic defence industrial base was called into question. Governments had to decide whether to allow mergers and acquisitions which would reduce competition and in particular whether to allow mergers and acquisitions which involved foreign partners. They were also in a situation where the change in the security environment made it harder to justify previous levels of support for the industry and 'competitive procurement policies aimed at value for money were introduced in a number of countries (Dunne and Macdonald, 2002).

The most striking change in industrial policy was in the US. During the Cold War industrial planning was undertaken through the Pentagon, but implicitly. In 1993 a merger wave was stimulated by the 'last supper' when the Pentagon Deputy Secretary Perry told a dinner of defence industry executives that they were expected to start merging. It ended when the Pentagon decided it had gone far enough and blocked the merger of Lockheed Martin with Northrop Grumman in early 1997 (Markusen and Costigan, 1999). This left the four major contractors in Table 5, with more recently, Northrop Grumman taking over aerospace and information technology company TRW to make it the third largest US arms producer after Lockheed Martin and Boeing (SIPRI, 2002).

Table 1:   US Defence Mergers.

Companies in 1993	Year	Companies after 1996
Boeing		
Rockwell		BOEING
McDonnel Douglas	1997	
Lockheed		
Martin Marietta	1994	LOCKHEED MARTIN
GE Aerospace	1992/3	
Loral		
General Dynamics	1992/3	
GM Hughes	1998	
E Systems	1995	RAYTHEON
Raytheon		
Texas Instruments	1997	
Northrop		
Westinghouse	1996	
Grumman	1994	NORTHROP GRUMMAN
TRW	2002	

In Europe the process was more complicated, since restructuring necessarily involved cross-border mergers, which raised political issues. The major players in Europe also had quite different ownership structures, including a substantial degree of state ownership in France. Both factors made a financially driven merger boom of the US type more difficult. Nonetheless, there was an increase in concentration, culminating in the acquisition of GEC defence interests by BAE Systems in the UK and the formation of the EADS (European Aeronautics, Defence and Space) company from DASA (a subsidiary of Daimler) of Germany, Aerospatiale-Matra of France and CASA of Spain. In 2002 the two largest military vehicle producers merged into one, Alvis.

II. The Corporate Options

Faced with the reduction in demand firms had five options on a civilian-military axis: convert, diversify, divest, cooperate or concentrate. Their strategic options were constrained by government's policy towards merger and by the nature of the financial systems within which they operated. In principle, the conversion of plants producing military products into ones producing civilian products was an option, but there are very few examples of a successful conversion strategy over this period. As experience in the post-Vietnam downturn in military demand had shown, conversion is incredibly difficult: the markets and cultures are so different in the military and commercial arenas. Smith and Smith (1992) discuss the difficulties and more general issues of corporate strategy and culture in the arms industry. Diversification involves the development of new commercial activities either through the organic growth of new businesses or the acquisition of existing businesses. This is more likely to work if the firm can build synergies between the military and civil parts of the business. Probably the most impressive piece of diversification was the UK defence company Racal, building the Vodaphone mobile phone business in the late 1980s, which it then spun-off. The remaining defence components of Racal were ultimately sold to Thompson CSF of France, to form the multinational Thales Company. There are far more examples of unsuccessful diversification. British Aerospace bought a construction company, a property company and a car company. There were plausible tactical justifications for each, but they did not work and BAe divested them and became more focussed as a defence company[1]. There was a widespread belief for a while that there were synergies between automobiles and aerospace, particularly defence aerospace, something on which Saab had based its advertising. Ford, General Motors and Daimler had all acquired defence arms. Ford and GM subsequently sold them and Daimler spun off DASA into the merger with Aerospatiale-Matra and CASA to form the multinational European Aeronatics, Defence and Space Company EADS.

Where competition regulations made it possible, divesting defence divisions by selling them to competitors was in many cases an attractive proposition, since they were worth more to the competitor who gained increased monopoly power. In the US General Dynamics was an early exponent of this strategy and shrank itself rapidly and profitably. In the UK, GEC sold its de-

---

[1] Feldman (2000) argues that BAe Enterprises, the venture capital arm had a potential for success that was never achieved because of the change in corporate strategy. Evans and Price (1999) describe that process of change.

fence divisions to BAe in 1999 and turned itself into a purely commercial company, Marconi (which failed spectacularly). Cooperation has always been common in aerospace and defence companies use joint ventures, collaboration and strategic alliances to gain the benefits of scale without losing independence. Wood and Sorenson (2000) describe a number of case studies of military aerospace collaboration. One of the success stories is the long-standing links between the state-owned French aero-engine company SNECMA and GE of the US. Joint ventures can be difficult to manage and companies prefer direct control, when they can get it. This drives the final strategy, concentration on the core weapons business. A group of companies have focused on defence, acquiring the defence divisions others divested, and often shedding civil activities. The concentrating companies, like BAe, have tended to diversify into other weapons systems to allow them to market a full product range rather than into civil.

Companies had realised the need to internationalise and had been acting upon it. Even prior to the present wave of restructuring companies were expanding supply chains internationally, building international joint ventures and taking strategic shares in foreign companies as an alternative to ownership. This trend has clearly accelerate with the support of governments and has led to marked changes in ownership structures. BAE Systems, formerly British Aerospace, now sells more to the US DoD than to the UK MoD and the French company Thales (formerly Thomson CSF), through acquisition of Racal, has become the second largest defence contractor in the UK (Skoens, 1998; SIPRI, 2000).

Both the argument in the previous section about the falling demand and rising fixed costs, and the discussion of the merger wave in this section, suggest increased concentration. Below we measure the increase in concentration using the SIPRI data on the top 100 arms companies, but before that it is useful to consider how economists explain changes in concentration.

III. Explanations of Concentration

Within industrial economics there are a number of approaches to the explanation of the size distributions of firms and the degree of concentration. This discussion follows Sutton (1998). One approach is statistical, following Gibrat's 1931 investigation of how the growth of firms is related to their size. We discuss and use this approach in section 5 and 6. This approach is criticised as being purely statistical, relying on stochastic processes, rather than economic analysis. From the 1950s the standard economic analysis used the structure, conduct performance approach. This started with from the underlying conditions of demand and supply which determined the structure of the industry as represented by, for example, barriers to entry, product differentiation and the degree of concentration. Then it analysed how concentration influenced conduct, e.g. price setting behaviour, choice of advertising intensity etc., and finally how structure and conduct influenced performance, e.g. profitability and consumer welfare. A major criticism of this approach was that features that it took as exogenous barriers to entry, e.g. the nature of the technology were in fact endogenously determined by firms through their R&D for instance. In the case of the arms industry the barriers to entry, national preference by larger states and the large fixed costs required to produce major weapons systems are largely exogenous to the firms involved. This critique of structure, conduct, performance, led to a range of game theory models, in which in the first stage firms determined their R&D or other sunk costs and then in the second stage competed with prices, given their first stage investments. The difficulty with such game theory models is that their predictions are very sensitive to assumptions about unobservable features of the environment, e.g. exactly how entry can happen.

In various work, Sutton suggests an alternative approach based on both game theory models and statistical assumptions. His approach differs from the usual approach in that it does not try to predict a unique equilibrium for the game or the whole size distribution, but to provide a lower bound on the concentration that one might observe in the market. It is based on the assumption that any observed industry is built up from a range of sub-markets. In the international arms industry the sub-markets are defined by the individual weapons and countries. He shows that certain basic principles, e.g. firms make enough profits to cover their fixed costs and no viable sub-market will be left unexploited, provide restrictions on the set of possible Nash equilibria that can be maintained and these restrictions provide a lower bound to concentration. In addition, fairly weak conditions on whether incumbents or entrants will meet a new sub-market opportunity also provides a lower bound. The independent sub-markets models gives a lower bound on concentration of

$$c_k = \frac{k}{n}\left[1 - \ln(\frac{k}{n})\right]$$

where c_k is the lower bound for the k firm concentration ratio and n is the total number of firms in the sample.

In general, the bound will depend on the nature of the linkages between the sub-markets and the strategies of the firms. Two parameters play an important role in these strategies. The first is σ, which measures the degree of linkage between submarkets. This linkage could come from substitution between products, with $\sigma = 0$ implying they are not substitutes and $\sigma = 1$ that they are perfect substitutes, or it could come from economies of scope. The internationalisation of the market during the 1990s is likely to have increased σ and this will tend to increase the lower bound on concentration. In this context government policies of national preference can be seen as inhibiting economic forces that would tend to increase concentration and the increased concentration observed over the 1990s reflects adjustment towards a more natural level of concentration as government obstacles were removed. The second important parameter is β, the elasticity of fixed and sunk costs to quality, in the relationship introduced above, where fixed costs are Fu^{β} and $u \geq 1$ is a measure of product quality. From these Sutton derives another parameter α (a function of β and σ) which is an escalation parameter: it measures how much extra sales one can make by outspending competitors on R&D. None of these parameters are directly observable, but they have implications for observables such as the R&D sales ratio and the degree of homogeneity of the industry.

Normally in highly R&D intensive industries, like defence, one would expect β to be low because the extra quality obtained per unit of R&D is high, making it profitable to invest in R&D. But this argument applies to R&D chosen by firms to give them a competitive advantage. In the arms industry R&D is chosen by governments to give them a military advantage. They may still invest even if it required a large R&D expenditure to give a small improvement in quality, because that small difference in quality could make the difference between winning and losing in combat. Within Sutton's framework, a low β combined with a low σ can produce high R&D sales ratios and a low degree of concentration. If this was the case and the fall in military expenditures caused governments to reduce their degree of national preference, this would cause σ to rise and the lower bound on concentration to increase. This would match the case of digital telephone switches analysed in Sutton (1998, ch 5). In the case of switches, however, the mechanism by which concentration increased was an escalation in R&D intensity. This meant switches moved from a low α industry to a high α one driving out the weaker players who could not keep up with the escalation. While there has been some evidence that military R&D expenditures have proved resilient, there has not been obvious R&D escalation of that sort in the defence industry during the 1990s.

The increasing size of fixed costs relative to the market and learning curves both increase the lower bound on concentration, Sutton (1998 ch 7) discusses this effect with respect to turbine generators and they are clearly applicable to the defence industry in the way discussed in section 2. In addition to the exogenous R&D problem, there is another difficulty with Sutton's approach for the defence case. Mergers and acquisitions play no role in the models and in the arms market of the 1990s they are crucial, driving a lot of the concentration.

IV. The Evolution of Concentration

To analyse the changing structure of the arms market the best available source of data is the SIPRI arms company database. SIPRI have collected information on arms sales, total sales, profits and employment for the 100 largest arms-producing companies since 1988. They send questionnaires to companies asking them for the information. In the case of the share of arms in total sales, companies may be unwilling to disclose this and in such cases estimates are used, with the assistance of a network of country experts.

As Table 2 shows the five largest companies in the SIPRI list accounted for 22% of arms production by the top 100 in 1990. This is very close to Sutton's independent sub-market lower bound for the five firm concentration ratio given above, which is 20%, similarly the 10 firm and 15 firm ratios are close to their lower bounds of 33% and 43%. At the end of the Cold War the international arms industry was not very concentrated. It is noticeable that the concentration in total sales was higher than in arms sales: commercial markets are more concentrated than military markets even though the commercial markets these firms were operating in were very different. In 2002, the five largest arms firms accounted for 40% of the total. This large increase in the share of the top companies is continued further down the sizes, as shown for the largest 10, 15, and 20. There was also an increase in concentration for total sales, but not by as much, since it started from a higher base. It is also interesting to note that in terms of total sales, including civil products, concentration was higher in 1990 than for arms sales and rose considerably less, leaving arms and total sales measures very similar in 2000. This may well reflect an increasing specialisation on defence sales by the major players.

Table 2:   Concentration.

Percentage share:	1990 % Arms	1995 % Arms	2000 % Arms	1990 % Total	1995 % Total	2000 % Total
Largest 5	22	28	42	33	34	40
Largest 10	37	42	58	51	53	57
Largest 15	48	53	66	61	65	68
Largest 20	57	61	72	69	73	76

One would expect an increase in concentration following a fall in demand, but this does seem a rather large increase given the size of the fall in demand. What seems more likely is that by its nature major weapons systems would naturally be a very concentrated market like pharmaceuticals, civil airliners, etc., but that the role of the national governments in attempting to maintain national defence capabilities has been to prevent the inevitable concentration. If the increase in concentration is to be seen as an adjustment to some equilibrium market structure, then this would be reflected in the dynamics of the sample. We would expect to find that the growth of the firms showed no clear pattern that suggested strategic successes of companies, but a general change across the whole size distribution.

The degree of change in the international arms industry is further illustrated in Table 3, which presents the arms sales data for companies that were in the top 10 in 1990 and or 2000. The change in the companies making up the top ten arms producers (in terms of arms sales) in 1990 and 2000, reflects the mergers that took place, in the industry. The degree of concentration that took place is also clear. The share of the top ten in the top 100 increased from 38% to 56%, with the average size of a top 100 company declining from $187 billion to $158 billion, while the top 3 companies almost doubled their arms sales.

Table 3: Change in the International Arms Industry.

			1990	2000	1990	2000	%Change
1	McDonnel Douglas	USA	1	-	9890	-	-
2	BAE Systems	UK	2	3	8710	14400	65.3
3	General Dynamics	USA	3	6	8300	6520	-21.4
4	Lockheed Martin	USA	4	1	7500	18610	148.1
5	General Motors	USA	5	49	7380	540	-92.7
6	General Electric	USA	6	20	6450	1600	-75.2
7	Raytheon	USA	7	4	5500	10100	83.6
8	Thales	Fr	8	8	5252	5160	-1.8
9	Boeing	USA	9	2	5100	16900	231.4
10	Northrop Grumman	USA	10	5	4930	6660	35.1
11	United Technologies	USA	13	11	4100	2880	-29.8
12	Litton	USA	19	9	3000	3950	31.7
13	TRW	USA	20	10	2980	3370	13.1

Developing the analysis to consider a wider set of companies we consider all companies that were in the top 100 list between 1990 and 1998. When computing growth rates over the period, however, only companies alive over that period can be considered. There are also missing values for some of the variables for some of the companies and hence the sample sizes will differ when we provide descriptive statistics for each of the variables. Starting from a list of companies that were in the top 100 in one or both of the years gave a sample of 125 companies. This includes companies that 'died' before 1998, companies that were 'born' after 1990, subsidiary companies and companies that have missing information. Taking out the companies that are subsidiaries owned by companies in the Top 100 and looking at only those companies that were alive in 1990, left us with a sample of 100 in that year of which 81 survived to 1998.

This sample shows an increase in concentration in Table 4. There was an increase in the average share of both arms sales and total sales between the two years as well as a marked increase in the spread of the distribution of shares, represented by the coefficient of variation. The Herfindahl index of concentration more than doubled for arms sales, increasing a little less for total sales.

Table 4:   Concentration Measures.

All companies	1990 Arms	1990 Sales	1998 Arms	1998 Sales
Number of companies	98	92	78	81
Average ($1995)	1875.4	11607.4	1808.9	14436.1
Coeff of Variation	1.09	1.61	1.80	1.98
Herfindahl	0.022	0.039	0.054	0.069
Survivors	Arms 1990	Arms 1998	Sales 1990	Sales 1998
Number of companies	63	63	60	60
Average ($1995)	1864.9	1634.0	11913.9	15500.2
Coeff of variation	1.09	1.59	1.67	1.98
Herfindahl	0.034	0.055	0.063	0.081

As Table 5 shows the fall in average arms sales over the period was just over 28%, but that this fall was not reflected in total sales, which grew by 7%, with employment falling by 25%. The average fall in the share of arms sales in total sales reported by SIPRI was 7%. The growth in arms sales was computed using the log difference between the two years which left a sample of 65 companies, the other computations differ in the number of companies included because of missing values.

Table 5: Growth 1990-98.

	Arms	Sales	Employ	Civil	Change in Arms share
Average	-0.284	0.074	-0.250	0.250	-6.6
Min	-2.940	-1.523	-1.233	-1.780	-72.0
Max	49.4	44.2	86.1	53.1	75.0
Coeff of var					
Number co.s	63	60	55	59	65

Table 6 presents a transition matrix that allows an analysis of the movements of companies across size classes over the period. Reading across the rows gives the number of firms in a particular size group in 1990 and down the columns, the number in 1998. Thus the diagonal represents the number of firms that stayed in the same size group over the period. The next to last columns gives the size groups in 1990 of those firms that exited the market prior to 1998. This shows that the majority of companies exiting were in the second and third size class, small to medium producers.

Table 6: Transition Matrix: Arms Sales, $00.

	0-5	5-10	10-20	20-30	30-40	40	Exit	Total
0-5	12	3	0	0	0	0	5	20
5-10	6	10	1	0	0	0	10	27
10-20	2	5	6	1	0	0	10	24
20-30	0	0	1	2	0	1	5	9
30-40	0	0	0	2	2	0	0	4
40	1	1	1	0	0	6	5	14
Total	21	19	9	5	2	7	35	98

Transition Matrix: Total Sales.

	0-1	1-5	5-10	10-15	15-20	20	exit	Total
0-1	9	2	0	0	0	0	3	14
1-5	0	20	0	0	0	0	14	34
5-10	0	1	7	1	0	0	6	15
10-15	0	1	1	0	1	2	3	8
15-20	0	0	0	2	0	2	2	6
20	0	1	0	0	1	9	4	15
Total	9	25	8	3	2	13	32	92

One interesting issue is the degree to which these changes in the size distribution represent changes in corporate strategy. As we have discussed companies could respond to the decline in arms sales by diversifying into civil production, as some did though with mixed success. Alternatively, they could diversify into arms production, which again some did. Classifying the companies as:

- Winners: increasing arms sales and increasing civilian sales.
- Diversifiers: declining arms sales and increasing civilian sales.
- Rearmers: increasing arms sales and decreasing civilian sales.
- Losers: decreasing arms sales and decreasing civilian sales.

Diversifiers could be converting plants, diversifying by organic growth or acquisition or divesting their arms sales. We used estimated civil production of the sample and considered the frequency distribution for these categories both for those companies with increasing arms shares and for those with decreasing arms shares, as shown in Table 7. Interestingly, 9 of the 11 companies that showed both increasing arms sales and increasing civil sales showed a decreasing share in their arms sales, meaning they became less important to the company. The diversifiers make up the largest group and the losers are evenly spread between increasing and decreasing arms shares.

Table 7: Classifying Companies.

	Increasing Arms Share	Decreasing Arms Share	Total
Winners	2	9	11
Diversifiers	0	33	33
Rearmers	6	0	6
Losers	4	3	7
Total	12	45	57
Exits			33
Sum			90

To consider the dynamics of the industry further we need to focus on the growth rates of the companies and to choose a framework for the analysis. This is undertaken in the next section.

V. Econometric Issues

A useful approach for analysing the growth of companies is an empirical analysis within the framework of testing Gibrat's law (Dunne and Hughes, 1994 and 1993; Sutton, 1997; Caves, 1998). This approach was used in the 1970s to analyse the reasons for an observed inexorable rise in concentration of manufacturing industry, which led to concern that this would continue and lead to increasing monopoly power (Hannah and Kay, 1977). In fact as the problem was identified things were already changing and there was a steady rise in the share of smaller firms in total output taking place.

Gibrat's law states that the probability distribution of growth rates was the same for all sizes of firms:

$$\frac{S_{it}}{S_{it-1}} = \varepsilon_{it}.$$

This can be tested by writing it as:

$$\log S_{it} = \alpha + \beta \log S_{it-1} + \varepsilon_{it}$$

and testing if $\beta = 1$. If $\beta < 1$ smaller firms are growing faster than the larger firms and if $\beta > 1$ the larger firms are growing faster than the smaller firms. This can also be reparameterised as a growth rate equation

$$\Delta \log S_{it} = \alpha + (\beta - 1)\log S_{it-1} + \varepsilon_t$$

in this case the test is for the coefficient on $\log S_{it-1}$ to be zero.

Another way of interpreting these regressions is to consider the model in log deviations form. Define

$$y_{it} = \log S_{it} - \log S_t$$

$$\log S_t = N^{-1} \sum_{i=1}^{N} \log S_{it}$$

then

$$y_{it} = \beta y_{it-1} + \varepsilon_{it}.$$

Squaring, summing over i and dividing by N, and taking expected values, noting that ε_{it} is independent of y_{it-1} gives

$$E(\frac{\sum y_{it}^2}{N}) = \beta^2 E(\frac{\sum y_{it-1}^2}{N}) + E(\frac{\sum \varepsilon_{it}^2}{N})$$

which gives the relationship determining the evolution of the variance of log firm size:

$$\sigma_t^2 = \beta^2 \sigma_{t-1}^2 + \sigma_\varepsilon^2.$$

This implies

or
$$1 = \beta^2 \frac{\sigma_{t-1}^2}{\sigma_t^2} + \frac{\sigma_\varepsilon^2}{\sigma_t^2}$$

$$\beta^2 \frac{\sigma_{t-1}^2}{\sigma_t^2} = 1 - \frac{\sigma_\varepsilon^2}{\sigma_t^2}.$$

The right hand side of this equation is the the R^2 of the cross-section regression, so

$$\frac{\sigma_t^2}{\sigma_{t-1}^2} = \frac{\beta^2}{R^2}.$$

This means that the evolution of the variance of log size, a measure of concentration, is determined by the ratio of the R^2 to β^2. Whether the variance increases or decreases depends both on β and the size of the stochastic shocks. If $\beta = 1$, as implied by Gibrat's law the ratio of current to previous variance is $1/R^2$ which must be positive so variance and concentration is increasing through time.

The way the model is formulated it is only possible to include companies that survive over the whole period. However, if the non surviving companies share certain characteristics, such as they are slow growing then this can obviously bias the estimation results. More formally, what we have is:

$$log S_{it} = \alpha + \beta \log S_{it-1} + \varepsilon_{it} \text{ if } S_{it} > 0$$
$$= 0 \text{ otherwise}$$

thus
$$E(\log S_{it} \mid \log S_{it-1}, S_{it} > 0) = \alpha + \beta \log S_{it-1} + E(\varepsilon_{it} \mid S_{it} > 0)$$

with
$$\varepsilon_i N(0, \sigma^2).$$

This can be written as
$$E(\log S_{it} \mid \log S_{it-1}, S_{it} > 0) = \alpha + \beta \log S_{it-1} + \sigma \lambda_i$$

where
$$\lambda_i = \frac{f(V_i)}{1 - F(V_i)} \text{ and } V_i = [\frac{\alpha + \beta \log S_{it-1}}{\sigma}]$$

with $f(..)$ the density function for the standard normal and $F(..)$ the distribution function for the standard normal. If there is sample selection bias and we were to estimate a simple OLS regression omitting $\sigma \lambda_i$ giving biased and inconsistent estimators.

For the two stage procedure let

$$d_i = 1 \text{ when } S_{it} > 0$$
$$d_i = 0 \text{ otherwise}$$

then we can set up a likelihood function
$$L = \Pi_{i=1}^{N} [\Pr(\varepsilon_i - V_i)]^{1-d_i} [\Pr(\varepsilon_i - V_i)]^{d_i}$$
$$= \Pi \; F\left[\frac{V_i}{\sigma}\right]^{d_i} \left\{1 - F\left[\frac{V_i}{\sigma}\right]\right\}^{1-d_i} .$$

As $F(-t) = 1 - F(t)$ this is the likelihood function for the probit estimation on d_i and $E(d_i) = V_i/\sigma$. So we estimate a probit:
$$\Pr(d_i = 1) = P(V_i).$$

Compute V_i and
$$\lambda_i = \left[\frac{f(V_i)}{1 - F(V_i)}\right].$$

For the second stage we use the consistent estimator of λ_i, $\hat{\lambda}_i$ to estimate
$$E(S_{it} | S_{it-1}, S_{it} > 0) = \alpha + \beta S_{it-1} + \sigma \hat{\lambda}_i$$
giving a consistent estimator of β.

It is also possible to use a maximum likelihood method, that uses this consistent estimator as a starting value to search for a solution on the highly non-linear likelihood function:
$$L = \Pi_{d_i=0} F\left(-V_i, \sigma^2\right) \Pi_{d_i=1} \left(S_{it} - V_i, \sigma^2\right)$$
now as $1 - F(-V_i, \sigma^2) = 1 - F(V_i, \sigma^2)$ which we call $1 - F_i$
$$L = \sum_{d_i=0} \ln(1 - F_i) - \frac{N-S}{2} \ln \sigma^2 - \frac{1}{2\sigma^2} \sum_{d_i=1} \left(S_{it} - V_i, \sigma^2\right)$$
which can be solved using an iterative process such as Newton Raphson.

VI. Estimation Results

To use the law of proportionate effects approach the first, 1990, and last year, 1998 of the sample are taken for each company and the following equation is estimated
$$\log S_{it} = \alpha + \beta \log S_{it-1} + \varepsilon_{it} .$$

Both $\log S_i$ in 1990 and in 1998 are close to normal. Skewness in the unconditional distribution in 1990 is 0.51 and in 1998 0.74; kurtosis is 2.48 and 3.00. Given the nature of the companies with their close relation to he national government it would seem worth introducing dummy variables to reflect the ownership of the companies. Dummy variables were created which take the value of one for the major arms producing companies and zero otherwise:

$$logS_{it} = \alpha + \beta \log S_{it-1} + \gamma_1 DUS + \gamma_2 DUK + \gamma_3 DFR + \gamma_4 DGR + \varepsilon_{it}.$$

As both an observation for 1990 and 1998 are needed for this regression only the companies that survive for the whole period and do not have missing values for the relevant variable in either year are included. For arms sales this gives around 84 observations and for total sales about ten fewer observations. The results are presented in Table 8.

Table 8: Estimates for Surviving Companies (dependent variable log sales).

N=63 for arms, N=60 for total.

	α	β	γ_1	γ_2	γ_3	γ_4
Arms	0.53	0.88	−0.18	0.48	−0.04	0.21
(t)	0.77	8.53	−1.16	2.96	−0.26	1.31
Total	0.05	0.99	0.07	−0.13	0.02	0.54
(t)	0.27	24.08	0.49	−0.75	0.13	2.74

The total equation fits better with an $\overline{R}^2$ of 0.91 compared to 0.65 for the arms sales. The hypothesis that $\beta = 1$ cannot be rejected in either case (with t ratio of −1.11 for arms sales and -0.22 for total sales). There was some evidence of heteroscedasticity, so robust standard errors were used. These results do seem to support the hypothesis that the probability distribution of growth rates was the same for all sizes of firms. There are, however, some country specific effects, though the only significant coefficients on the dummies are for the UK in the total sales regression and Germany in total sales. The results suggest a growth in concentration in the sample of companies, but with no difference in growth rates across size classes. This is true for both arms sales and total sales. There is some evidence that the UK companies had a higher growth rate than the other countries in total sales and Germany a higher growth in total sales. There is no evidence of any US specific effect. This is somewhat strange given the rapid concentration in the

US. However, separate regressions on the US and non US samples for the 59 companies with both total sales and arms sales data in both periods suggests some differences. For the US companies the estimate of β, (standard error of β) was 0.78 (0.21) with a standard error of regression of 0.87, for non-US companies the estimates were 0.98 (0.07), with a standard error of regression of 0.39. Non-US firms stayed the same, small US firms grew relatively faster, size of arms sales in 1990 predicted size in 1998 much better for the non US firms than for the US firms. This difference deserves further investigation but we will return to the combined sample.

As we have discussed it is possible for the results to be biased by sample selection effects. Estimating a probit model with survive/not survive as the dependent variable and the value of the size variable in 1990 proved to be a rather poor model. As it is possible that survival may be a nonlinear function of size a squared term was entered

$$\Pr(d_i = 1) = \Phi(\delta_1 + \delta_2 s_{it-1} + \delta_3 s_{it-1}^2).$$

This worked better though the probabilities are still poorly defined, especially for the arms sales, as shown in Table 9. Investigation of the factors that determine survival requires further investigation.

Table 9: Probit Survival Estimates.

	N	Survive	δ_1	δ_2	δ_3
Arms	100	65	10.5	-2.73	0.18
(t)			1.19	-1.12	1.10
Total	97	63	9.43	-2.09	0.12
(t)			1.72	-1.63	1.60

Using these probit results to provide the Mills ratio for the sample selection procedure gave the results in Table 10.

Table 10: Sample Selection Estimates.

N=65 for Arms N=63 for Total

	α	β	γ_1	γ_2	γ_3	γ_4	σ	$\bar{R}^2$	$\frac{\beta^2}{R^2}$	$t_{\beta=1}$
Arms	0.38	0.86	-0.17	0.52	-0.05	0.22	0.60	0.65	1.07	-1.36
(t)	0.54	8.11	-0.89	1.97	-0.22	0.78	0.53			
Total	0.14	1.00	0.08	-0.12	0.04	0.55	-0.21	0.90	1.09	-0.07
(t)	0.35	22.2	0.58	-0.60	0.19	2.62	-0.40			

In none of the four cases is sigma significantly different from zero, suggesting that the results are not sensitive to sample selection bias over this period. These estimates from the Heckman two stage procedure are consistent, but not fully efficient. As outlined above maximum likelihood estimates can be obtained from LIMDEP, which use the Heckman procedure to provide starting values and these are presented in Table 11. The results are little different to the previous ones, apart from γ_2 the UK dummy coefficient becoming insignificant in the arms sales equation.

Table 11: Maximum Likelihood Estimates.

	N	δ_1	δ_2	δ_3
Arms	98	11.3	-2.96	0.20
(t)		1.30	-1.26	1.24
Total	92	3.11	-0.66	0.04
(t)		0.52	-0.48	0.49

	α	β	γ_1	γ_2	γ_3	γ_4	σ	ρ	$t_{\beta=1}$
Arms	0.49	0.88	-0.18	0.49	-0.04	0.22	0.57	0.24	-1.28
(t)	0.55	9.24	-0.64	1.14	-0.11	0.42	4.27	0.13	
Total	0.16	1.03	0.18	-0.04	0.04	0.59	0.60	-0.96	0.19
(t)	0.25	15.0	0.96	-0.16	0.15	2.32	8.26	-20.6	

Sales of arms and total sales may interact. To allow for this we introduce, lagged total sales, S in the arms sales, A, equation and lagged arms sales in the total sales equation. This gives the equations:

$$\log A_{it} = \alpha + \beta \log A_{it-1} + \delta S_{it-1} + \gamma_1 DUS + \gamma_2 DUK + \gamma_3 DFR + \gamma_4 DGR + \varepsilon_{1,it}$$

$$\log S_{it} = \alpha + \beta \log S_{it-1} + \delta A_{it-1} + \gamma_1 DUS + \gamma_2 DUK + \gamma_3 DFR + \gamma_4 DGR + \varepsilon_{2,it}.$$

The results are given in Table 12.

Table 12: Explaining log Sales, N=59.

	α	β	δ	γ_1	γ_2	γ_3	γ_4
Arms	0.61	0.90	−0.02	−0.20	0.48	0.03	0.22
(t)	0.75	10.0	−0.29	−1.22	2.81	0.19	1.29
Total	0.56	1.05	−0.15	0.15	−0.07	0.10	0.63
(t)	1.39	21.7	−1.96	0.99	−0.36	0.77	2.95

As before, the total sales equation fits much better than the arms sales equation, $\bar{R}^2 = 0.91$ against 0.61 for arms. The hypothesis that the coefficient of the lagged dependent variable is unity is not rejected in either case, $t(\beta = 1) = -1.15$ for arms and 1.05 for total sales. Lagged total sales is negative but not significant in the arms sales equation, lagged arms sales is negative and significant in the total sales equation. Companies with large relative arms sales in 1990 grew slower than other companies of the same size. When the arms sales equation is split by US and non-US as before, the the non-US relationship continues to have a much smaller standard error, total sales have a significant positive effect for non-US companies. For US companies total sales have a negative and insignificant effect, but including them raises β to just above unity, rather than 0.78 when they are excluded.

Conclusions

At the end of the Cold War, the international arms industry was relatively unconcentrated by comparison with comparable high technology industries like commercial aerospace or pharmaceuticals. In fact it was quite close to the Sutton lower bound. The main reason for this was probably the tendency for the major military powers to prefer to procure from national defence industries. The decline in the total size of the market and the tendency for R&D requirements for major weapons systems to rise produced an increase in concentration, with the five firm concentration ratio rising from just over 20% to over 40%. The way concentration increased differed in the US and Europe. However, the industry is still not very concentrated by comparison with comparable industries and the economics suggest that concentration will continue. This is likely to raise some difficult political issues as countries face powerful international arms monopolies. The econometric work we conducted did not reject the hypothesis that for a company its growth rate of arms sales was independent of its initial level of arms sales, but there is clearly scope for further work.

References

Brzoska, Michael, and Lock, Peter., eds., (1992), *Restructuring of Arms Production in Western Europe*, Stockholm International Peace Research Institute and Oxford University Press, Oxford.

BVC (2000), Bureau of Verification and Compliance, *World Military Expenditure and Arms Transfers*, 1998, US Department of State.

Caves, R E (1998) Industrial Organisation and New Findings on the Turnover and Mobility of Firms, *Journal of Economic Literature*, Vol. XXXVI, December, pp1947-1982.

Dunne, Paul, and Alan Hughes (1994), Age, Size, Growth and Survival: UK Companies in the 1980s, *Journal of Industrial Economics*, Vol XLII, No 2, June, 1994, pp 115-40.

Dunne, Paul, and Alan Hughes (1993), The Changing Structure of Competitive Industry in the 1980s Chapter 4 in Driver and Dunne (eds) (1993) *Structural Change in the UK Economy*, pp 80-117.

Dunne, Paul and Gordon MacDonald (2002), "Procurement in the Post Cold War World: A Case Study of the UK", Chapter in Claude Serfati (ed) *"The Future of European Arms Production"*. Cost A10 Action, European Community Office for Official Publication, Brussels.

Dunne, Paul (1995) The Defence Industrial Base, Chapter 14 in Keith Hartley and Todd Sandler (eds) (1995) *Handbook of Defense Economics*, Elsevier, pp 592-623.

Evans, Richard and Colin Price (1999), *Vertical Take-off*, Nicolas Brealey Publishing, London.

Feldman (2000), *The Rise and Fall of British Aerospace Enterprises*, Mimeo, National Institute for Working Life, Stockholm, Sweden.

Hannah and Kay (1977) *Concentration in Modern Industry: Theory, Measurement and the UK Experience*, Macmillan, London.

Kirkpatrick, David (1995) The Rising Unit Costs of Defence Equipment: The Reason and the Results, *Defence and Peace Economics*, 6 (4), 263-288.

Levine Paul and Ron Smith (2000) Arms Export Controls and Proliferation, *Journal of Conflict Resolution*, 44, 6, 885-895.

Markusen, Ann (1997) *Understanding American Defence Industry Mergers*. Paper presented to a conference on the Globalisation of the Defence Industry and the Arms Trade, Middlesex University Business School, September 1997.

Markusen, Ann R and Sean S Costigan (eds)(1999) *Arming the Future: A Defense Industry for the 21st Century*, Council on Foreign Relations Press, New York.

Martin, Steven, R. White, and Keith Hartley (1996), Defence and Firm Performance In the UK, *Defence and Peace Economics*, 7, 325-337.

SIPRI (various years) *Armaments, Disarmament and International Security*, Stockholm International Peace Research Institute, Oxford University Press.

Skoens, E. et al (1998) Arms Production. Chapter in SIPRI Yearbook 1998, Oxford University Press.

Smith, Ron (1990) Defence Procurement and Industrial Structure in the UK, *International Journal of Industrial Organisation*, 8, pp185-205.

Smith, Ron and Dan Smith (1992) Corporate Strategy, Corporate Culture and Conversion; Adjustment in the Defence Industry, *Business Strategy Review*, Summer 1992, 45-58.

Sutton J (1997) Gibrat's Legacy, *Journal of Economic Literature*, Vol. XXXV, December, pp 40-59.

Sutton, J. (1998) *Technology and Market Structure*, MIT Press.

Wood, Pia Christina and David S Sorenson (eds) (2000) *International Military Aerospace Collaboration*, Ashgate Publishing Aldershot.

Acknowledgements

We are grateful to SIPRI for the use of their data, in particular to Elisabeth Skoens and Reihilde Weidacher. The conclusions we draw are, however, our own and should not be attributed to SIPRI. Smith is grateful to the ESRC for support under grant L138251003, and the others under grant R00239388.

Chapter 6
ARMAMENTS GROUPS AND THE FINANCIAL MARKETS: AN "UNLIMITED WARFARE" CONVENTION IN THE MAKING?

Luc Mampaey, Claude Serfati

Introduction

This article analyses the role of finance in the transformation of the US military-industrial system (MIS) and its new configuration at the beginning of the 21st century. The term "system" is proposed as it implies an entity that is composed of interdependent elements and has a reproductive logic of its own. This approach was developed in previous work on the "French armaments meso-system" [Chesnais and Serfati, 1990; Serfati, 1995; Mampaey, 2001]. It goes beyond an approach based on industrial "sectors" (or branches of industry). A sectoral focus does not permit an accurate portrayal of the unique nature of armaments production as regards both its customer (a sole buyer or monopsony) and its place in macroeconomic reproduction (armaments are neither capital goods nor consumer goods). Nor does it reflect the strong intermeshing of industrial groups and state institutions. The American MIS is dominated by four components: the armaments groups and firms, the Department of Defense (DoD), Congress and the executive. The system is driven by its own power, which has enabled it to take permanent root in the American economy and society and to establish self-reproductive mechanisms there, but also by the present-day capitalist dynamic ("globalization") which assigns the United States a unique role in defending the world order [Serfati, 2001].

The major transformations of the American MIS have taken place in three spheres. The institutional shareholders and the "financial community" have played an active part in the restructuring and the strategies of the big armaments groups; today, they have very clear majority control in that respect. Secondly, the relationship between military and civil technologies has changed (notably as regards information and communications technologies) in a way that provides new opportunities for the armaments groups. Finally, the political institutions (particularly those answering to the executive) have greatly strengthened their relations with the industrial groups, particularly since the election of George W. Bush, and even more so since 11 September 2001. These "internal" transformations of the MIS are part of a new international economic and geopolitical context. US national security doctrine, formulated under the Clinton administration but finalised in 2002, takes account of this by placing democracy and the defence of the free market and free trade at the heart of the country's "vital interests". On this basis, it justifies the preventive – in other words, *discretionary* – use of military force [The White House, 2002]. The authors of the present paper believe that the transformations within the MIS are far-reaching enough to justify the assertion that, for the armaments industry, the period that began with the Second World War has now ended. The hypothesis advanced in this article is that the American military-security system, whose development has greatly accelerated since 9/11, results from this combination of internal transformations within the MIS and shifts in international relations.

This article will first demonstrate that the very important merger and acquisition trend of the 1990s was organised in close correspondence with the demands of the "markets" and the recommendations of the financial analysts. The industrial restructuring led to the creation of mega-groups. The aim of this vertical integration was to narrow down access to Pentagon contracts. The great majority of these moves were accepted by the competition authorities - a direct breach of the principles (and theory) upon which such decisions are supposed to be based (maintenance of competition, industrial efficiency etc.). The second part of this article will analyse the financial performance of the US defence groups. The indicators cited will show that these groups provide handsome rewards for their leaders and shareholders. Obviously, they are not at all in the same bracket as the junk bond firms or the dotcoms whose ratings and temporary gains often depended on the number of times they were clicked by surfers. The big armaments groups are built on much more solid "fundamentals". The emphasis on security, a much broader concept than "defence", led to the creation of the Department of Homeland Security in 2002. This is the opening of a new phase of *political centralization* which may prove just as important as the threshold that was crossed with the creation of the Department of Defense (DoD) at the end of World War II. With security concerns now so much to the fore, the defence groups also have new opportunities to develop information and security technologies. The "social bloc" formed by finance, armaments and politics is fostering the emergent military-security system. The conclusion to this article will look at how the financial markets are beginning to assume that new wars and military operations are inevitable and are thus, in a way, forging a consensus of "unlimited warfare". This "convention" - whose essence, according to John Maynard Keynes, "lies in assuming that the existing state of affairs will continue indefinitely, except in so far as we have specific reasons to expect a change"[2] – is based not on self-referential mimicry but on the hope that military supremacy will, for as long as possible, shelter the American economy from the consequences of production and consumption patterns which are "unsustainable" for a large portion of the planet.

I. Industrial Restructuring Under the Thumb of Finance

I.1. Finance Moves Into Armaments

Changes in the ownership of big companies are one of the major characteristics of the past 25 years [Plihon, 2000]. Investment funds (mutual and pension funds) have become the main shareholders in industrial production groups. US domination of this field is very strong. In the OECD countries in 1998, 60% of the assets of institutional shareholders (meaning investment funds, insurance companies and a few other financial institutions) were of American origin.

Box 1 : A New Stock Exchange Identity for Armaments.

Investors' new infatuation with the armaments industry, since the collapse of the "new economy" and even more so since the 9/11 attacks, is reflected in the decision of several exchanges to establish separate indexes exclusively for the arms sector. The Amex Defense Index (DFI), launched on 21 September 2001 by the American Stock Exchange (Amex), is a response to this investor expectation. It contains 15 stocks (see Table 1), including the five top-ranking contractors, Lockheed Martin, Boeing, Raytheon, Northrop Grumman and General Dynamics. The DFI is a very broad sample of the highly capitalised firms in the armaments sector.

We estimate that the firms in the DFI represent around 80% of the DoD's spending on procurement and RTD&E, and that they are therefore sufficiently representative of the sector as a whole. For the purposes of our analysis, the DFI is compared with broader-based indexes, namely Standard & Poor's 500 (S&P500), the Nasdaq and the Dow Jones Industrial Average, or with sectoral indexes.

Institutional shareholders were very active in the restructuring implemented by the US armaments industry during the 1990s. Today, they have a massive presence among shareholders of the prime contractor groups. Table 1 shows

---

[2] John M. Keynes, *The General Theory of Employment, Interest and Money*, Chapter 12, Section 4.

the shareholder structure of the 15 defence groups that make up the Amex Defense Index (DFI). It should be noted that the institutional investors control a considerably larger proportion of the capital within the DFI than in the firms on the S&P500 index. On average, the institutional investors hold a 65.33% share in the S&P500 firms, but an average of 79.24% in the 15 firms making up the DFI, and more than 80% in 7 of these DFI companies. In Lockheed Martin, the world's leading armaments producer, the institutional investors' holding is all of 95%. None of the companies which make up the Major Market index (the 20 "blue-chip", or XMI) is controlled to this extent by institutional investors (the XMI average is 66.08%).

Such data on the holdings of the main US investment management institutions take account only of their direct holdings in the armaments groups. To these should be added their holdings via the funds that they manage. The financial institutions have, in fact, developed many relationships which take the form of shareholdings, delegated management mandates etc. The lack of transparency due to the intermeshing of financial networks and the density of non-commercial (interpersonal) links between the institutions does nothing to heighten this awareness.

Table 1: Ownership Structure of Armaments Groups in the US.

Name	Symbol	% Capital Held by Institutional Investors 3-mai-05
Amex Defense Index (DFI)		
Lockheed Martin Corporation	LMT.N	95,00%
FLIR Systems Inc.	FLIR.O	95,00%
Drs Technologies Inc.	DRS.N	92,91%
Alliant Techsystems Inc.	ATK.N	89,16%
Northrop Grumman Corporation	NOC.N	85,94%
Stewart & Stevenson Svcs Inc.	SVC.N	84,90%
The Titan Corporation	TTN.N	81,48%
General Dynamics Corporation	GD.N	79,08%
EDO Corporation	EDO.N	78,70%
L-3 Communications Hldgs Inc.	LLL.N	78,47%
United Industrial Corporation	UIC.N	75,79%
Raytheon Co.	RTN.N	74,01%
Boeing Co.	BA.N	66,33%
Rockwell Collins Inc.	COL.N	61,21%
Engineered Support Systems Inc.	EASI.O	50,59%
Amex Defense Index (DFI) *average*	^DFI	79,24%
Major Market Index (XMI) *average*	^XMI	66,08%
S&P 500 *average*	^GSPC	65,33%

Note: The table is based on the DFI index composition in May 2005, i.e. before the acquisition of Titan by L-3 Communications (August 2005), the acquisition of Engineered Support Systems by DRS Technologies (January 2006) and the acquisition of Steward & Stevenson by Armor Holdings Inc. (May 2006).
Sources: *The Wall Street Journal* and *Reuters*.

I.2. Vertical Concentration and Relational Power

The continuous decline in military spending since 1986 (and which went on until 1998) convinced the Department of Defense (DoD) that it could no longer guarantee contracts to as a high a number of prime contractors as in the "fat years" of the Reagan administration. So in January 1993, DoD Deputy Secretary William J. Perry called together the leaders of the main groups and asked them to merge their activities. The result was particularly spectacular, as Figure 1 shows.

Figure 1: Concentrations in the US Armaments Industry, 1993-2006.

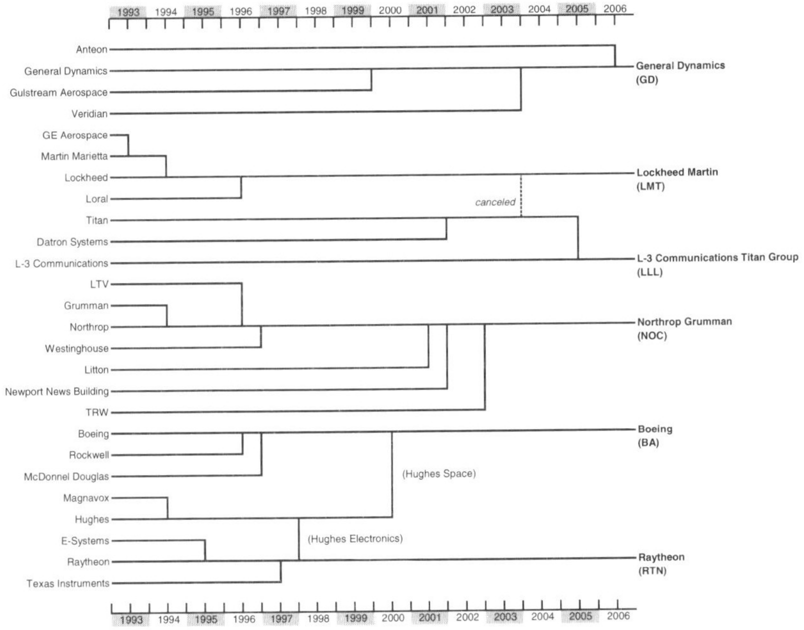

Source: Table adapted and supplemented by the authors, on the basis of *The Economist*, 20 July 2002.

The DoD left the concentration process up to the shareholders – at least, it did so until, in 1998, the Department of Justice issued an unfavourable opinion on Lockheed Martin's plans to acquire Northrop Grumman for US$8.3bn. Since 2001, mergers between major contractors have accelerated again, with Northrop Grumman's acquisition of Newport News Building and TRW, in 2002, at respectively $2.6bn and $7.8bn, and the acquisition of Veridian by General Dynamics in 2003 (at $1.2bn.). In 2005, L-3 Communications acquired Titan for $2.65bn. More recently, General Dynamics announced the acquisition of Anteon ($2.2bn), DRS bought Engineered Support Systems ($1.88bn) and Armor Holdings acquired Stewart & Stevenson ($755m).

The institutions that make up finance capital have thus, with the consent of the DoD, been active agents of the concentration process within the armaments industry. The institutional investors have been assisted by firms of analysts and advisers, the investment banks and the "shapers of sentiment" on the financial markets (for an analysis of the new configuration of US finance capital resulting from the see Roturier et Serfati, 2003]. The objective was to maximise the value that could be added to stocks by ceding/acquiring assets. More and more industrial groupings were cobbled together. The "financial community" worked up an enthusiasm for this "industrial meccano", altogether worthy of the one put together in France over the past three decades by state agencies and the CEOs of groups (whether nationalised or not). Top group executives also helped to assemble this meccano, which provided them with major financial incentives (stock options, amongst other things).

In the period 1992-2002, the value of merger and acquisition operations reached $136bn [SIPRI, 2003, updated by the authors]. Advisers and executives advocated strengthening the vertical integration of the defence groups, asserting that this would lead to greater industrial and technological efficiency. At the beginning of the 1990s, arms production saw many moves towards disengagement from activities considered non-core. Groups involved mainly in automotive production (General Motors, Ford, Chrysler) and IT and electronics (IBM, Unisys, Texas Instruments, General Electric), as well as certain groups that are very much present in other public markets, such as Westinghouse (nuclear and engineering) and ATT (telecommunications), ceded their defence assets. These were acquired mainly by the big arms system integrating groups, who are the main suppliers to the DoD. Thus, the concentration process within the US armaments industry was vertical, since these groups, which design and assemble armaments systems, bought subsystems and complex components.

Does this process match the conclusions drawn in the literature on business management? That literature emphasised that, since the beginning of the 1980s, a strategic objective of the groups was to "recentre" on the trades that make up their "basic skills". This recentring process went through three stages: disengagement from activities regarded as secondary or unprofitable during the 1980s, then external growth and, finally, transnational concentrations [Batsch, 2002]. The vertical-type concentration observed in the armaments industry brings together within a single whole such different skills as those needed for systems integration, the production of equipment which itself is of many different types (electronics, propulsers etc.) and finally the production of modules (or "components"). It does not correspond to the dominant strategic model, unless one considers that the technological chain of arms production as a whole is in itself a specific trade, which would explain the "recentring" on "armaments trades" by the contractor groups and others' disengagement from these trades. This would come down to recognising as a discrete activity not only systems integration but also subsystem production and even the production of the modules that the integrating groups have acquired.

Once again, it may be seen that technological trajectories are largely determined by institutional factors and the action of social groups [Serfati. 2001a]. And indeed, the academic literature has not failed to emphasise, in contradiction to this vertical integration, that since the 1990s, technologies designed and produced for civil purposes have frequently been applied to the production of components and subsystems integrated into the new generations of armaments systems[3]. "Dual technologies" (for both military and civil production) became a common topic during the 1990s. Some even expressed the belief that these technologies, together with other factors (for example, reforms in procurement) would lead to the gradual dissolution of the military-industrial systems. A kind of MIS attrition through "technological obsolescence", with the civil firms taking over on the frontiers of technology.

In fact, the priority placed on vertical concentration by the contractor groups reflected, rather more prosaically, a wish to strengthen what industrial economics calls "market power". Control over the whole of the technological chain needed for production of armaments systems strengthens the barriers to the entry of possible competitors. It makes it very difficult for new integrating groups to emerge which might achieve the status of top-rank contractors. Thus, it places civil firms, which are producing often complex subsystems, in a position of dependence vis-à-vis their defence group clients. Yet the biggest profit margins are generated by systems integration activities. They are based at least as much on technological and organisational skills as on the cosiness and opacity produced by the relationship of bilateral monopoly that exists in the defence industry (one seller - the integrating group; and one buyer - the DoD). The top-ranking groups' strengthening of their "relationship power" (a more accurate term than "market power" in this particular industry) was, together with added share value and the fees paid to consultants, the main driving force of this "industrial meccano".

---

[3] Many second-rank suppliers (subsystems) and third-rank suppliers (components) produce both for military and for civil users. At this level, a certain degree of diversification does exist.

I.3. "Re-enclavement" and Industrial Overcapacity

Finally, far from achieving the goal of the discreteness of armaments production, the restructuring of the 1990s led to a "re-enclavement" of the US armaments industry [Markusen, 1997] and led the contractor groups into a very strong dependence on armaments production and on contracts with the Pentagon. The share of the military in their turnover reached considerable proportions for the foremost US armaments groups[4] (Table 2).

Table 2: Revenue, Income and Employment in the Principal US Armaments Groups
(2003, revenue and income in millions of dollars, employment in units).

Name	Symbol	Total Revenue (millions USD) 2003	Defense Revenue (millions USD) 2003	Defense Share (%) 2003	Net Income After Taxes (millions USD) 2003	Employees (units) 2003
Amex Defense Index (DFI)						
Lockheed Martin Corporation	LMT.N	31.824,00	30.097,00	94,57%	1.053,00	130.000
Boeing Co.	BA.N	50.256,00	27.227,81	54,18%	685,00	157.000
Northrop Grumman Corporation	NOC.N	26.396,00	18.839,89	71,37%	758,00	122.600
Raytheon Co.	RTN.N	18.109,00	16.904,40	93,35%	535,00	78.000
General Dynamics Corporation	GD.N	16.369,00	12.591,24	76,92%	982,00	67.600
L-3 Communications Hldgs Inc.	LLL.N	5.061,59	4.369,19	86,32%	277,64	38.700
Alliant Techsystems Inc.	ATK.N	2.366,19	2.102,17	88,84%	120,46	13.100
Rockwell Collins Inc.	COL.N	2.542,00	1.270,00	49,96%	236,00	14.500
The Titan Corporation	TTN.N	1.756,21	1.085,92	61,83%	-13,24	9.900
Drs Technologies Inc.	DRS.N	1.001,25	940,15	93,90%	31,75	3.750
Engineered Support Systems Inc.	EASI.O	572,70	555,20	96,94%	27,67	2.412
EDO Corporation	EDO.N	460,67	414,97	90,08%	13,99	1.931
Stewart & Stevenson Svcs Inc.	SVC.N	1.066,97	404,99	37,96%	25,71	3.600
United Industrial Corporation	UIC.N	310,95	248,76	80,00%	3,86	1.600
FLIR Systems Inc.	FLIR.O	311,98	233,98	75,00%	41,56	480
Total DFI	^DFI	158.404,50	117.285,68	–	4.778,39	645.173

Note: (1) The ranking of the firms is based on the defence revenue.

(2) *ibid.* table 1.

Sources: *Defense News* and *The Wall Street Journal*.

---

[4] The process in the UK is fairly similar. The military activities of the EADS group represent only 20% of its turnover (thanks to production of the Airbus), but in France, this should not be allowed to hide the fact that the main contractors are focussed on the military (starting with Thales).

Promises that the restructuring would bring improvements in industrial performance proved hollow. Even today, the top-ranking contractor groups still have major production overcapacities and, as regards reducing costs to the customer (the Pentagon), their results are far removed from the objectives that served to "legitimise" these mergers [Gholz, Sapolsky, 1999]. Thus, it may be observed that the analysts and management advisers have shown a level of competence rivalled only by the insight that led them to revere Enron as a model of excellence. The restructurings of the armaments groups have, in fact, further worsened their bureaucratic behaviour, while benchmarking studies show they are lagging seriously behind in the industrial efficiency stakes [Velocci. 2003].

At the end of 1996, for fear that these groups might gain excessive power, the DoD set up a working party to look into the issues and consequences surrounding this vertical concentration, which ran counter to established theory. Nonetheless, the DoD went along with the great majority of the requests made (concerning the perplexity that the defence "case" caused amongst the "regulation economists", see Kovacic et Smallwood. 1994). Between March 1994 and August 2001, out of 169 transactions examined by the regulatory authorities in the defence industry, only 2 were turned down, while for 16 others, permission was subject to certain modifications in the merger/acquisition operation. An examination of the mergers/acquisition shows that "in marked contrast to its pursuit of anti-trust challenges in a number of high tech and other cases, the U.S. antitrust authorities have been remarkably hands-off in their treatment of mergers and consolidation in the domestic U.S. defense industry" [Crandall, 2002]. Confidence in industrial "rationality" was summed up thus by the Deputy Under-Secretary in charge of industrial policy, during one of his testimonies to the Armed Services Committee of the House of Representatives: "we believe that the companies are sufficiently motivated by their interest in defense and the commitment of their shareholders to support the innovation and the costs reduction without excessive governmental intervention" [Ciardello, 19 March 2002]. And yet, the remarkable concentration already illustrated in Figure 1 did lead to a strong reduction in the number of contractors per type of equipment and to the formation of groups that are, de facto, in a monopoly position within major segments [GAO, 1998]. This does not seem to have worried the Pentagon, but it delighted the "markets". The institutional shareholders (pension funds, mutual funds), always on the look-out for innovations if they are the kind that might push shares up and pull in a bit of added value, backed the industrial restructuring recommendations made by the "financial community" of analysts, consultants and CEOs.

The formation of giant defence groups in the US enabled American industry to consolidate its world domination a little more. Certainly, it widened the gap between the Americans and the European groups, their only real competitors, and for a whole series of reasons, the process now in motion represents a transatlanticisation of armaments production [Serfati, 2003]. We are certainly not in the situation of world monopoly envisaged by certain American researchers [Kapstein, 1994]. However, on the one hand, the European armaments groups depend to an important extent on American R&D budgets, and on the other, the strengthening of intellectual property laws by the Office of Defense Trade Control threatens to limit the use that they could make of skills acquired through cooperation programmes or joint ventures. More generally, military programmes are still very important elements of industrial policy and in some technological fields (those linked to ICT but also biotechnology), their role may even expand.

II. Solid "Fundamentals"

II.1 Self-fulfilling Prophecies

The attraction of the "markets" to the armaments industry did not start with the "bargain effects" produced by 9/11. Between 1990 and 1997, the time of the major restructurings, the share value of the 20 top defence companies almost quadrupled, whereas the industrial index S&P 500 merely doubled [Delétang, 1998]. And yet, during this period, the cut-backs in military budgets that had begun in 1986 continued. Thus, neither the alleged "peace dividends" reaped from this reduction in military spending and the demise of the USSR nor the presence (from 1992) of a Democratic administration, which is generally more prudent about military expenditure, dampened the optimism of the "markets" about the restructurings then underway. This is scarcely surprising, as on the one hand, the "industrial logic" of the concentrations was to reinforce the relational power of the main contractor groups and thus to increase the volume of orders for the big contractor groups, and on the other hand, the groups' shareholders and CEOs were anticipating an increase in spending on R&D and the production of weapons systems.

These prophecies, too, were "self-fulfilling". Yet they had nothing in common with the "bubbles" seen on the financial markets. The status assigned to the big armaments groups is obviously dissimilar to that of the firms that issue junk bonds or of the "Internet convention" whose stock market valuations and temporary gains during the "new economy" period were often based on the number of clicks by surfers [Boyer 2002]. The "fundamentals" of the big contractor groups, rooted in the permanence of the defence role, are altogether more solid.

Nonetheless, from 1997 onwards, the stock market value of armaments companies began to fall, and this drop was for the most part concentrated within the major groups. This new downward slide, coming after the strong rally just described, was partially due to the disastrous results produced by the megamergers. But there are also other reasons for the drop in the share value of the big defence groups. The exuberance which broke out on the US financial markets after the Asian crisis (1997), and which is now seen to have been totally disproportionate to the real situation of American firms, manifested itself in an infatuation with new economy companies, and the "old economy", of which defence shares are part, was temporarily put on the back-burner. But then, this drop in the market value of the big groups served as a reminder that the armaments group shareholders and the "financial markets" were impatient to see their military budget hopes come true.

It is interesting to note that the Department of Defense registered some very official disquiet about the market fall. Its officials attributed the collapse of some values to the "short-termist" behaviour of the "markets", and they emphasised that there is no justification for such behaviour in the case of a "long-term" industry such as defence. At the same time, they declared that the falls posed a threat to the vigour of an "vital industry for the national security of the United States" [Wall, Velocci, 1999]. And in fact, from 1998 onwards, the decline in the defence budget halted, on the initiative of the Clinton Administration. Starting in 1999, the military budget, and particularly spending on R&D and procurement (Figure 2) showed a spectacular rise, as the Administration proposed an increase of $110bn over the period 1999-2003. The upward trend in military budgets therefore clearly predates the election of George W. Bush and 9/11. It took some time before the programme of increased military spending decided by Clinton reassured the markets and no longer seemed just a lucky accident (Figure 3). The rise in share values finally resumed a few months after 9/11, at a time of collapse on Wall Street and even more so on the Nasdaq.

Figure 2: **Distribution of Military Expenditure in the US, 1960-2009**
(*DoD Budget Authority*, in billions of constant dollars, at FY 2004 prices).

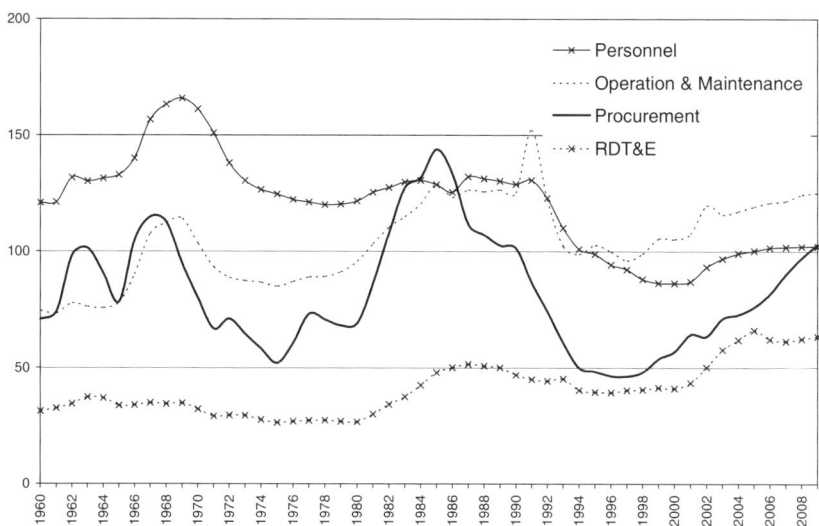

Source: U.S. Department of Defense [2003]. *National Defense Budget Estimates for FY2004*. Office of the Under Secretary of Defense (Comptroller), March 2003.

II.2. War Dividends

Since 2001, financial analysts have gradually provided the armaments sector with a separate identity, whereas until recently it was submerged within broader sectors and indexes (see Box 1). And indeed, the attraction exercised by the armaments groups is undeniable. Figure 3 compares the performances of the DFI index (composed of 15 major firms in the armaments sector), with those of the four main US stock indexes: the Dow Jones Industrial Average (DJ Industrial – a general index of industrial shares), Standard & Poor's 500 (S&P500), the Nasdaq (technological shares), and the Major Market Index (the 20 "blue-chip", or XMI). The base for this comparison is an index equal to 0 on January 2, 1998 (the DFI was launched on September 21, 2001 by the American Stock Exchange but data for the index is available back to September 30, 1996). The "Twin Towers effect" is clearly perceptible: the rise in this new, specifically "defence" index was rapid and sustained up to April 2002, but then fell back in the ensuing months. Upward movement returned in March 2003, when the war against Iraq was launched. The certainty of a "short war" at the military level, which had also been the wish of the IMF's chief economist[5], coupled with the prospect of military engagements in the offing in consequence of the new doctrine of national security, rekindled investor confidence and even pulled all of the Wall Stress and Nasdaq values along behind it – although at a goodly distance.

Figure 3: **Comparison of the Dow Jones Industrial, Nasdaq, S&P500, Major Market Index and DFI Indexes from January 2, 1998 to December 31, 2005 (January 2, 1998 = 0).**

Source: The authors, from NYSE and NASDAQ.

We have reconstituted the data that permit a comparison across the period 2000-2005 (Table 3). The progression in the values of the groups making up the DFI index is much stronger than for the other specific and general market indexes. Over this five-year period, 11 of the 15 firms in the DFI showed gains of over 100% (ranging from 134% to 1,142%), whereas the general performance of the US market during past five years, as measured by the

---

[5] The economist declared that a short-term military action in Iraq would probably have only a minor impact on the world economy, and could even produce a "positive effect" by eliminating uncertainty over the situation. Quoted in A. Friedman, *IMF Chief sees upside of a short war in Irak*, International Herald Tribune, 20 September 2002.

Dow Jones US Total Market Index on 3 May 2005, is a negative value at −17.09%. It should be noted that the highest-performing armaments firms are strongly involved in information and communications technologies (ICT).

Table 3 also reveals the extraordinary attractiveness of the armaments sector when it is compared with the *Amex Major Market Index* (XMI). The Nasdaq reached its historical peak on March 2000, at 5060.34 points, before heading into the steep plunge down to a low of 1116.76 points on 10 October 2002. Imagine a well-informed, far-seeing investor, or simply a lucky one: smelling disaster for the "new economy", he prudently turns back towards the "old economy" of the armaments industry. On a portfolio containing one share in each of the companies on the DFI index, he would have achieved, 5 years and 2 months later (3 May 2005), a gain of 165.85%. If, on the other hand, he had played safe and gone for the 20 blue-chips – top-ranking values supposed to combine high returns with low risks – which make up the *Amex Major Market Index* (XMI), the operation would, by the same date, have made a loss of −2.39%.

Table 3: The Exceptional Performances of the Armaments Groups.

Name	Symbol	Market Capitalization millions USD 3-mai-05	Gain/Share from March 10, 2000 to May 2, 2005 %
Amex Defense Index (DFI)			
Boeing Co.	BA.N	49.183,16	82,86%
Lockheed Martin Corporation	LMT.N	27.061,19	263,77%
General Dynamics Corporation	GD.N	21.139,21	166,50%
Northrop Grumman Corporation	NOC.N	19.691,95	133,74%
Raytheon Co.	RTN.N	17.007,99	94,12%
L-3 Communications Hldgs Inc.	LLL.N	8.273,68	216,83%
Rockwell Collins Inc.	COL.N	8.173,98	98,44%
Alliant Techsystems Inc.	ATK.N	2.615,70	336,92%
United Industrial Corporation	UIC.N	1.957,30	207,23%
FLIR Systems Inc.	FLIR.O	1.852,16	991,02%
The Titan Corporation	TTN.N	1.523,78	-47,48%
Engineered Support Systems Inc.	EASI.O	1.462,95	1141,99%
Drs Technologies Inc.	DRS.N	1.208,91	372,11%
Stewart & Stevenson Svcs Inc.	SVC.N	694,32	154,11%
EDO Corporation	EDO.N	597,49	382,23%
Result for a DFI portfolio	**^DFI**	**162.443,78**	**165,85%**
Major Market Index (XMI)			
General Electric Co.	GE.N	383.717,10	-17,59%
Exxon Mobil Corp.	XOM.N	363.052,98	47,45%
Johnson & Johnson	JNJ.N	204.082,97	93,31%
Wal-Mart Stores, Inc.	WMT.N	199.543,62	-1,08%
Procter & Gamble	PG.N	136.604,75	102,42%
Altria Group	MO.N	134.418,82	243,23%
IBM	IBM.N	123.225,38	-26,80%
Chevron Texaco Corp.	CVX.N	109.430,88	30,67%
Coca Cola Co.	KO.N	104.593,53	-4,70%
Merck & Co.	MRK.N	74.852,90	-39,95%
American Express Co.	AXP.N	65.769,60	25,27%
3M Company	MMM.N	58.849,02	88,22%
The Walt Disney Co.	DIS.N	54.050,83	-25,19%
E.I. Du Pont de Nemours and Co.	DD.N	46.968,67	2,81%
Dow Chemical Co.	DOW.N	44.124,49	42,42%
McDonalds Corp.	MCD.N	37.285,84	-7,15%
International Paper Co.	IP.N	16.815,13	-6,86%
AT&T Corp.	T.N	15.319,69	-77,58%
General Motors	GM.N	15.060,06	-65,56%
Eastman Kodak	EK.N	7.177,25	-53,78%
Result for a XMI porfolio	**^XMI**	**2.194.943,50**	**-2,39%**

Note: The ranking of the firms is based on the market capitalization.

Source: Prepared by the authors, based on *The Wall Street Journal*, data updated on 3 May 2005.

II.3. High Stock Exchange Performances, Limited Risks

Shareholders' satisfaction with the defence groups had already been noted in previous studies. Higgs and Trevino calculated that, over a long period (1970-1989), the stock market performances of the defence groups (measured by share price) were markedly superior to those of the S&P 500 index. This holds true however many defence firms (from 5 to 50) are taken into account. For instance, while the S&P 500 index progressed by 12.51% per year over the period 1970-1989, stocks in the 10 foremost DoD contractors progressed by 17.46% per year, and those of the top 50 contractors by 16.24% per year [1992]. Trevino and Higgs explained these good performances on the exchanges by a rate of return on capital invested in production by armaments groups that was superior to the rate of return on the average capital of firms making up the S&P.

The data collected lead us to draw different conclusions for the recent period (1998-2002). Certainly, as we have seen, their performances on the exchanges are above average. But according to our calculations[6], most of the defence groups do, as regards rates of economic profitability based on data from the firms' own accounting, put in performances that are inferior to the average for firms on the S&P. There may be several reasons for this situation. It is in part the consequence of the disastrous results produced by the acquisitions (it was mainly the groups which made the most acquisitions that show the most mediocre rates of economic profitability). It is also doubtless due to the costs generated by the very high remuneration of leading defence group executives. The scandals surrounding Enron, WorldCom etc. have placed particularly large question marks over the top management of the American groups, who are (rightly and properly) considered responsible for strategic errors but are also accused of bringing in lavish remuneration structures, well cushioned against falls in share value. However, this questioning does not yet seem to have reached the leaders of the groups contracting to the Pentagon. A study shows that, in 2002, the median income of a CEO in the defence groups was $5.4m. That is 45% more than the median incomes of all CEOs ($3.5m). This difference is due mainly to the considerable increases that the defence group CEOs obtained in 2002 (+79%, as against +6% for all CEOs) [Hartman and Martin, 2003].

---

[6] They are not reproduced in this paper.

Table 4: **Remuneration of Armaments CEOs** (in Thousands of US Dollars)

Firm	Name of CEO	2001	2001	% rise
LMT	Vance D. Coffman	16,556	25,337	**53**
BA	Philip M. Condit	3,929	4,145	**5**
RTN	Daniel P. Burnham	2,588	8,922	**245**
NOC	Kent Kresa	7,352	9,222	**25**
GD	Nicholas D. Chabraja	5,719	15,245	**167**
median "Armament" income (1)		2,992	5,358	79
median "Industry" income (2)		3,490	3,700	6
difference Armament/Industry (%)		**-14**	**45**	

Note: This table is based on a study in *Business Week* (21 April 2003) which looks at 365 big American companies, 37 of which are in the armaments sector.
Source: Hartman and Martin, 2003.

> **Box 2: Stock Market Valuation - Risks and Returns.**
>
> *No doubt there are other reasons for this gap, observed between 1997 and 2002 – notably as regards the measurement of economic profitability (for an analysis of the methodological problems and a comparison of the evaluation sources, see the group report of the Commissariat général du plan [the French economic planning commission], chaired by D.Plihon [2002]).*
>
> Tobin's q ratio, as we have calculated it for the years 1998 to 2002, is based on the approximation given by the formula suggested by Chung and Pruitt [1994], according to which q is equal to the ratio of the sum of the market value of own capital (market capitalization) and of the book value of the debt, to the book value of the economic assets. A q equal to 1 therefore indicates identical sharemarket and book valuations. Although the theoretical basis of this is subject to discussion, a high value for q is often interpreted as a sign that a speculative bubble is forming.
>
> The risk represented by a share may be measured by its volatility. This may be represented by the coefficient β (beta), a measure of the systematic (or non-diversifiable) risk of a share – in other words, of the risk linked to market movements and therefore not reducible through a better diversification of the portfolio, contrary to the specific risk linked to the company itself. Shares with β coefficients above 1 are more volatile and are therefore considered to be higher-risk than shares with coefficients below 1. The β coefficient of a portfolio is equal to the arithmetic average of the β coefficients of the shares making up the portfolio.

Two statements may be made concerning the importance of the gap between economic profitability and stock market performances for the period 2000-2004 (Table 5). Firstly, it concerns all the groups, although to differing degrees, since the Tobin's q ratio (see Box 2), which expresses this gap precisely, varies from 1.07 to 4.08 in 2004. Secondly, the gap between the sharemarket and book valuations became in most cases more and more marked during the period 2000-2004: the average value of Tobin's q for the DFI companies as a whole rose from 1.43 to 2.02 between 2000 and 2004.

However, the level reached by the q ratio does not indicate the formation of a "bubble" around defence shares. Nor does it reflect excessive risk-taking, as confirmed by the calculation of a commonly used indicator (see Box 2). Table 5 does indeed indicate that the β coefficient of a portfolio made up of the 15 stocks in the DFI index comes out at an average of just

0.32 in May 2005, which would mean that risk-taking in the case of armaments is lower than for an investment in the XMI ($\beta = 0.74$) – despite, be it recalled, a markedly higher return (Table 3). This fact therefore seems to disprove the correlation – positive, in principle – between return and risk as established by financial theory.

The gap observed between the economic profitability of the groups contracting to the DoD and their stock market performance seems rather to show that the markets' assessments are guided more by industrial considerations (efficiency, etc.) than by the security offered by these groups, based as it is both on their solid fundamentals and on their vital role, which makes them too strategic to fail.

Table 5: Risks and Stock Market Appreciation of Armaments Groups in the US.

Name	Symbol	Bêta (β)		Tobin q				
		23-nov-04	3-mai-05	2004	2003	2002	2001	2000
Amex Defense Index (DFI)								
United Industrial Corporation	UIC.N	0,60	0,55	4,08	4,62	4,03	2,59	1,73
FLIR Systems Inc.	FLIR.O	-0,12	0,31	4,02	3,30	3,87	3,82	1,31
Engineered Support Systems Inc.	EASI.O	0,12	0,25	3,42	3,76	2,68	1,99	1,33
Rockwell Collins Inc.	COL.N	0,94	0,93	3,03	2,71	2,22	1,88	0,57
General Dynamics Corporation	GD.N	0,56	0,46	1,78	1,72	1,98	1,99	2,39
EDO Corporation	EDO.N	-0,21	-0,19	1,77	1,59	1,49	2,19	1,14
The Titan Corporation	TTN.N	1,83	1,18	1,75	2,10	1,39	1,67	1,57
Lockheed Martin Corporation	LMT.N	-0,11	-0,37	1,69	1,60	1,73	1,50	1,23
Boeing Co.	BA.N	0,69	0,78	1,60	1,50	1,36	1,41	2,01
L-3 Communications Hldgs Inc.	LLL.N	0,26	0,16	1,60	1,37	1,39	1,69	1,76
Alliant Techsystems Inc.	ATK.N	-0,23	-0,32	1,56	1,56	1,77	1,51	1,84
Stewart & Stevenson Svcs Inc.	SVC.N	1,07	1,10	1,49	1,16	1,04	1,17	1,35
Raytheon Co.	RTN.N	0,40	0,42	1,29	1,14	1,15	1,05	0,87
Drs Technologies Inc.	DRS.N	-0,14	-0,23	1,10	1,10	1,27	1,57	1,13
Northrop Grumman Corporation	NOC.N	-0,15	-0,30	1,07	1,02	1,05	1,11	1,14
Amex Defense Index (DFI) *average*	^DFI	0,37	0,32	2,08	2,02	1,89	1,81	1,43
Major Market Index (XMI) *average*	^XMI	0,00	0,74	0,17	0,67	0,69	0,66	0,66
S&P 500	^GSPC	1,00	1,00	–	–	–	–	–

Note: The groups are ranked according to Tobin's q in 2004.
Sources: The authors, from *The Wall Street Journal Online* and *Reuters*.

III. A New "Social Bloc": Finance, Armaments and Politics

III.1. A New Institution, the Department of Homeland Security

The transformations in the military-industrial system (MIS) are sufficiently important for us to consider that, as far that system is concerned, the period that began with the Second World War has now drawn to a close. It is our hypothesis that an American military-security system is developing and that it has significantly accelerated since 11 September 2001[7]. Its creation results

---

[7] For a different assessment, see Duménil and Lévy, 2003. Analysing "the context and the foundations of [the] new military strategy of the United States" (p.78), they write in the section devoted to the "military-industrial complex" that it "represents a force that is not negligible, but it is not the heart of the capitalist

from a combination of international transformations within the MIS and shifts in international relations, with the doctrine of "preventive war" as a major component of this.

We have mentioned the industrial restructuring and the new relations between the armaments groups and finance. Now, mention must be made of the creation of the Department of Homeland Security (DHS) immediately after 9/11 (although it had been proposed for several years by bipartisan think tanks). This reflects a degree of political centralization around government that is unprecedented in the history of the United States. The DHS combines the activities of 22 agencies and 1,700,000 employees. From its creation in 2002, it was allocated a budget of $38bn, relating both to military aspects (22% of the total) and to civil ones (for example, public health, accounting for 12% of the total, or protecting transport infrastructure: 20% of the total). The DHS plan to provide commercial civil aircraft with anti-missile defences[8] – at a probable cost of $10bn to equip some 6,800 planes – is a revealing glimpse into the new "security" approach.

The creation of the DHS should be seen in the context of the type of international economic and geopolitical relations that have existed over the past decade – i.e. globalization dominated by financial capital and the central position occupied by the United States [Serfati, 2001]. It is inseparable from the new doctrine of national security, which had already been formulated under the Clinton administration but which reached completion with the publication by the White House, on 17 September 2002, of the report on "The National Security Strategy of the United States of America" [White House, 2002]. It justifies the preemptive – in other words, *discretionary* – use of military force to deal with a very diverse range of threats against the country's "vital interests". The defence of the market economy and of the concept of "free trade", "a moral principle even before it became a pillar of economics", features among these vital interests [ibid, p. 18].

Two elements suggest that a new threshold has been crossed. The document of 17 September 2002 is considered to be just as important as the publication of document NSC-68 (14 April 1950), which provided the basis for the Cold War and the "containment" of the USSR [Kirshner, 2003]. The NSC-68, and the military credits that were voted in, enabled the military-

---

system in the United States." (p.92) . On the one hand, because the ranking of the armaments groups, on the basis of their market capitalisation, is modest, and on the other because "the profit share of the military manufacturing sector is difficult to evaluate, but is very weak." As the present chapter confirms, the central place that we attribute to the military-security system within American capitalism rests upon a series of geopolitical, economic (financial and technological) and socio-political factors whose effects are now highly cumulative.

[8] Dow Jones Newswires, 15 May 2003.

industrial system (the "complex") constituted by the DoD at the end of the Second World War to take permanent root in the American economy and society. The "militarization of government", i.e. the predominance of the defence and security agencies (DoD, State Department, CIA, Presidential Security Adviser, NSC, Joint Chiefs of Staff) began during that period [Jablonski, 2002, p. 8]. The second element is the creation of the DHS, whose role is already being compared to that played after World War II by the DoD and the National Security Council (the President's advisers on issues of national security).

III.2. Information and Security Technologies

Together with changes in the links of finance and politics to armaments, the third factor favouring the emergence of a military-security system concerns security's role in the field of information and communications technologies (ICT). Noting the potential of these technologies, the US military have, since the end of the 1980s, developed the notion of *informational dominance*. Major R&D programmes devoted to ICT and space were launched by the DoD. They were less affected by the reductions in the military budget (1986-1998) than were those aimed at armaments production. The entrance barriers which protect the big groups (cf. the first section) are strengthened by the types of skills needed to implement the new doctrines put into practice in Serbia, Afghanistan and Iraq. "Network-centric warfare" (NCW)[9], which underlies the new US military doctrines, works to the advantage of the main contractor groups whose "comparative advantage" derives generally from their skills in systems integration. The implementation of NCW does indeed demand more organizational architecture, more integration of "systems of systems" and, of course, increased protection and security for the networks and, therefore, the production of highly securized software and hardware. Only groups well used to the heavy constraints posed by armaments systems and the DoD's demanding specifications are able to master the necessary skills [Dombrowski *et al*, 2002].

The defence groups are also well positioned on the new "security" markets driven by demand from civilian clients (enterprises and households), but also by a new category of public procurement orders from the different states and local authorities within the USA. These markets hold considerable promise. They are also tempting to the civilian CIT groups, who possess a high level of skills in systems integration, as well as to the small enterprises present in CIT "niches" that are useful for security. These small businesses

---

[9] NCW bases military engagement on a decentralized network of forces who share information rather than on "platforms" (aircraft, ships etc.).

are attracting the attention of the top-ranking contractor groups, who have stepped up their acquisitions of, or participation in, start-ups. Competition from the civilian groups could become more threatening when the procurement of security systems bypasses the DoD. That is where the armaments groups can use the "comparative advantage" that results from their relational power, for instance their unrivalled influence with Congress and the agencies in charge of financing the R&D programmes aimed at "homeland security". The defence groups thus find themselves in a particularly favourable posture on certain innovation trajectories for information and security technologies oriented towards commercial markets [Serfati, 2004].

IV. An "Unlimited Warfare" Convention in the Making?

As may be observed over the past two decades, the financial markets base their behaviour on "conventions", in accordance with mechanisms that A. Orléan has analysed, drawing upon the reflections of Keynes [1999]. The collapse of the Nasdaq from 10 March 2000 onwards marked the end of the "Internet convention", which was indissociable from the "new economy", and ushered in some topsy-turvy times on the US financial markets.

The economic and political situation in which the US finds itself today is very different to that of the 1990s. The "new economy" is a thing of the past, as is the "happy globalization" which brought strong, widespread growth and promoted international trade through the opening of frontiers, the deregulation of markets and the privatization of industries. In this context, the revival plan for the American economy proposed by the Bush administration, based on massive tax cuts for the high-income households, a spectacular rise in military spending and a gigantic budget deficit, shows the processes that are at work both within US domestic relationships and the country's relations with the rest of the world. Domestically, the organizations and institutions that make up America's financial capital have every reason to show satisfaction[10] with a plan that goes hand in hand with an absence of effective measures to limit the insatiable appetite of the "markets" and the resulting malfeasance. No explanation is needed as to why the Bush plan is a dream come true for the armaments groups.

The macroeconomic revival effects – which, be it noted in passing, are seriously disputed even by "moderate" Keynesians [Tobin, 2002] – presuppose the attainment of conditions that are even more governed by the rela-

---

[10] This amounts to a "virtuous circle for rentiers": well-to-do households can subscribe to loans taken out by the State in order to finance this gaping deficit, thanks to the savings that they are able to build up as a result of the tax cuts of which they are the main beneficiaries.

tions that the US establishes with the rest of the world. In particular, a massive revival of capital flows would be needed. Such flows (which have slowed down greatly since 2002) finance the external deficit and enable the United States to remain the "consumer of last resort". It is also necessary to ensure the maintenance of interest payments on debt (essentially by the countries of the South) and on other types of unearned income which, based as they are on property rights (intellectual, petroleum etc.), flow into the US. These transfers in the United States' favour are even more difficult to ensure than in the 1990s. Yet they are a determining condition for the payment of pensions to wage-earners and of dividends and interest to shareholders, as well as for efforts to avert another collapse of share prices.

The war against Iraq, despite the context in which the decision was taken (relative isolation of the United States), the difficulty of maintaining order and the very high financial cost of the operation, did not stop the upward trend on Wall Street and the Nasdaq during 2003 (Figure 3). This disproves the conventional assertion that the financial markets feel revulsion at the use of military violence. During the 1990s, the exuberance seen in the American financial centres had not yet been dented by the multiplication of "new wars" linked to globalization (SIPRI [2003] counted, for the period 1990-2001, a cumulative total of 57 major conflicts on 45 different territories, i.e. about one-third of the planet). It is true that, viewed from American territory, they may seem far away. However, "the stock market is not sentimental", as the *Financial Times* commented in its stock market section in an explanation of why the markets boomed when the armies of the United States (and NATO) attacked Serbia on 12 April 1999.

After the wars in Afghanistan and Iraq, the US "markets" may be "internalizing" within their behaviour the inevitability of new wars and military operations. They may, in fact, be forging a sort of "unlimited warfare" convention in which the *discretionary* use of armed force by the United States becomes their new horizon. This new convention, unlike those of the 1990s, is not based on self-referential mimicry relating to the unlimited commercial potential offered by technology and the American model's presumed seduction of the rest of the world. Rather, it is based on very real "fundamentals" such as the gigantic size of military expenditure and the technological drive on the security front, which underlie the conviction that military interventions by US armies, alone or within alliances, are going to become more frequent. This convention does not have the power to prevent anticipations that are at first excessively optimistic and then pessimistic, because they are governed by the behaviour of the "animal spirits" which are at work within the financial markets and which result in alternating bubbles and crashes of varying size. More prosaically, this convention is based on the hope that military supremacy may, for as long as possible, keep the American economy sheltered from the consequences of a pattern of production and consumption that is "unsustainable" for a large portion of the planet.

References

Batsch L. (2002), *Le capitalisme financier*, Repères n°356, La Découverte, Paris, 2002.
Boyer R. (2002), *La croissance, début de siècle, De l'octet au gène*, Albin Michel, Paris.
Chesnais F. et Serfati C. (1990), « L'industrie militaire, une locomotive du développement industriel ? » dans Chesnais F. (Editeur), *Compétitivité internationale et dépenses militaires*, Economica, Paris, p. 169-216.
Chung K.H. and Pruitt S.W. (1994), « A Simple Approximation of Tobin's Q », *Financial Management* (Autumn), p.70-74.
Ciardello V. (2002), "Global Changes in the Defense Industrial Bases : Challenges and Opportunities" , 31 January, DUSD, mimeograph.
Crandall M.S. (2002), "Antitrust in the Digital Age: An Overview", *ICAF Economics Instrutional Paper*, janvier, National Defense University.
Delétang F. (1998), « La consolidation de l'industrie de défense américaine : un défi pour l'Europe », *L'Armement*, N° 61, March 1998.
Dombrowski P.J., Gholz E., Ross A.L., "Selling Military Transformation: The Defense Industry and Innovation", Orbis, Summer 2002, p.523-536.et al, 2002.
Duménil G; Lévy D. (2003), « Néolibéralisme-Néomilitarisme », *Actuel Marx*, n° 133, p. 77-99.
Gholz E. and Sapolsky H. (1999), "Restructuring the U.S. Defense Industry", in *International Security*, Winter 1999.
Hartman Chris and Martin David (2003), *More Bucks for the Bang: CEO Pay at Top Defense Contractors*, United Fair Economy, 28 April, 2003.
Higgs R. and Trevino R. (1992), "Profits of U.S. Defense Contractors", in *Defense Economics*, 1992, Volume 3.
Jablonski D. (2002), "The State of the National Security State", *Parameters*, Winter 2002-2003, p. 4-20.
Kapstein E.B. (1994), "America's Arms-Trade Monopoly", *Foreign Affairs*, May-June, p. 13-19.
Kirshner J., Strauss B., Fanis M., Evangelista M. (2003), *Iraq and Beyond: The New U.S. National Security Strategy*, Peace Studies Program, Cornell University, Cornell Occasional papers, January 2003.
Kovacic W.E., Smallwood D.E. (1994), "Competition Policy, Rivalries, and Defense Industry Consolidation", *Journal of Economic Perspectives*, vol.8, n° 4, Spring, p. 91-110.
Mampaey L. (2001), "Ownership and regulation of the defense industrial base : the French case", in Serfati C., *The restructuring of the European defense industrial base – Dynamics of change*, European Commission, COST Action A10, Director-

ate-general for Research, EUR 19977, Office for Official Publications of the European Communities, Luxembourg.

Markusen A. (1999), "The Post Cold War Persistence of Defense Specialized Firms", in Susman G.I. et O'Keefe S. (ed.), *The Defense Industry in the Post Cold-War Era: Corporate Strategies and Public Policy Perspectives*, Elsevier, Oxford.

Orléan A. (1999), *Le pouvoir de la finance*, Editions Odile Jacob, Paris.

Plihon D. (2000), « L'économie des fonds propres : un nouveau régime d'accumulation financière », dans Chesnais F. et Plihon D., *Les pièges de la finance mondiale*, Syros, Alternatives économiques, Paris, p. 17-37.

Plihon D. (2002) (Rapport du groupe du Commissariat Général du Plan), *Rentabilité et risque dans un nouveau régime de croissance*, La Documentation Française.

Roturier P. et Serfati C. (2003), « Enron, la 'communauté' et le capital financier », *Revue de l'IRES*, 1er trimestre.

Serfati C. (1995), *Production d'armes, croissance et innovation*, Economica, Paris.

Serfati C. (2001a), "The adaptability of the French armaments industry in an era of globalization", N° 2, August, *Industry and Innovation*, p. 221-239.

Serfati C. (2001b), « Le système militaro-industriel américain à l'ère de la mondialisation », n° 36, *Economie et société*, série P (Relations économiques internationales), p. 801-820.

Serfati C. (2003), « Coopération européenne et intégration transatlantique des industries d'armement : le cas de l'aéronautique » in Klein J., Buffotot P., Vilboux N. (Sous la direction de) *Vers une politique européenne commune en matière de sécurité et de défense : défis et opportunités*, Economica, Paris.

Serfati C. (2004), *Impérialisme et militarisme au 21° siècle*, Editions Page 2, Lausanne.

Sipri (2003), *Sipri Yearbook 2003*, Stockholm.

The White House (2002), *The National Security Strategy of the United States of America*, 17 September, no publisher.

Tobin J. (2002), "Macroeconomic Strategy in War Times", *ECAAR News Network*, vol.14, n°1, p.1-2.

U.S. General Accounting Office (1998), *Defense Industry Consolidation: Competitive Effects of Mergers and Acquisitions*, GAO/NSIAD-98-112, March 4, 1998.

Velocci A.L. (2003), "Grading the Industry", *Aviation Week & Space Technology*, 21 July 2003.

Wall R. Velocci A.L (1999), "Hamre's Stock Concern Draws Mixed Reaction", *Aviation Week & Space Technology*, 15 November.

PART IV:
THE MACRO-REGIONAL CASE OF THE GREEK-TURKISH CONFLICT AND THE "GREATER MIDDLE EAST"

Chapter 7
REASONS FOR TURKEY'S MILITARY PRESENCE IN CYPRUS AND ITS POTENTIAL EFFECTS ON REGIONAL STABILITY

Andrew Michael

I. Historical Background

Historically, many Turkish government officials, the MGK, and Turkish nationalists have argued that Cyprus belongs to Turkey.[1] Cyprus was under Ottoman rule for over 300 years (1571-1878). Under the Treaty of Berlin (1878), Turkey transfered Cyprus to Great Britain. The latter gained the right to occupy and administer Cyprus, while the Sultan nominally continued to maintain his sovereignty over Cyprus (Spyridakis, 1974). In 1914, Great Britain annexed Cyprus thus ending any claims of sovereignty the Sultan had over the island. In the Treaty of Lausanne (July 24, 1923), Turkey renounced all claims to Cyprus, which remained under British rule.[2] Thus, any arguments that have been made since then, that Cyprus belongs to Turkey, lack statutory validity and are most likely to have been nurtured by feelings of nationalism.

It is important, however, to consider the nature of Turkey's interest in Cyprus. According to Sonmezoglu (1991), during the period 1950-60 Britain encouraged Turkey's involvement against the Greek Cypriots' revolution for liberation against their British colonial ruler and their desire for unification (enosis) with *motherland* Greece. Furthermore, the British encouraged Turkey's policy of taksim to counter the Greek Cypriots' demand for enosis.[3] Sonmezoglu argues that this policy was inappropriate and impractical because Greeks and Turks lived in mixed cities and "there was no clear geographic basis for creating two federal states" (Yavuz 1992:137).

It is not clear what Turkey's policy on Cyprus was prior to the 1950s. Many Greek Cypriots (GCs) believe that Turkey was not interested in the Turkish Cypriots (TCs) of Cyprus and would not have become involved if it were not encouraged by Britain. Others (Yelsida 1979, Mchenry 1981) argue that Turkey was always concerned about Cyprus. Sonmezoglu,

---

[1] For a review of historical events that may provide insight regarding the legitimacy of this claim see Spyridakis, Sonmezoglu, and Stanley Kyriakides.
[2] Article 20 'Turkey hereby recognises the annexation of Cyprus proclaimed by the British Government on the 5th November, 1914' in Great Britain, *Treaty of Peace with Turkey Signed at Lausanne on July 24, 1923*, London: HMSO, p. 23.
[3] According to Sonmezoglu, in 1954, Turkey argued for taksim (or taxim), a policy to promote self-determination separately for the Greek and Turkish communities.

however, believes that Turkey had no policy on Cyprus before the 1950s. Similarly, Sukru Gurel (1985) argues that "although there was public interest and concern for Cyprus among the bureaucratic elite of the Turkish Foreign Ministry, there was no government policy until London 'forced' Ankara into the conflict" (Yavuz 1992: 137). What is clear, however, is that Turkey began to support an independent state for the Turkish Cypriots as early as 1954.

In February 1959, an agreement was reached in Zurich and London between Britain, Greece, Turkey, and the leaders of the two communities. "The Zurich and London agreements declared Cyprus a free [independent] state whose territorial integrity was to be guaranteed by the U.K., Greece and Turkey" under the Treaty of Guarantee (Spyridakis, 169).[4] The Agreements precluded both enosis and *any type of partition* of the island.

In 1959, the GCs elected Archbishop Makarios III as the first president of the new republic. The Republic of Cyprus was declared an independent state, on August 16, 1960. Early on, it became clear that the constitution was not workable. On a number of occasions, the Turkish vice-president vetoed legislation that would have generated needed funds for economic development. This frustrated the GCs who began to resent the TCs' lack of cooperation. During 1960-1974, tension began to grow resulting in inter-communal clashes.

On Monday, July 15, 1974, the military junta in Greece orchestrated a coup d' etat that was executed by Greek colonels with the help of disillusioned Greek Cypriot revolutionary veterans.[5] The purpose of the coup was to kill president Makarios and replace him with someone who would be more cooperative with the Greek junta. President Makarios, however, was able to escape to London. Five days later, on Saturday, July 20, Turkey invaded Cyprus.

The official position of the Turkish government at the time (and until today) is that it was intervening militarily as it was obliged to do so under the Treaty of Guarantee to restore constitutional order and to protect the TC minority. During the first phase of this invasion Turkish troops looted, raped and killed civilians. A cease-fire was eventually secured. However, this lasted only until August 14, 1974 at which time, the second phase of the Turkish invasion began. When this second military operation was over, about 37% of the northern part of the island came under control of the Turkish occupation troops. The TCs migrated to the any rational

---

[4] One of the provisions of the constitution allowed for 950 Greek, and 650 Turkish troops to be established on the island.
[5] Many of the commanding officers in the Cyprus National Guard were Greek colonels.

contemplation of this outcome suggests that their concerns northern part of the island occupied by Turkish troops, whereas 200000 GCs were forcefully uprooted from their homes to move to the areas controlled by the Cyprus government in the south, thus becoming refugees in their own country.[6]

Since then, negotiations have taken place between the presidents of Cyprus (who have been elected by GCs) and the TC leaders Rauf Denktash and more recently Mehmet Ali Talat. For years negotiations led nowhere resulting in an impasse. In the latest initiative, the United Nations Secretary General, Kofi Annan, submitted a plan for a comprehensive solution to the Cyprus problem. Although the majority of TCs voted in favor of the plan, the majority of GCs (75%) voted against it. Given that it is the GCs who for years have wanted a solution, were not addressed and their rights not secured. The GCs voted against the plan for a number of reasons of which I state only two. First, they felt that it did not provide enough security from future military advances by Turkish troops. Second, not all of the GC refugees were to be allowed to return to their homes.

II. The MGK, the TSK, and the Turkish Government: Conflicting Agendas?

The Cyprus government has proposed a complete demilitarization of the island. According to this proposal, all Greek and Turkish troops would be removed from the island and a EU (or NATO) armed force would replace them to reassure both Greek- and Turkish-Cypriots of their security. This proposal was made during the last UN initiative but was rejected by the Turkish government and therefore was not part of the Fifth Annan Plan that was voted upon in the April 2004 referenda. This begs a number of questions. Why does the Turkish government (read MGK) insist on maintaining a military presence on the island and why does it insist on having the right to take military action to restore stability if it decides that there is such a need? Does this military presence indeed contribute to stability on the island or is it an additional (yet possibly unnecessary) cause of Greco-Turkish tension in the region? These questions must be considered in view of the fact that Cyprus is now a member of the EU.

In discussing whether Turkey's military presence in Cyprus is a stabilizing factor or a cause of tension, it is important to consider who makes foreign policy decisions in Turkey and what are the objectives of these

---

[6] The fact that the Turkish Armed Forces violated the cease-fire and proceeded with the second phase of their military operations proves that their intentions were not to restore order and peace but rather to enlarge the territorial gains of their invasion.

decision makers? If it is Mr. Erdogan's government, arguably there is the potential for an alternative Turkish stance on the Cyprus issue to enhance Turkey's road to EU membership. Such a stance could reduce tension. If it is the MGK and the Turkish General Staff (TGB) of the Turkish Armed Forces (TSK), then one must consider the interests that they are trying to serve. Oddly, the goals of the Turkish government may not necessarily be the same as the goals of the MGK and TGB. Richter (1996) states that Turkish foreign policy is "neither influenced by parliamentary terms nor by the changes of government. [The aims of its] foreign policy are pursued over decades and never given up no matter which party rules...Strategically foreign policy aims are not to be discussed" (p. 29). Perhaps foreign policy is not determined by civilian governments but rather by the TSK, TGB and MGK.

Mr. Erdogan's government has been working hard to create those conditions that will eventually allow Turkey to reap the benefits of EU membership. Thus, it may be assumed that the Turkish government's objectives are in line with the interests of the majority of Turkey's citizens. One must also consider the Armed Forces' goals and interests. Do these goals necessarily serve the interests of the Turkish nation? Of course, such thoughts are blasphemy for those Turkish citizens who consider the TSK to be the defenders of the Turkish nation. But is it not possible that the current interests of the Turkish nation may not align with those of the TSK and the MGK? As Ian Lesser (2000:16) states, "The Turkish military...have been resistant to reforms, including economic reforms, which they view as threatening to the security, integrity, and welfare of the state."

Assume that one accepts the view that Turkey's membership in the EU will be beneficial to the Turkish nation. Since civilian control of the military is a prerequisite for EU membership it should lead to the MGK playing a smaller role in policy formulation and decision-making.[7] This in turn would mean that the generals' importance would diminish. To the extent that these generals desire to retain power and control (and I argue that they do), to that extent they may feel that their personal interests are in jeopardy.[8] Hence, one might expect that they would attempt to justify the need for them to have power, and to take any actions that will help them to retain power.[9]

---

[7] On November 7, 2000, in announcing the conditions that Turkey had to fulfill before accession talks could begin, the EU Commission explicitly stated that Turkey's National Security Council had to be converted into a consultative body (Richter, 2001).

[8] The members of the TGB may also be motivated by a high need for power and achievement, and perhaps a need to satisfy their personal egos that may be nurtured by nationalist feelings. If this is true, it could explain their regional strategic objectives.

[9] In the past such attempts ended in military coups (e.g. May 1960 and September 1980).

One way of achieving this would be to convince public opinion that their powerful existence is necessary for the protection of the Turkish nation.[10] This could be achieved by stirring up feelings of nationalism, playing on the fears of past events, claiming that the Turkish minorities need to be protected, and by continuously referring to external and internal threats (real and illusionary) that would make the average citizen feel that there is indeed a need for a powerful TSK and a strong military presence in sensitive geographic regions.[11] As an example of such rhetoric, I present here an excerpt from a news conference held by the Turkish Chief of the General Staff Hilmi Ozkok in Ankara (broadcast by Turkish TRT 2 television on April 13, 2004):

> *I have repeatedly expressed my views on Cyprus's strategic importance for Turkey...Cyprus's importance for the TSK is based on two fundamental principles...our responsibility for the security of our Cypriot kinsmen...[and] the importance of Cyprus's strategic importance for Turkey's security....These two basic principles have continuity, because stability and balance in Cyprus and in the eastern Mediterranean can be ensured only in this way....Only powerful states have been able to retain their presence in Anatolia...If you consider the incidents that have been going around us for years...you will see that not only has the need for a powerful armed force not diminished, but it has grown...Esteemed members of the media, our army which is a steely expression of Turkish unity, Turkish power and capability, and Turkish patriotism, is the invincible guarantee of our land and of the systematic efforts we have been making to achieve Turkey's ideals....The TSK is the steely guarantee of the existence, sovereignty and integrity of the Turkish Republic....[However], the TSK is being portrayed as the greatest obstacle for change. According to [various] circles, the only thing to do is to try to undermine and weaken the TSK at every opportunity that arises...Who would benefit from the weakening of this force? (BBC Monitoring European).*

According to Gerassimos (2003:64), the formation of the MGK essentially legalized the military's "intervention at will into the country's economic,

---

[10] On December 2, 2000, the General Staff published a White Book on Turkey's defence strategy. This paper emphasized the indispensability of the MGK. Sibel Yuksek, "White Book by Ministry of National Defence" Sabah (2 December 2000).

[11] Following this line of reasoning, one may argue that the perceived "Greek threat" today is an illusion that the MGK and the TSK continuously perpetuate in order to justify and retain their power in Turkish society and to justify their decisions and actions such as maintaining a military force in Cyprus.

social, cultural, foreign, and political affairs." After the September, 1980 coup, the President's and MGK's powers were enhanced (Gerassimos). "As a result, the MGK, although not responsible to the Parliament, became almost the 'highest, non-elected, decision-making body of the [Turkish] state" (Cumhuriyet, 1989, January 19). Gencer Ozcan argues that during the 1990s the military's role increased because of the "increased threats from Kurdish separatism and Islamic fundamentalism" (Richmond 2003: 168) Mehmet Ali Birand points out that whereas in the past the TSK "would follow developments and intervene when the conditions presented themselves, now...they determine the direction of day-to-day policies at the source" (Turkish Daily News, 2001, August 31).

Gerassimos cites a number of reasons to explain why the military's political supremacy has been uncontested and augmented. He believes that the political leaders are reluctant to challenge the military officers because there is a "high level of cohesion and unity inside [their] ranks" (p. 65). Moreover, Roper (1999) points out that major powers are unwilling to put any pressure on the officers due to Turkey's significant geo-strategic and geo-economic importance to the West. Coupled with the military's increasing financial power (Parla, 1998) and the authoritarian political culture (Jenkins, 2001:19) Gerassimos believes that these factors will preserve and strengthen the military's "hegemonic political supremacy over the civilians in the years to come" (p. 66).

Analysts have argued that there is a quiet internal struggle between the MGK, and Mr. Erdogan and progressive (pro-EU) politicians. The two sides may even disagree on their policy toward the Cyprus problem. On a number of occasions, however, Mr. Erdogan and Mr. Gul have stated that no such disagreements exist on the Cyprus problem.[12] However, it is possible that such statements are made to prevent the opposition parties from exploiting the matter for political gains. Turkey's goal of becoming a EU member has rendered the Cyprus problem a controversial issue to deal with. Whereas, certain politicians appear to be willing to adopt a new and more flexible stance on the Cyprus issue for sake of EU membership, many nationalists are unwilling to concede anything that Turkey's military might would allow them to keep.

In describing the Turkish elite, the former Vice-Premier of the "TRNC" Mustafa Akinci, once stated that, "two schools of thought exist in Turkey. One of them supports changes, democracy, and accession to the EU and the

---

[12] See for instance, 'Turkish premier denies differences with military [or] president on Cyprus', BBC Monitoring European, January 8, 2004, p. 1.

other believes that Turkey should not join the EU [if it means withdrawing troops from Cyprus] and democracy is unnecessary." Richter also mirrors the above views when he states that, "the military in Ankara are not ready to give up what they won by the force of weapons" (p. 37).

It is difficult to prove exactly how the TSK's and MGK's power is exercised and to what extent. However, one may infer their intervention in politics by observing various events. For instance, the day after Mr. Erdogan's Islamist Justice and Development (AKP) party had won the elections on 3 November, 2002, Mr. Erdogan expressed the view that the Cyprus problem could be solved based on the Belgium model. Two days later, Mr. Erdogan "was called to the Turkish Foreign Ministry for a 'briefing'…and speaking afterwards to the media, he sought to modify his original statement, saying that Belgium could serve only as an 'inspiration'" (2002, *The Cyprus Weekly*). One can only speculate what was actually said during that meeting. Perhaps Mr. Erdogan was told that it is not the elected Turkish government (but rather the TSK/MGK) that makes decisions on foreign policy issues such as the Cyprus problem. Similarly, when the UN Secretary General initially submitted the first version of the "Annan Plan" on 22 November, 2002, the "Turkish military bluntly told the government at the National Security Council meeting on 29 November that it would not be allowed to determine Turkish policy on Cyprus. Privately, military officials insist[ed] that the threat [would] be backed by force if necessary, since it believes that a strong military presence in northern Cyprus…is vital to Turkey's strategic needs" (IISS as cited in Andreou et al., 2003: 294).[13]

Copley (2004) and Gorvet (2003) believe that during the last few years, the military's power seems to have declined. In August 2003, Turkey's parliament passed the 7th European Union Harmonization Package that included a number of reforms aimed at reducing the military's influence in politics.[14] In theory, the reforms are supposed to have limited the MGK's powers so that it has only a purely advisory role. Moreover, the MGK's structure has been changed so that the military has less control over it. However, have the reforms genuinely reduced the MGK's power or was this highly publicized event a publicity tactic to impress decision making bodies in the EU? The events have yet to confirm that the military's strength has weakened. The MGK and the TSK are still very powerful and the Turkish

---

[13] Hence, at least at that time, there was a serious conflict of interest between the AKP's government and the military regarding the Cyprus issue and any Annan (UN) plan that would not satisfy the MGK's demands.

[14] One of the decisions taken by the Turkish government was to reduce by 60 percent the 2004 budget of the MGK General Secretariat (BBC Monitoring European, Nov. 2, 2003).

government cannot pursue objectives that the former do not approve. The TGB still plays an important role and its influence should not be underestimated (Gorvet).

III. Reasons for Turkey's Military Presence in Cyprus

For the past thirty years, the Turkish Ministry of Foreign Affairs, successive Turkish government officials, Turkish scholars, and the TGB through the MGK, have reiterated the view that the Cyprus problem was solved in 1974 by Turkey's *peace restoring military intervention*. According to this view, there is no Cyprus issue. Peace and order were restored and have been maintained since then. They have argued that the presence of the Turkish troops has been instrumental in preserving this peace and order, as well as necessary for the protection of the TCs from nationalist GCs. For years, the TC leader, Rauf Denktash, had argued that the Greek- and Turkish-Cypriots cannot live together peacefully because the GCs have always wanted to harm and eliminate the TCs. Hence, according to this view, it is best that the Greek- and Turkish-Cypriots live separately, and that the *de facto* division of the island should be recognized *de jure* with the recognition of the existence of two separate states. This request has also been made over the years by various Turkish Prime Ministers, other government officials and the TGB in the MGK.

The question that needs to be considered is whether these reasons are still significant, honest, or justifiable given Cyprus' accession to the EU and the new sociopolitical climate that has emerged. Given the social and economic security that would exist in a European demilitarized Cyprus, Fouskas (2003: 112) argues that the Turkish side's argument for the need for two sovereign states to protect "the Turkish Cypriot community from Greek nationalists, does not make much sense." He draws attention to the fact that due to its close geographic proximity, Turkey does not have to maintain a military presence on the island to exercise political sovereign power in Cyprus. He thus concludes that Turkey's insistence on maintaining "troops in Cyprus is not connected with the security of the Turkish Cypriots, but with Turkey's long-term strategy of gaining strategic control of the whole of Cyprus [via a 'partnership state']" (p. 113).

Since April 2003, the occupation regime (or if one prefers, the TC administration) has permitted Greek- and Turkish- Cypriots to cross the

Green (cease-fire) Line.[15] Since then, Greek- and Turkish- Cypriots have intermingled on a daily basis without any problems. Many TCs have begun to work for GC firms and many have received medical treatment at "Greek-Cypriot" public hospitals without having to pay for these services.[16] More importantly, there have not been any serious incidents of violence between the GCs and TCs since the "crossings" began. This proves that the claims made by Mr. Denktash and Turkey over the years that GCs and TCs cannot live peacefully together were simply a tactic to keep the two communities separate with the aim of insisting on a bizonal, bicommunal solution to the Cyprus problem and ultimately the creation of two separate states.

IV. Turkey's Strategic Interests

In addition to the alleged need to protect the TCs, the MGK stresses that Turkish troops are needed in Cyprus to protect the strategic interests of Turkey. The Turkish Armed Forces have always been against any Cyprus settlement that would result in the withdrawal of Turkish troops from the island (Turkmen, Nov. 2000). Papasotiriou (1998:13) states that "the combination of geopolitical benefits that accrue to Turkey from the occupation of northern Cyprus is so important to Turkish strategic thinking, that Turkey has extremely high incentives to maintain the present situation in the Cyprus problem."

Various views have been expressed regarding what exactly are Turkey's strategic interests. These include:

1. To exclude Greece from the Eastern Mediterranean (Fouskas) and to prevent Cyprus from coming under the complete control of Greece; a situation that would result in "the strategic encirclement of Turkey by sea" (Papasotiriou 1998:12).
2. To use Cyprus as an instrument of pressure against Greece in order "to draw a median line in the Aegean" (Fouskas 2003:111).
3. To deal with the potential "threat from Syria over the formerly Syrian province of Hatay" (Papasoteriou:13). Efraim Inbar argues that the Turkish-Israeli alliance is "based upon a common perception of threat from Syria, Iran, and Iraq" (Richmond, 2003: 168).

---

[15] Greek and Greek-Cypriot analysts believe that this move was made for two reasons, one tactical and the other economic. At that time, the Turkish-Cypriot side felt cornered as the international community felt that it was Mr. Dentash's intransigence that had repeatedly led to an impasse in the intercommunal talks. Moreover, the TRNC's economy needed a life saving injection that did in fact occur as a result of expenditures of the Greek Cypriots during their one day visits to the northern part of the island.

[16] This service is provided even though TCs do not pay taxes to the Cyprus government.

Turkey's presence in Cyprus allows it to "control...air and sea routes critical for the defence of Israel and the advancement of US interests in the South-eastern coastal strip of the Mediterranean" (Fouskas:111).[17]

4. To be able to simultaneously deal with multi-front threats (Greek, Syrian, Kurdish, and even Russian).

Elekdag (1996) points out that with the threat from Russia diminished due to the end of the Cold War, Turkey established a new security policy in the mid 1990s that was based on a new military doctrine whereby Turkey's Armed Forces had to be able to fight two and a half wars simultaneously, i.e. against Greece, Syria, and the Kurdish Workers' Party (PKK). Copley (2004) also argues that the Kurds in northern Iraq, and a possible direct Iranian access to the Mediterranean via the northern part of Iraq and Syria, are the TGB's greatest perceived threats. Mango (1994) also considers the Kurdish issue as Turkey's "biggest single political problem" (Coufoudakis 1997: 157).

Constantinides (1996: 323) also states that Turkey's foreign policy has been influenced by the Kurdish movement that has challenged and threatened its status as a unitary state and that Turkey's Balkan policy is linked to its ambitions "to play a role of regional leader in three strategic areas: the Middle East, the Balkans, and the ancient Soviet Republics of the Caucasus-Central Asia." He sees an increasing number of the ruling Turkish elite supporting the development of "an imperial neo-Ottoman external policy" with respect to the Balkans and Middle East. He argues that this foreign policy (which David Bachard has labeled Neo-Ottomanism) is based on the Imperial Ottoman tradition and cites the invasion in 1974 and occupation of the northern part of Cyprus "as the beginning of an effective neo-Ottoman orientation of Turkish foreign policy" (p. 332).[18] Constantinides further argues that Turkey plays on the issue of protecting and caring for Turkish minorities (e.g. in Bulgaria and in Thrace) in order to promote Neo-Ottomanism and cites occupied northern Cyprus as one more example of the "strategic use that Turkey makes of the minorities" (p. 331). Mango, however, rejects the view that Turkey's occupation of the island is an example of Turkish expansionism and portrays Turkey as a "regional role model" (Coufoudakis 1997: 157-158).

---

[17] This further enhances Turkey's importance to the US, which in turn perpetuates US support for Turkey. This support reveals itself as pressure on the EU countries to promote Turkey's EU membership, an unwillingness to condemn Turkey's poor human rights record, and an acceptance of the status quo in Cyprus in violation of UN resolutions.

[18] The term Neo-Ottomanism was initially used by David Barchard in "Turkey and the West," London, Rutledge & Kegan Paul.

V. Consequences of the Status Quo

What are the consequences that have resulted from the presence of Turkish troops in Cyprus? The insistence of Turkey to retain troops on the island has been a major impediment to a solution of the Cyprus problem. The status quo has hurt both the GCs and TCs and has necessitated large public military expenditures by Cyprus, Greece, and Turkey. Close to 30000 Turkish Cypriots have emigrated mainly to Germany and Britain due to the poor economic state of the "TRNC" and the increased number of illegal Turkish settlers from Eastern Anatolia that has led to substantial demographic changes.[19] Relations between Greece and Turkey have been strained over issues regarding the Cyprus issue, the Turkish minorities in Thrace and due to disputes in the Aegean sea over territorial waters, the continental shelf, and air space (Constantinides, 1996).

The Turkish invasion and continuing presence of Turkish troops on the island has led to increased military expenidtures in the region by Cyprus, Greece and Turkey (Dunne et al., 2003; Karagol & Palaz, 2004; Kollias et al., 2004; Kollias & Paleologou, 2003; Sezgin, 2004). Cyprus's high military burden is due to the perceived threat that Turkey one day may wish to engage in military operations to occupy the whole island. During 1990-1995, Turkey ranked first and Greece ranked fifth in imports of conventional weapons (Dunne et al., 2003).[20] Between 1985 and 1999, Greece's defence burden (i.e. its military expenditure as a percentage of GDP) was much higher than the EU and NATO averages, and in 1999 it was 4.8 percent (Kollias and Paleologou, 2003).[21]

Greece has increased its expenditures to maintain a balance of power with Turkey, to protect its national interests and sovereignty, and to prevent further military operations by Turkey against the Greek Cypriots (Dunne et al., 2003). Kollias and Paleologou (2003) have found empirical evidence that Greece's military expenditure during the period 1960-1998 was positively and significantly influenced by external security concerns related to Turkish defence expenditure. As Kollias points out, "Turkey is perceived by Greek security and defence policy as the main and most imminent source of external threat to its sovereignty and national interests" (as cited in Kollias & Paleologou 2003: 438). Dunne et al. have also found this perceived Turkish threat to be "one of the long-run determinants of Greek

---

[19] Many TC do not get along very well with the Turkish settlers. They see the latter as being different from them despite their Turkish background.
[20] Based on SIPRI data.
[21] Based on SIPRI data.

military spending" (p.456). More importantly, they have found "some evidence that military spending crowds out other forms of government spending in Greece" (p. 459).

Turkey has justified its military expenditure as necessary to protect itself from the Greek threat as well as other perceived threats in the region. Various studies have sought to determine the effects of Turkey's defence expenditures on its economic growth. Studies by Sezgin (2004), Dunne et al. (2001), and Karagol & Palaz (2004) have found that Turkey's military expenditure has negatively affected Turkey's economic growth. Sezgin (2004: 203) has also found "Turkish arms imports [to] have contributed to Turkey's indebtedness."

The aforementioned suggest that Turkey's military presence in Cyprus has created large economic costs for Cyprus, Greece and Turkey. Furthermore, this military build-up has cultivated feelings of insecurity and at times has led to increased tensions. This became very apparent when the Cypriot government had announced its decision to buy Russian S-300 missiles. Turkey threatened that it would sink any ships transporting the missiles to Cyprus. Under great pressure from the USA and other countries and to avoid further tension and conflict, the Cypriot government decided to deploy the missiles to the Greek island of Crete. However, one may argue that Turkey's military might and presence on the island do contribute to regional stability by deterring Greece from engaging in any sort of military confrontation with Turkey.

Many would argue that the current state of Greco-Turkish relations is less hostile than it was compared to even just a few years back. However, during this recent period of seemingly improved relations between the Greek and Turkish governments, the TSK have continued to provoke Greek sentiments. Over the years, Turkish jet fighters have constantly entered Greek air space without following due procedures which include the submission of flight plans. However, Turkey disputes Greece's air space.[22] Nevertheless, if indeed Turkey wants to reduce tension in the Aegean and contribute to better relations, tactful diplomacy would suggest that such provocations should be avoided, especially during a period of time when the Greek governments of Mr. Karamanlis (and in the past Mr. Simitis) have strongly supported Turkey's bid to join the EU. Instead, violations of Greek air space have intensified during the last three years occuring on a monthly basis. Violations even occurred in December 2004 when Greece and Cyprus chose not to veto a decision that granted Turkey a date to begin its EU

---

[22] Greece argues that its national airspace extends to 16kms. Turkey recognizes only 10kms.

Accession Talks. Similarly, on April 12, 2005, as the Foreign Ministers of Greece (Mr. Moleviatis) and Turkey (Mr. Gul) were *announcing confidence building measures* (italics added) to reduce the causes of tension and conflict, 28 Turkish jet fighters violated Greek air space ten times in the northern and central parts of the Aegean!![23] Such provocative actions, far from contributing to stability, create unnecessary tension and skepticism about Turkey's true intentions and role in the region.

VI. A Future of Stability?

Turkey's insistence on maintaining its troops in Cyprus was one of the main reasons that the latest UN initiative for a comprehensive solution failed. The fifth version of the Annan Plan included provisions that were unacceptable to the Greek Cypriots. For instance, although the Plan provided for a gradual demilitarization of the island, it did not guarantee complete demilitarization. Moreover, it would allow Turkey to use military force when it deemed necessary to restore order in the Greek Constituent State that was to be created! The presence of military troops on the island could be considered of secondary concern since the Turkish Armed Forces can quickly be deployed from Turkey to Cyprus. What is of greater concern for the Greeks in this Plan is Turkey's intervention rights. Given that the Turkish government (i.e. the MGK) has repeatedly rejected the proposal of the Cyprus government for a complete removal of *all* Greek and Turkish troops and the replacement of the Cyprus National Guard with an EU force, it is clear that the real reasons for Turkey's demands for the creation of two states and its continuing military presence on the island has nothing to do with the protection of the Turkish Cypriots.

Copley (2004: 5) argues that Prime Minister Erdogan "was clearly instructed by the TGB to continue to escalate Turkish demands on the Annan Plan" so that the Greek Cypriots would reject it.[24] This was done because the TGB and MGK felt that the Annan Plan's provision for a gradual (yet partial) demilitarization jeopardized Turkey's long term strategic interests because it failed to take into account the TGB's concerns regarding a perceived Iranian threat which is a potential obstacle to its neo-Ottomanist expansion in the Caucausus and Central Asian Turkic regions.

---

[23] Greece and Turkey agree on confidence-building measures, (2005, April 15), *The Cyprus Weekly*, p. 19.

[24] This also suggests that Turkish Cypriot leaders are not free to make their own decisions regarding the Cyprus issue. Therefore, when any Turkish official states that it is the leaders of the two communities that must work together to negotiate a solution, he is making such remarks to create the impression that the Turkish government is not the key to the solution. This of course, is far from reality.

Therefore, to the extent that neo-Ottomanism is true, Turkey's military presence in any region is likely to create destabilizing conditions.

The Annan Plan legalizes violations of human rights of Greek Cypriots created by the Turkish invasion. Such violations would perpetuate feelings of distrust and possibly create new threats. For the Cyprus issue to be resolved and for Greco-Turkish relations to be normalized, a solution must be found that serves the national interests and strategic concerns of all parties involved, while simultaneously restoring the human rights of all Cypriots. For sure, a non-solution is not the solution. In addressing the Turkish parliament on February 17, 2004, Turkish Foreign Minister Abdullah Gul said:

> *Our intention and our desire is to have the two sides agree on a document and for the two peoples to accept it. That would be the ideal solution. If that happens, our region will be not one of hostility and confrontation, but to the contrary, one of cooperation, solidarity and common interests. The eastern Mediterranean will be a region of cooperation (BBC Monitoring European, February 17, 2004).*

Mr Gul's words imply that the status quo does not foster regional stability but rather hostility and confrontation. However, while referring to the outcome of the EU Copenhagen Summit of December 12-13, 2002, in the same address, Mr Gul also stated that, "it was the Greek Cypriot side's unilateral accession to the EU this year and the great problems that this would usher that made us assume [finally after 30 years!] the political will to settle this [i.e. the Cyprus] issue." Hence, Mr. Gul's own contradictory remarks in this address to the parliament support the view that Turkey has never really wanted to change the de facto division of the island and therefore (to use Mr. Gul's very own words) has never cared about reducing the regional tension, hostility and confrontation. The only reason why Turkey tried to appear supportive of efforts made for a solution was to secure a date from the EU for the beginning of Accession Talks.

On February 27, 2004 in a monthly press briefing held at the Office of the Chief of the General Staff (OCGS), Major-General Sabri Demirezen stated that:

> *The Turkish Armed Forces(TSK) have always supported the search for a **fair and lasting solution** [bold added] to the Cyprus problem...and that every effort necessary to ensure that a solution which safeguards the security interests of the Republic of Turkey, as well as those of the*

[self-declared] Turkish Republic of Northern Cyprus was being made (BBC Monitoring European, Feb. 27, 2004).

Unfortunately, the TSK has never wanted a change to the de facto division let alone a *fair and lasting* solution. Two months after the above monthly media briefing, the TSK's Chief of Staff, General Hilmi Ozkok, while referring to the benefits of the proposed Annan Plan, stated that, "those [Greek Cypriots] who will come to the north will be able to take back only one third of *their* (italics added) properties." If only one-third of the Greek Cypriot refugees are allowed to take back *their* own properties, how fair can such a solution be? Can such a solution be a foundation for stability and peace?

The apparent stability on the island is fragile. No doubt a fair compromise must be reached. Such a compromise is likely to be achieved with less difficulty if foreign policy decisions are taken by the TC leaders and not by the MGK or even the Turkish government. This paper suggests that the members of the Turkish General Staff are unwilling to compromise their own personal interests. These interests conflict with those of the people of Cyprus, Greece, *and* Turkey. These interests conflict with long term peace in the Eastern Mediterranean. To the extent that neo-Ottomanism is for real, Turkey's military presence in Cyprus is a cause of tension and will not result in regional stability in the long term.

References

Andreou, A.S., Mateou, N.H. and Zombanakis, G.A. (2003) 'The Cyprus puzzle and the Greek-Turkish arms race: Forecasting developments using genetically evolved fuzzy cognitive maps', Defence and Peace Economics, 14(2), 293-310.

Constantinides, S. (1996) 'Turkey: The emergence of a new foreign policy and the neo-ottoman imperial model', Journal of Political and Military Sociology, 24 (2), Winter, 323-34.

Copley, G.R. (2004) 'Cyprus: Blaming the Victims, Missing the Point', Defense & Foreign Affairs Strategic Policy, 32(7/8), July/Aug, p. 4-7.

Cost of invasion is now 6.8bn pounds (2004, July 23) The Cyprus Weekly.

Coufoudakis, V. (1997) 'Turkey-The challenge of a new role' [book review] Journal of Political and Military Sociology, 25 (1), Summer, 157-59.

Dunne, J.P. et al. (2003) 'The demand for military spending in the peripheral economies of Europe', Defence and Peace Economics, 14(6), December, 447-60.

Elekdag, S. (1996) 'Two and a half war strategy', Perceptions, 1, 33-57.

Fouskas, V.K. (2003) Zones of Conflict: US Foreign Policy in the Balkans and the Greater Middle East, London: Pluto Press.

Gerassimos, K. (2003) 'A brief overview of the evolution of civil-military relations in Albania, Greece, and Turkey during the post-WWII period', Journal of Political and Military Sociology, 31, 57-70.
Gorvet, J. (2003) 'Monitoring the military might', Middle East, 338: 18.
Gurel, S. (1985) Kibris Tarihi, Instanbul: Kaynak Yayinlari.
International Institute for Strategic Studies (IISS) (2002), Strategic Comments, 8(10).
Jenkins, G. (2001) 'Context and Circumstance: The Turkish Military and Politics', Adelphi Paper, 337, London: Oxford University Press.
Karabelias, G. (1999) 'The evolution of civil-military relations in post-war Turkey, 1980-95', Middle Eastern Studies, 35, 130-32.
Karagol, E. and Palaz, S. (2004) 'Does defence expenditure deter economic growth in Turkey? A cointegration analysis', Defence and Peace Economics, 15 (3), June, 289-298.
Kollias, C., Naxakis, C. and Zarangas L. (2004) 'Defence spending and growth in Cyprus: A causal analysis', Journal of Defence and Peace Economics, 15(3), June, 299-307.
Kollias, C. and Paleologou, S.-M. (2003) 'Domestic political and external security determinants of the demand for Greek military expenditure', Defence and Peace Economics, 14(6), December, 437-45.
Lesser, I.O. (2000) 'Changes on the Turkish Domestic Scene and their Foreign Policy Implications', in Zalmay Khalilzad et al. (eds.), The Future of Turkish-Western Relations: Towards a Strategic Plan, Arlington VA, RAND, p.16.
Mango, A. (1994). Turkey-The Challenge of a New Role, Westport: Praeger.
Mchenry, J.A. (1981) The Uneasy Partnership on Cyprus, 1919-1939: The Political and Diplomatic Interaction Between Great Britain, Turkey, andthe Turkish Cypriot Community. Unpublished doctoral dissertation, University of Kansas.
Papasotiriou, C. (1998) 'Regional and international conditions for a viable solution to the Cyprus problem', The Cyprus Review, 10, 11-18.
Parla, T. (1998) 'Merchantile Militarism in Turkey, 1960-1998', New Perspectives on Turkey, 18.
Richter, H. A. (2001) 'Ankara's policy towards Cyprus and the European Union', The Cyprus Review, 13, 29-45.
Roper, J. (1999) 'The West and Turkey: Varying roles, common interest', International Spectator, 34, (1).
Richmond, O. (2003) 'Turkey in World Politics' [book review], The Cyprus Review, 15, 167-71.
Sezgin, S. (2004) 'An empirical note on external debt and defence expenditures in Turkey', Defence and Peace Economics, 15(2), April, 199-203.
Sonmezoglu, F. (1991) The Cyprus Problem: Attitudes and Positions of the Sides Involved, Intanbul University Press.
Spyridakis, C. (1974) A Brief History of Cyprus (Rev. ed.). Nicosia: Zavallis Press.
Turkish chief of staff briefs media on Army's stand on Cyprus, duty to nation (2004, April 13, p.1), BBC Monitoring European, London.
Turkish foreign minister addresses parliament on Cyprus issue (2004, February 17, p. 1), BBC Monitoring European, London.

Turkish military support fair, lasting solution in Cyprus (2004, February 27, p. 1), BBC Monitoring European, London.

Turkish National Security Council budget to be cut by 60 per cent (2003, November 2, p.1), BBC Monitoring European, London.

Turkmen, I. (2000, Nov. 30) Moving away from rational policy, Hurriyet.

Yavuz, M.H. (1992) The Cyprus Problem: Attitudes and Positions of the Sides Involved [book review], The Cyprus Review, 4(2), Fall, 135-8.

Yelsida, B. (1979) Problems of National Political Integration in Cyprus, MA Thesis, San Francisco State University.

Chapter 8
MILITARY TENSION AND DEFENCE SPENDING DYNAMICS BETWEEN GREECE AND TURKEY

Christos Kollias, Susana-Maria Paleologou

Introduction

The Greek-Turkish conflict is well documented in the international relations literature (*see inter allia* Sonmezoglou and Ayman, 2003; Dokos and Tsakonas, 2003; Yiallourides and Tsakonas 2001; Constas,1991; Larrabee, 1992). Since both countries yearly allocate a substantial part of their income to defence they have also attracted considerable attention in the defence economics literature a comprehensive and critical survey of which can be found in Brauer (2002, 2003). In comparative terms, vis-à-vis other NATO and EU countries, their defence burden (i.e. the share of military expenditure in GDP) is the highest among the members of NATO and the EU. In 2002 it stood at 4.3% in Greece and at 4.9% in Turkey. Furthermore, in contrast to the predominant trend in the post bipolar era, their defence budgets have increased in real terms by approximately 31% in the case of Greece (from $4013 mil. to $5241 mil. in constant 2000 prices) and by 55% in the case of Turkey (from $6373 mil. to $9888 mil. in constant 2000 prices) during 1990-2003.

Several factors can be hypothesized as possible explanatory determinants of military spending. Variables such as GDP, external threat(s), spillins from allies, domestic political factors, the interests of the military industrial complex have been used in empirical research seeking to identify the determinants of such expenditures by states (Sandler and Hartley, 1995). Given the tense bilateral relations of Greece and Turkey, particular attention has been paid to external security variables that could help in explaining their respective defence outlays (*inter allia*: Sezgin and Yildirim, 2002; Kollias and Paleologou, 2003; Ocal, 2002). Indeed, a number of studies have empirically investigated whether the hypothesis of a Greek-Turkish arms race can find a modicum of empirical verification. Overall the reported results are mixed since apart from the methodological issues involved in such empirical studies; their findings depend among other things on the methodology used and the time period covered by the tests (Brauer, 2002; 2003; Kollias, 2001).

Despite the marked improvement in their bilateral relations in recent years, spurred by the so called *earthquake diplomacy* and Greece's support to Turkey's EU candidacy, the major issues that have in the past brought the two countries to the brink of war on a number of occasions remain unresolved and could potentially lead to a deterioration in their relations in the future. As Gunluk-Senesen (2001, 2004) observes, in the post bipolar period, Greek-Turkish bilateral relations have gone through the usual cycle "*tension – negotiation – tension*". In fact, as pointed out therein, some major events have marked this period such as the Imia crisis in 1996, the proposed deployment of the S-300 missiles in Cyprus in 1997-98, the declaration of the joint defence area by Greece and Cyprus in 1993, the issue of the extension of Greek territorial waters to 12 miles and the Ocalan affair in 1999. Such events mark the downturns of the bilateral relations cycle. Others, such as the lifting of the Greek veto in 1995 to Turkey's accession to the customs union and again in 1999 the lifting of the veto to the EU candidacy by Turkey, the Madrid Declaration in 1998, the signing of a number of bilateral treaties, mark upward turns in the cycle. In fact, ever since the rapprochement spurred by the earthquakes, Greek-Turkish bilateral relations have gone through an unprecedented improvement (Evin, 2004; Anastasakis, 2004; Tsakonas, 2001a; 2001b; Sonmezoglou and Ayman, 2003; Dokos and Tsakonas, 2003).

Yet, despite this marked improvement two of the issues that divide the two countries – Cyprus and the Aegean – and have in the past brought them well beyond the bellicose rhetoric and sabre rattling stage to the brink of a military confrontation remain unresolved. These issues are emotive for both sides and touch upon fundamental aspects of their respective national strategy and security policies as well as threat perceptions embedded in their respective peoples. As long as such issues of strategic importance for both countries remain unresolved it is possible that they will continue to drive their respective defence budgets irrespective of the progress achieved in terms of finding a less tense *mondus vivendi*, replacing the usual bellicose rhetoric that has often dominated their interaction with a climate of cordiality and good will (Anastasakis, 2004; Evin, 2004). This paper investigates the possible impact of one of these issues on their respective military spending. It focuses on the Aegean dispute and in particular the disputes over sovereign airspace length using a military tension index.

I. The Military Tension Index

As already pointed out, recent years have witnessed a marked improvement in the bilateral climate and interaction between the two countries. This progress has led to the signing of a number of bilateral agreements on issues such as culture, energy, ecology, trade, illegal migration and organized crime, economic and regional cooperation, tourism etc. Although these are important and to some extent unprecedented steps that can facilitate a sustainable, long term improvement in their relations, they nevertheless could be classified as issues that fall within the sphere of *low politics*. When it comes to issues that fall within the sphere of *high politics* and form the strategic core of their relations marginal or no progress has been achieved. Given this, it could be argued that in their respective security agenda and concomitant defence planning, mutual concerns over each other's long term strategic intensions remain as important long-term determinants of their military spending.

Defence planning takes place with a medium to long term time horizon and probably is unaffected by fluctuations in bilateral relations that do not appear to lead to strategic shifts and to sustainable long term solutions to the issues that form the strategic core of bilateral relations and are the source of tension and friction. Current defence capability is the result of decisions made by defence planners in the past. Current defence decisions determine future defence capability and future balance of military strength between rivals. Defence planning and decisions are made under conditions of uncertainty. If no observable change in the rival's long term strategy is evident, then defence planners will tend, at least partially, to decide upon past experience. If the rival's behaviour and/or actions in the past were – or were perceived to be – aggressive and hostile, then a "*better safe than sorry*" attitude will tend to dominate current defence planning and decisions irrespective of the climate in which current bilateral discourse is conducted. If a rival has behaved aggressively in the past, defence planners will tend to assume that there is no reason to expect it will not do so again in the future if the issues that caused this aggressiveness remain unresolved. Even more so, if the rival has in the past relied or used its military strength either to extract concessions or to advance its interests by force.

The dispute concerning the length of Greek sovereign airspace over the Aegean is one of the issues that falls within the sphere of high politics and forms the strategic core of Greek-Turkish bilateral relations. The dispute causes on a daily basis dog fights between military aircrafts. Such encounters of fighter planes (often armed) maintain the two air forces on high alert with the concomitant impact on the level of military tension. This practice has remained unaffected by the substantial improvement of recent years albeit it no longer leads to bellicose exchanges between the two governments. Since the current improvement has thus far not affected strategic core issues such as the length of sovereign Greek airspace one could suggest that such issues dividing the two countries continue to partially drive and determine military spending and arms procurement decisions. To examine empirically the possible impact on defence expenditure the military tension index used here consists of the number of Greek airspace violations over the Aegean by the Turkish Air Force. Such activities maintain and increase the underlying military tension which, one can reasonably argue, has a positive impact on the defence budgets either increasing them or at least rendering them more inelastic and therefore less prone for cutbacks. Indeed, as it can be seen in Figure 1, Greek and Turkish military spending has exhibited a steady upward trend, growing in real terms by 20% and 113% in Greece and Turkey respectively during 1985-2003.

Figure 1: **Greek and Turkish Military Spending 1985-2003** (in constant 2000 US $ mil).

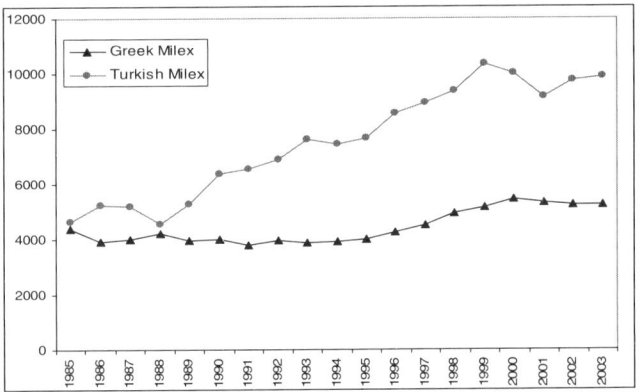

In brief and without delving into the technical substance which is well beyond our scope here, the essence of the issue at hand is as follows. Greece claims a 10-mile airspace over the Aegean and this claim is disputed by Turkey that "recognizes" only a 6-mile airspace i.e. a length equal to that of Greek territorial waters. At the same time Turkey has declared a casus belli policy if Greece extends its territorial waters in line with the international treaty that allows countries to claim a 12-mile territorial water zone with the corresponding 12-mile airspace. Thus, the reported violations, i.e. the index used here, to a large extend, but not exclusively, concern the entrance of Turkish air force planes into the area between the six and ten mile zone. In essence, what is being proposed here is that once one of the two parties in a dyad of states perceives the actions of the other as infringements of its sovereign territory (in this case airspace) such actions, irrespective of the grounds on which they are justified, generate tension and in particular, military tension since branches of their respective armed forces are involved. In this case in almost daily dog fights mostly in the six to ten mile zone mentioned earlier. Clearly of course, the same in reverse applies for the other member of the dyad that may very well perceive the length of national airspace claims by the other party, again irrespective of the grounds on which they are justified, as inhibiting its right to free and unobstructed access to international airspace. Therefore, given the differences between the two parties on the length of the airspace, this issue becomes a source of tension and friction that has a military dimension build into it. One could then reasonably argue that this could have an impact, albeit perhaps indirect, on defence policy and therefore military spending. Here, it should be stressed again, that the aim of this study is not of course to delve into the technical and legal substance of this issue but rather to merely point to the fact that the inability to make substantial headway let alone resolve it, results in military tension that in turn may at least partially drive defence spending.

Figure 2:   Number of Violations of the Greek Airspace.

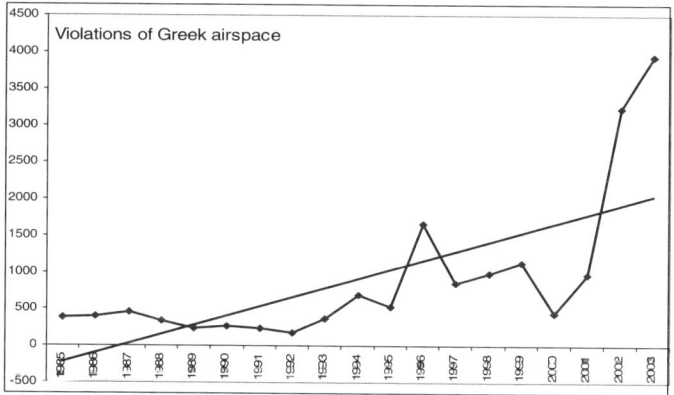

Turning back to the proposed tension index, a graphical representation reveals that, in the last fifteen years or so, the proposed index has followed an upward trend, seemingly unaffected by the rapprochement of recent years (Figure 2). Indeed, allowing for a fall in 2000 the number of violations has increased substantially especially in 2001-03 as it can be seen in the relevant figure. However, before proceeding with the use of this proposed tension index in our empirical tests a number of points of clarification are in order. In particular, it should be pointed out that this index, published by the Greek Ministry of Defence, is not independently verified by outside actors such as for example NATO sources. This of course raises issues concerning the validity of this index along with the methodological problems associated with the definition of what in fact constitutes an airspace violation. It should however be mentioned that the Greek Air Force HQ directly relays real time data of Turkish Air Force activity in the disputed airspace to NATO HQ in Brussels. Allowing for the undoubtedly important methodological and reliability weaknesses of this data series, it is nevertheless possible to use it in order to capture empirically the underlying divisions and concomitant tension in bilateral relations since it can be argued that it encapsulates military threat perceptions.

II.   Empirical Findings

In this section we proceed to examine whether we can establish empirically a relationship between military tension as reflected by the violations time series (Figure 2) and defence expenditure by Turkey and Greece. Although this by no means would unequivocally establish the presence of an armaments race between the two states it nevertheless will offer empirical verification in support of the argument that the defence budgets of our dyad are at least partially determined by the tension that is generated from issues that form the strategic core of their relations. To this effect the following equations were tested for the period 1985-2003:

$$GMILEX_{it} = \alpha_0 + \beta_1 GMILEX_{it-1} + \beta_2 VL_{it-1} + \varepsilon_{it} \quad (1)$$
$$TMILEX_{it} = \gamma_0 + \gamma_1 TMILEX_{it-1} + \gamma_2 VL_{it-1} + e_{it} \quad (2)$$

where *(GMILEX)* and *(TMILEX)* are the Greek and the Turkish military expenditure respectively, and *(VL)* is the number of yearly violations of the Greek air space by the Turkish air force. However, we need to treat the possible presence of endogeneity formally since the number of violations of the Greek air space might be endogenous. When there are endogeneity problems the traditional OLS methodology results are biased. We first used the standard Ordinary Least Squares (OLS) regression technique and then we take into account that the airspace violations variable might be endogenous. For this reason we use the instrumental variable (IV) technique. Our empirical results reveal that the variable is endogenous only in the case of Greece. The

OLS regression procedure requires the residuals and the RHS variables of an equation to be uncorrelated. Thus, OLS yields biased estimates when the RHS variables are influenced by the LHS variable and consequently the residual of the equation. We test for the endogeneity of the Greek air space violations variable in equations (1) and (2) by using a Hausman (1978) procedure via the IV estimation. If we find the presence of endogeneity we then use an instrumental variable for *(VL)*. The Hausman test considers the difference in two estimates. The first estimate must be consistent and asymptotically efficient under the null hypothesis but inconsistent under the alternative hypothesis. The second estimate is not asymptotically efficient under the null hypothesis but consistent under both the null and the alternative hypotheses. In our case the null hypothesis is that the *(VL)* variable is exogenous. The results are reported in Table 1 below. The OLS coefficients will be unbiased, consistent and efficient if the null hypothesis is satisfied. If the alternative hypothesis holds, which is the existence of endogeneity, then the OLS estimation is biased and only IV estimation provides unbiased estimators. We report the estimators from the IV method in Table 2, although we will rely on OLS for efficient estimators if there is the case that the null hypothesis of the Hausman test is not rejected. The Hausman test is a single-equation F-test. In order to perform the Hausman test we need to include an instrumental variable in equations (1) and (2). The null hypothesis of the F-test is that the coefficient of the instrumental variable is equal to zero. If we do not reject the null hypothesis then we can not reject the OLS as the method to estimate the models. For each equation we use as instruments the lag of the *(VL)* variable, which determines the Greek defence spending.

Table 1: Results of the Hausman Test.

Equation of:	Variable
	Violations (VL)
Greek Defence Expenditure *(gmilex)*	$F(1, 15) = 5.931^*$
Turkish Defence Expenditure *(tmilex)*	$F(1, 15) = 0.021$

* statistically significant at 5% level

In Table 2 the IV estimates of equations (1) and (2) are presented. The significance of the *(VL)* variable is not altered only in the case of Turkey. The results are consistent with the Hausman test for endogeneity which suggested that the *(VL)* variable in the case of Greece is endogenous and in the case of Turkey is exogenous. Thus only in the case of Turkey the OLS estimates given in Table 2 are unbiased, consistent and efficient.

Table 2: Instrumental Variable Estimation of the Impact of Airspace Violations on Military Spending, 1985-2003.

Dependent Variable	Greek Military Expenditure (gmilex)		Turkish Military Expenditure (tmilex)	
Intercept	1.18 (1.57**)	1.61 (2.16*)	0.57 (0.70)	0.69 (0.90)
VL (-1)	0.03 (2.40*)	-	-0.009 (-0.25)	-
VL (-2)	-	0.06 (3.01*)	-	0.003 (0.07)
Dep. vb. (-1)	0.83 (8.56*)	0.76 (7.68*)	0.95 (8.78*)	0.92 (9.23*)
R^2	0.93	0.94	0.90	0.90
$\overline{R}^2$	0.92	0.93	0.89	0.89
SEE	0.03	0.03	0.08	0.08
DW	2.06	2.65	1.87	1.86
LM χ^2 (1)	0.26	2.50	0.02	0.03
Normality χ^2 (2)	0.75	2.62	1.14	1.34

Notes: R^2 is the coefficient of determination; $\overline{R}^2$ is the adjusted coefficient of determination; SEE are the standard errors of the regression. DW is the Durbin-Watson statistic; Lagrange multiplier test of the residual autocorrelation; Normality test is based on a test of skewness and kurtosis of the residuals. * Statistical significant at the 5% level; ** Statistical significant at 10% level.

Table 3: Seemingly Unrelated Regression Estimation of the Impact of Airspace Violations on Military Spending, 1985-2003.

Dependent Variable	Greek Military Expenditure (gmilex)		Turkish Military Expenditure (tmilex)	
Intercept	1.42 (1.64)**	1.71 (2.35)*	0.42 (0.59)	0.33 (0.43)
VL (-1)	0.04 (2.48)*	-	-0.02 (-0.48)	-
VL (-2)	-	0.06 (3.15)*	-	-0.0081 (-0.21)
Dep. vb. (-1)	0.79 (7.08)*	0.74 (7.74)*	0.97 (10.30)*	0.97 (9.91)*
R^2	0.89	0.94	0.91	0.90
$\overline{R}^2$	0.88	0.93	0.90	0.88
SEE	0.04	0.03	0.08	0.08
DW	1.71	2.66	1.98	1.92

Notes: R^2 is the coefficient of determination, $\overline{R}^2$ is the adjusted coefficient of determination, SEE are the standard errors of the regression. DW is the Durbin-Watson statistic. *Statistical significant at the 5% level; **Statistical significant at 10% level.

The seemingly unrelated regression estimation (SURE) consists of a series of endogenous variables that are considered as a group because they are linked to each other. The IV estimators yield consistent parameter estimates when the equation systems are simultaneous. However, IV estimators yield inefficient estimates, because they apply only to a single equation within the system equations. Thus, they do take into account that one or more predetermined variables are omitted from the equation to be estimated, but they do not take into account the fact that there may be predetermined variables omitted from other equations as well. An alternative source of inefficiency arises because single-equation estimation does not account for the cross equation correlation among errors. The problem of loss of efficiency can be resolved by using the SURE model, which consists of a series of equations linked because the error terms across equations are correlated. The SURE method involves generalised least squares estimation and improves the efficiency by taking into explicit account the fact that cross-equation correlations may not be zero. These results are reported in Table 3. As we can see the previous results obtained with the IV estimation are not altered. Overall they seem to suggest that only in the case of Greek military expenditure there exits a positive and significant effect from the violations tension index. In the case of Turkish defence spending, the coefficient sign is negative but totally insignificant in both the instrumental variable estimation as well as the results obtained from the SURE methodology. These findings may be interpreted as one sided threat perception behaviour on the part of Greece and are in line with those reported by Kollias (2004). In other words the activities of the Turkish air force are perceived by defence planners in Greece as evidence of aggressive strategic intentions vis-à-vis the national interests of Greece. The insignificant impact of the tension index on Turkish military spending is however more difficult to explain. Possibly, the presence of *noise* i.e. other strategic considerations such as internal security may render establishing such a relation difficult.

Concluding Remarks

The recent improvement in Greek-Turkish bilateral relations has not affected issues that form the core of their strategic differences and have in the past brought the two countries close to a military confrontation. Despite the marked progress, their respective defence expenditures have continued to increase in real terms. Using a military tension index this study tried to examine whether the major issues such as the Aegean airspace that remain unresolved can help in partly explaining Greek and Turkish military expenditures. It should be stressed here that the violations index was not used to examine the presence of an armaments race between the two countries in the action re-action sense, but rather to see whether it is possible to trace and establish a perception behaviour linkage in the case of defence spending. On the basis of the obtained results it seems that only a one-sided linkage was established in the case of Greece. Thus, in its case one may attempt to partly explain military spending in terms of this underlying military tension as captured by the aforementioned index. Again, without entering into the substance of the airspace issue, from a Greek defence planner's perspective, the violations of Greek airspace by the Turkish air force offers ample evidence that there has been no marked change in the long term strategy of Turkey as perceived by Greek security policy makers and defence planners. Finally, and irrespective of the empirical findings reported herein it should be also added that as long as such issues of strategic difference exist between the two countries, both will continue in the future to allocate substantial resources to defence thus depriving themselves and their peoples from the possible benefits of a peace dividend.

References

Anastasakis, O. (2004) "Greece and Turkey in the Balkans: Cooperation or rivalry?" *Turkish Studies*, 5(1), 45-60.
Brauer, J. (2002) "Survey and review of the defence economics literature on Greece and Turkey: what have we learned?", *Defence and Peace Economics*, 13(2), pp. 85-107.
Brauer, J. (2003) "Turkey and Greece: a comprehensive survey of the defence economics literature" in C. Kollias & G. Gunluk-Senesen [eds], pp. 193-241.
Constas, D. [ed] (1991) The Greek-Turkish conflict in the 1990s, Macmillan.
Dokos, Th. and P. Tsakonas (2003) "Greek-Turkish Security Relations Reconsidered: A View from Athens", in C. Kollias & G. Gunluk-Senesen [eds], pp. 9-35.
Evin, A. (2004) "Changing Greek perspectives on Turkey: an assessment of the post-earthquake rapprochement", *Turkish Studies*, 5(1), 4-20.
Gunluk-Senesen, G. (2004) "An analysis of the action-reaction behaviour in the defence expenditures of Turkey and Greece", *Turkish Studies*, 5(1), 78-98.
Gunluk-Senesen, G. (2001) "Turkish defence expenditures in view of the ups and downs in Turkish-Greek relations: is there a reaction", *Hellenic Studies* 9(2),73-89.
Kollias, C. (2004) "The Greek-Turkish rapprochement, the underlying military tension and Greek defence spending", *Turkish Studies*, 5(1), 99-116.
Kollias, C. (2001) "A look at the methodological issues involved in the Greek-Turkish arms race hypothesis", *Hellenic Studies*, 9(2), 91-114.
Kollias, C. and Gunluk-Senesen G. [eds] (2003) *Greece and Turkey in the 21st Century. The Political Economy Perspective*, New York: Nova Science Publishers.
Kollias, C. and S. Paleologou (2003), Domestic political and external security determinants of the demand for Greek military expenditure, *Defence and Peace Economics* 14(6), 437-445.
Larrabee, S. (1992) "Instability and change in the Balkans", *Survival*, 34, pp. 31-49.
Ocal, N. (2002) Asymmetric effects of military expenditure between Turkey and Greece *Defence and Peace Economics* 13(5), 405-416.
Sandler, T. and K. Hartley (1995) *The Economics of Defence*, Cambridge University Press.

Sezgin, S. and J. Yildirim (2002) "The demand for Turkish defence expenditure" *Defence and Peace Economics* 13(2), 121-128.

Sonmezoglou, F., and G. Ayman (2003) "The roots of conflict and the dynamics of change in Turkish-Greek relations", in C. Kollias & G. Gunluk-Senesen [eds], pp: 37-48.

Tsakonas, P. (2001a) "Turkey's road map to the European Union: implications for Greek-Turkish relations and the Cyprus issue", *Hellenic Studies*, 9(1), 71-100.

Tsakonas, P. (2001b) "Turkey's post-Helsinki turbulence. Implications for Greece and the Cyprus issue" *Turkish Studies*, 2(2), 1-40.

Yiallourides, C., and P. Tsakonas [eds] (2001) *Greece and Turkey after the end of the Cold War*, New York & Athens: Caratzas Publishing.

Chapter 9
THE "BROADER" MIDDLE EAST AND NORTH AFRICA: TRANSCENDING BEYOND THE TRADITIONAL *REALPOLITIK*-SECURITY MECHANISMS

Galip Isen

I. Stretched to Fit the "Greater" Middle East

"Middle East" entered lexicons during WW II, with America's rising global predominance. Previous European hegemons preferred "Near" East. Both epithets allude to a presumed "Western" prominence defining the world in zones of interests (Mansfield, 1991: 1-2, Rainer, 1996: 40). U.S. President George W. Bush's "Greater" Middle Eastern Initiative (GMEI) further complicates the terminology. It arbitrarily re-defines a geography by ascribing locality to a perturbing political problematic: America is troubled by "terrorism". It believes terrorism to emanate from the Middle East. When terrorism moves into Afghanistan, down a simple chain of logic, so do the borders of the Middle East. Hence, the modifier "greater".

The area in question resembles a hive of woes threatening regional stability but also considered dangerous for the interests of the Western world[1]: Most countries "possess bloody borders" (Huntington, 1993: 46), have ailing economies and except Israel and Turkey, are ruled by non-democratic regimes. Illiteracy is staggering. Ethnic, religious and gender discrimination is rampant. There are insufficient means of educating and training young, unemployed, unskilled populations for high-tech knowledge societies. The increase in disenfranchised, disenchanted individuals is considered a path to extremism and "terrorism". Illegal migration and transnational crime are ubiquitous. Anti-Americanism and xenophobic sentiments escalate in the shadow of events in Iraq, Afghanistan and Palestine, aggravated by U.S. support of Israel and regional despotisms (*see*: Wittes, 2004; Ottaway, Carothers, 2004).

The GMEI envisioned the integration of the *enlarged* Middle East, comprising Pakistan, Afghanistan, Iran, Turkey and the Arab countries with the West through a liberalization of values and markets. G8 allies, too, were invited to "encourage" local governments for launching democratic reforms, expanding human rights, political liberties and participation; enabling ra-

---
[1] Dar Al Hayat, 13 February 2004. Data based on 2002-2003 UN 2002 Arab Human Development Report (AHDR). NATO's web site added *terrorism, fundamentalism, migration* and *ecological deterioration* among future threats in mid 1990's. New non-military risks include crime, health and corruption.

tional, efficient and accountable governance; moderating political discourse; empowering women; spreading literacy; promoting civil society; speeding economic development; boosting investments and enterpreneurial spirit; raising standards of living; improving education. Political stability thus achieved would reduce the pull of extremism, abate terrorism and enhance security (Wittes, 2004). The G8 Summit at Sea Island included Northern Africa and re-baptized Bush's project the *"Broader Middle East and North Africa Initiative"* (BMENAI)[2].

II. Everywhere is the Middle East!

If poverty, dictatorship, ignorance and violence[3] are global security risks, the *"greater"* Middle East practically encompasses the *entire* Third World[4]. None of the inventoried ills is unique to the Middle East. Other Third World societies excluded from the modern *eucosmos*[5], including non Mideastern Moslem societies, fare little better (*see*: Alam, 2002; Fox, 2001).

---

[2] The BMENAI consists of two documents; a *"Partnership for Progress and a Common Future with the Region of the Broader Middle East and North Africa"*[2] and a *"G8 Plan of Support for Reform"*. The Palestine conflict, omitted in the GMEI, was acknowledged as a cause of problems. The provision to "encourage" change was eschewed on grounds that viable reforms only generate internally. Henceforth, BMENAI will be the preferred abbreviation unless Bush Administration's original GMEI document is meant.

[3] Conflict and violence in the Middle East are not worse than elsewhere (Fox, 2001). In Colombia, America's back garden, the "oldest and most durable democracy in Latin America", 300,000 were killed in 40 years of civil war funded from the cocain trade. More labor leaders were murdered than in any country. In Peru, an electoral crisis resulted in street battles among supporters of presidential candidates in the early 2000's. Two guerilla groups financed by drugs trade, continue warring against the government (CIA Fact Book, 2001). According to the 2001 Human Rights Watch Report "everyday violation of human rights-including police abuse, torture, and lack of access to effective justice systems" remained constant in Latin America while policy makers paid little attention. By 2005, Venezuelan leadership was challenging Bush and in 2006 the ex-Sandinist, Marxist Daniel Ortega won the presidency in Nicaragua.

[4] As well as a considerable population within the modern world – blacks numbering 35 million make up 12.3 percent of America (2000). Approximately one-fourth live in poverty. The median income of an African American household is slightly more than half of whites'. The gap widens. Unemployment is twice as much, higher education half. Black Americans have shorter life expectancy and less access to health care. More than one million black men are incarcerated. The vast majority of African Americans practice Baptist and Methodist Christianity in *separate* churches. They are also the predominant Muslim group in America (Encarta 2000 figures).

[5] Iran holds with Venezuela in economic growth, Malaysia is ahead of Thailand, Egypt is ahead of Ukraine, Turkey slightly behind Russia, Pakistan a little behind-and Indonesia somewhat ahead of India, Bangladesh is just behind Vietnam, Tunisia is well ahead of Georgia and Armenia and Jordan is significantly ahead of Nicaragua. Nearly every Islamic country experienced a decline in population growth compared to Latin America. Islam's weakness is the lag in democracy and gender equality but evidence from human rights watch groups does not paint a prettier picture for most Latin American or ex Soviet countries either (*see*: Alam, 2002). A World Values Study by Harvard scholar Pippa Norris and Ronald Inglehart of Michigan University (2002-RWP02-015) showed only an infinitesimal difference between Moslem and non Moslem subjects' approval of democratic principles and institutions. According to various empirical studies, although religion seems to be particularly important in the Middle East, it is only partially effective in conflicts which are otherwise mostly similar to those occurring elsewhere (Fox, 2001).

Washington's motive in singling out the "greater" Middle East and priming it for a re-launched campaign of "modernization" seems to be the stabilization of the region in the hope of preventing further incidents like 9-11 (Ottaway, Carothers, 2004: 1). However, analyses by several American and foreign scholars,[6] some published before 9-11, attribute "terrorism" to America's imperialistic-hegemonic policies and partisan preference of Israel[7] over Palestinians/Arabs. A uni-dimensional linkage of BMENAI and America's "war against terror" thus obfuscates the "Middle East problem" by reducing focus to a single phenomenon. Even superficially, the premises of the GMEI branch beyond terrorism to a complex of geostrategic prerogatives, control of oil, territorialism and hot conflict. None of these concerns is new. The significance of every problem, from *jihad* or oil to shifty allegiances, is transposed because of the historic phenomenality of the region. Even the 200 year-old "Jewish Question" at the base of the Arab – Israeli conflict cannot be labeled an all–comprising issue.

III. A Way of Looking at the World

"Facts become fiction without adequate frames of reference describing what facts are" – *theory* is linked to the experience at the source of the structures of meaning (Laing, 1967: 17). A "problem" or empirical concern can only be defined in relation to the comprehensive experience from which theories and *Weltanschauungen*[8] spring. Deductions from empirical observation, distended from the *historiogenesis* of facts can obscure the matrices of meaning in which experience "makes sense". The events folding out today in the

---

[6] Some writers on the right claim Washington's foreign policy precipitates terrorism and urge avoiding entanglements abroad as in Bosnia, Kosovo or Somalia. For others, terrorism is a form of covert warfare, a *casus belli* justifying military reprisal (see: Carpenter, 1996,: Carr, 1997; Houghton, 1997; *see also* Guelke,995: 160 Phillips, 1994; Feingold 2002, Ignatieff, 2002). For moderates, most attacks target U.S. *military* presence "*abroad*". What America calls terrorism may be seen by others as anti-imperialist struggle. Radicals as Noam Chomsky (2001), Howard Zinn (2001) or Edward Said (2001) have long denounced American foreign involvement as interventionist, imperialistic and even terrorist-ic. Following 9-11, even sympathetic Moslem reaction was often supplemented by admonitions against Washington's imperialist inclinations, pro Israeli and anti Arab-Moslem policy and support of local autocracies (Rubin, 2001; Brown, 2001).

[7] "There is absolutely no escaping the fact that the recruiting sergeant for Al Qaida is the alienation caused by the Palestinian question". Pat Cox (2003), the President of the European Parliament Liberals.

[8] A comprehensive definition of W*eltanschauung* is provided by Sigmund Freud in Chapter 32 of The New Introductory Lectures to Psychoanalysis (1932): "...*Weltanschauung,* (is) ... an intellectual construction which gives a unified solution of all the problems of our existence in virtue of a comprehensive hypothesis, a construction ... in which no question is left open and... everything in which we are interested finds a place." Literally, "looking on to the world", a W*eltanschauung* is a cognitive style that provides the individual with a theoretical image of the world and describes the criteria of constructing "reality" (Isen, Batmaz, 2000: 134). According to Paul Ricoeur, a perspective, a point of view is "primal" finitude in that it delineates one's open reception of the world (Mcquarrie, 1976: 192).

BMENA gain significance for its historicity. *"Question d'Orient"* emerged out of the competition among fledgling capitalist colonial powers. The long demise of the Ottoman Empire; Napoleon's invasion of Egypt, British and European reaction, Jewish nationalism, the return to "promised lands", Arab – Muslim reciprocation, the interference of major powers in search of geostrategic and economic supremacy and later, expedient energy are few aspects of that historicity (*see*: Mansfield, 1991: 43, 159-166; Rich, 1992: 44-47).

In this paper, singular phenomena as terrorism, oil policy, geopolitics, liberalization or modernization are attached in the context of *globality*. Globality denotes the *one-ness* of the world. It refers to the inherent historic process of organic functional integration and articulation of diverse units all over the world in a *whole* that is motivated by the universal economic *and* cultural dynamics of capitalism[9]. Globality is a holistic, dialectical process that contains idiosyncrasy, conflict, difference and transcendence as well as harmonious integration. It differs from "globalization" which roughly corresponds to the worldwide unification and identification of transnational markets and communications. States gradually feel forced to relinquish their absolute hold on decision making, not to a higher authority, but in a process where interests have become impossible to define relative to national boundaries. The outcome of the articulation, whether it is smooth (as in the case of the capitalization of Japan) or controversial (as in the case of Iran's Islamic Revolution) has repercussions[10] on the totality of the relationship between the "part" and the whole (Isen, 2004: 234).

The big words of yesteryear's politics are radically altered in a holistic and historical *Weltanschauung* of globality. For instance, "geopolitics", an epistemic key to the process of colonialism and a Cold War priority, is now devoid of its content as some piece of strategic or resource rich real estate possessed by one nation that may also serve critical ends sought by others. Oil, too, is rather a commodity, not the strategic "weapon" it used to be after

---

[9] Which also comprise the non-capitalist world, of course. Capitalism is usually understood as a mere economic system of activities operated privately for profit - manufacture, logistics, commerce; banking, etc– (Cameron, 1977: 290-291). Here capitalism denotes not a strictly economic, but an historical social system, a *world system*. As defined by Immanuel Wallerstein (1996), a capitalist world-economy is built around a division of labor that permits it to sustain and reproduce the system and a *geoculture* that defines its *weltanschaaung* legitimating social structures and seeking to contain discontentment. Capitalism's *differentia specifica* is endless capital accumulation through *institutions* that link geographically disparate activities and optimize profits globally (*see*: Wallerstein, 1997).

[10] These repercussions may non-linearly turn to conflict from harmony. Japan's smooth passage to *keiretsu* capitalism from *zaibatsu* oligarchy, for instance, paralleled its role leading to WW II and its aftermath, the American hegemonic progress.

the *Yom Kippur War*[11] (Isen, 2004: 242-243; Han, 2004: 329, 359-363). The BMENA constitutes a critical geography not solely because of geostrategy or resources but because the area delineates a psycho-cultural and temporal fault line enveloping a plethora of Third World issues into a single specific problematic. It represents the most active, the longest and oldest frontier in the *unique* conflict of essence in five centuries: the antinomy of being or not being *modern*.

IV. The Fault Line of Modernity

Modernity is a uniquely European[12] phenomenon. It corresponds to the progress of capitalism as a *world system*. Beside presuming constant technological progress and innovation, modernity represents the "triumph of human freedom and eternal liberation" (Wallerstein, 1995: 471-472). Modernity epitomizes a typical way of mind and life, values and praxes around more or less common and homogeneous, markedly urban, social, political, economic and psychological structures underlying a whole civilization. Originally a Roman word, modern became synonymous with reason, science and progress during the Enlightenment. The "rational" man was "liberated" from religious and metaphysical dogma and assigned a centrality in the natural order of things. The secularization of reason rendered a vision of the individual, previously hypostatic to the divine, as capable of reaching truth by analytical thinking. Analytic secular rationality coupled with a consciousness of self and the uniqueness of individuality, led to the pursuit of such ideals as emancipation, participation and sharing power, wealth and welfare (Alexander, 1995: 66; Barzun, 2000: 125-126, 271, 522, 714; Tipps, 1973: 200-201; Wallerstein, 1995; 1997). Beside seeking technical and pragmatic[13] innovation, modernity thrives on a constant flux of originality, dissent and diversity where ideas are concerned. Therefore it is also a pluralistic project of "unity in diversity", liberating the individual's mind, will and faith by standing open to choice (Barzun, 2000: *xv*, 4-9, 1250).

Reason is the faculty of making sense of experience by constructing causality patterns. Many animals are capable of reasoning (Bonner, 1983: *passim*; Cameron, 1977: 10; Macquarrie, 1973: 140-141,). It is a mode of adapting and relating to things in the life environment. By "defining" reality,

---

[11] Geopolitics or oil is still fairly important but hardly the backbone of world polity.
[12] Europe is used here "more as a cultural than a cartographical expression referring to North America as well as Western Europe" (Wallerstein 1997). Anglophone Oceania can also be considered part of this cultural geography.
[13] *Gr.* relating to things.

reason renders possible the recognition and solution of problems. Anything from common sense to theology, the supernatural, the unknowable, the charismatic, the moral or the metaphysical can guide reason in assigning cause and effect. Modern *rationality* differs in that its reasoning methods and processes are based on mathematical principles[14]. *Ratio* is especially concerned with relativity. The rational-modern mind applies relativity to analytical processes in the study of nature and the realm of human relationships that constitute society.

While *rational* cognition and praxis are based on relativity, forms of non-modern *Weltanschauung* tend to rely on *absolutes*[15] – absolute truth, norms, power and as a corollary, absolute and hierarchical forms of socio-political organization. They are not loath to seek socio-political legitimacy in reference to divine, dogmatic, traditional, metaphysical templates or the decisions of "superior" arbiters. A distinguishing characteristic of the "*modernity schism*" lies less in descriptive "social indicators"[16] as the gross revenue of a society or the technological equipment at its disposal but in a rather diffuse cognitive style: Throughout the non-modern social geography of absolutes, the individual is systemically sublated to some hyper-static socio-psychological value system (honor, shame, love, family etc.) or a political objective or an ideology (chief, idol, nation, religion etc.). The state is crystallized as the primary, sometimes the only political and economic estate[17] (Schick, Tonak, 1998: 80). The central position of the polity apparatus determines power hierarchies and constricts the range of individual liberties.

The emancipative democratic and civil aspects of modernity remain a Western privilege, while non-Europeans attempt to acquire the wealth, technology, skills, machines and weapons that are "part of being modern" and reconciling them with their traditional culture to "become modern without being Western" (Huntington, 1993: 41-42). This distinction may be attributed to an *a-historical* interpretation of modernity as a developmental state

---

[14] Mathematics long predates 15th century modernity. "Zero" is an oriental invention and "*algebra*" is an Arabic word. However mathematics as a covenant of knowledge and logic is nowhere as central to construing the world as in modernity: mathematical exactness, certainty and clarity have been superior tools of reference and thus an epistemological basis for "objectiv-*izing*" secular knowledge (see: Macquarrie, 1973: 132-133).

[15] As a rough generalization, for the non-modern mind, mathematics serves to "order" things in absolute categories while it functions to "compare" them in the modern cognitive style. Averroes's mathematical "rationalism" was rejected as heresy both by the Christian church and the followers of Imam Ghazali. The Arabic name for rationalists was "*mut'azil*", meaning "the isolated, those who stand alone".

[16] Most oil rich countries import and use latest technology but continue to remain customers of such products with no advance in technology production.

[17] This is a generalization of Schick and Tonak's (1998) observation of early Republican Turkey.

any society can achieve by emulating *Eurogenic* techniques and behavior patterns.

Modernization theory[18] emerged in post WW II academic circles to plot the charts of that emulation. It was assumed by an eschatological reductionism of history that the "new" nations of decolonized Asia, Africa and Latin America could progress toward democracy, industrialization and market economy regardless of their different cultural and historical backgrounds, provided they accept Western universals[19] (Bostanoglu, 1999: 110-114, 118-122; Alexander, 1995: 67; Manzo, 1991: 6; Shafer, 1988: 45; Bottomore, 1977: 377; Almond, 1970: 232). If those states could perform efficiently, not only would they develop economically, but also "modernize politically and achieve stability". They would form competitive, pluralistic, participative multi-party systems while Western-trained political and bureaucratic elites ensured the success of the program, facilitated by the education of young, urbanized masses (Manzo, 1991: 13; Bostanoglu, 1999: 113-118). Modernity though, proved less an inevitable trajectory than a continuum differentiating Europe from the rest of the world. Thus, modernity evolved as a "temporal denominator" that separated Eurogenic societies into a particular zone where a specific, mathematic-ized experience of time–space[20] exists.

Modernization theory disregarded the peculiar characteristics and structures of modern and modern-*izing* societies. Despite Washington's prescriptions, the height of the Cold War was marked with protest, dissent, revolutionary rhetoric and anti Americanism in the developing world. The Non-

---

[18] Or the theory of comparative politics.

[19] A recent example of history writing with modern capitalist society as the "*telos*", Francis Fukuyama's *The End of History* deserves mention. Before Fukuyama, Edward Shils (1962) declared "modern means being Western" and Reinhard Bendix defined modernization as going through all the social, political and economic processes Western civilization did since industrialization (Shafer, 1988: 55). Such pundits of modernization theory as Gabriel Almond and Powell (1966: 302) clearly indicate the West-ward orientation of political change in "developing" societies. Eisenstadt (1966) defined modernization as a social, economic and political progression toward western systems (Higgott, 1983: 16).

[20] Immanuel Wallerstein (1988) challenged the modern - positivist conception of time and space as separate and objective verities and proposed them to constitute a single category of experience. Time and space are invented "realities" and can be explained differently as dependent on their relevance to the analysis at hand. He extrapolated five dimensions of "TimeSpace", as a combined dimension of reality: episodic-geopolitical, cyclico-ideological, structural, eternal, and transformational; leaving the field free for still more. Instead of time and space as "out there", to be measured and made "objective", he argued that construed TimeSpace is an instrument of general explanations of rules of behavior, "but only within the context of specific long-term structures" or "historical systems" (Wallerstein, 1998: 71-88). The concept of time – space is employed here to denote the idealization of temporal organization of collective experience in a particular geography by a culture that (according to Wallerstein) is particular to an historical system – modern or non-modern, of which Islam is one. It refers to the hierarchies of priorities and imperatives around which social life is organized. Time-space imposes, tells or suggests to individuals what the society expects them to do with their lives, i.e., spend their time. Ideas of time-space are irrevocably related to interest and power structures – they serve to challenge as well as perpetuate them.

Aligned movement emerged, in many parts of the world, "socialist" governments took to power. As of the mid and latter 1960s, "stability" and "order" replaced democratization as keywords of the theory. Various scholars[21] argued that developing countries did not possess institutions to cope with the pressures of social mobility and political participation; and that modernization could progress more rapidly under authoritarian[22] regimes. Throughout the Third World, coups d'etat, dictatorships, autocratic, oppressive regimes, supported or at least condoned by Washington, became the norm (Bostanoglu, 1999: 115; *see*: Wallerstein, 2000: 107-108).

V. BMENAI: A Shortcut Through History?

The BMENAI resembles a re-hashed early 21st century formulation of modernization theory. It expressly assumes that social change effected by infusion of Western institutions, technology and mores can work a shortcut between history and future. To the American *Weltanschauung*, the epoch-deep dichotomy of modern and *non*-modern *still* appears as a problem that can be resolved by political *gentrification* of Third World cultures.

During the Cold War, American Middle East policy consisted of aiding Israeli defense, keeping oil flow constant, promoting some kind of a peace process and more recently, seeking cooperation against terrorism. Political reform received little more than lip service (Achcar, 2004; Asmus, McFaul, 2004). The rift between modernity and non-modernity was subsumed to strategic exigencies. In the name of stability, the U.S. maintained excellent ties with dictatorships, monarchies and sheikhdoms in Jordan, the UAE, Morocco or Egypt. Iran, under the Shah, was a staunch ally. Authoritarian rule by the word of the Qur'an never impeded U.S. policies toward Saudi Arabia until "sharia" was "recognized" as a threat because of Osama bin Ladin's discourse and the alleged links between the Wahhabi[23] establishment and Al Qaeda[24]. Washington consorted with Saddam Hussein during the Iran – Iraq

---

[21] Most notably, Samuel Huntington (1968; 239) who championed the military as the "apostles of order" versus the the "apostles of revolution". He maintained "students and monks cannot run a state but colonels can".

[22] Authoritarian regimes were distinguished from totalitarian (mainly, communist) by Jeane Kirkpatrick (Dictatorships and Double Standards, *Commentary*, 1978) in that they allowed more civil autonomy from state and ruling party ideology and could evolve toward democracy, and therefore deserved U.S. support as long as they helped fight and vanquish communism.

[23] Saudi Interior Minister Prince Nayef whose tacit support to Al Qaeda is well reported, favored *jihad* against all who were not proper Sunni Muslims. Nayef, was cited as a main obstacle before reform in Saudi Arabia (see: Doran, 2004).

[24] The U.S. sponsored Osama during his tenure in Afghanistan fighting Soviets with the *Taliban*, who were American allies, too.

war (Adams, 2001; Pipes, 1991: 16). It was only after terrorism was "established" as a threat that Pres. G. W. Bush declared[25] a shift in the policy of tolerating friendly tyrants for the sake of stability (Achcar, 2004; Wittes, 2004). Along came the GMEI which practically replicated[26] the priorities of modernization theory.

The GMEI indicated less a change of *Weltanschauung* than just another "practical" response to political exigency. For now at least, the U.S., reverted to the original formula of political modernization after stability paradigms failed. Europeans acquiesced to the BMENAI, too, because they acknowledged an imminent threat[27] on their periphery[28]. The "new" policy is still motivated by a dose of trial and error pragmatism. At a juncture when, beside other Moslem societies, even in oil rich Saudi Arabia, assumed to be politically stable and loyal, the economy has deteriorated, social malaises have surfaced and radical Islamic activism has surged, Washington has realized that "democratization today can eliminate military preemption tomorrow" (Asmus, McFaul, 2004). Opaque politics can harbor potentially dangerous alliances and transparent governance can possibly be more efficient for controlling events. Disrobed of altruistic rhetoric, the BMENAI materializes as a project for maintaining a vital geography reasonably stable, peaceful and secure through some rule of law but also dependent and sealed, so the modern *eucosmos* will not be contaminated by its political, cultural or demographic effluence.

VI. The Economy of Culture for Security

The resurrection of modernization theory as policy may be an indication that America has better acknowledged the role of *culture* in matters of security.

---

[25] Air Force Graduation Ceremony address, June 2, 2004.
[26] Promotion of democracy, free elections, good participatory governance, transparency, practice of human rights without harassment or restrictions in civil society organization, free media, women's and girls' enfranchisement, fighting corruption, operation of NGOs; development of judiciary and legal systems; building a knowledge society, expanding digital technology in education, community and business; to improve literacy, reform textbooks and schools; expand economic opportunities and cooperation with the West, enhance the private sector and enterpreneurism, integrate finance (including a Greater Middle East Development Bank partnership) to liberalize and expand financial services (Dar Al Hayat, 2004).
[27] The G8 working paper reflected that if the GME continued to "add every year to its population of underemployed, undereducated, and politically disenfranchised youths" this "will pose a direct threat to the stability of the region, *and to the common interests of the G-8 members*."
[28] The BMENA is a passageway of illegal immigration and organized crime for Europe. A commentary on *WorldSecurityNetwork*, the official site of the U.S think tank, German Marshall Fund stated "It is from this region that the most imminent threats to Western security are likely to emanate in the 21st century. It is here that the dangerous mix of extremist ideologies, terrorism, and access to weapons of mass destruction is most likely to occur. And it is certainly no accident that the most dangerous part of the world where the war on terrorism will be won or lost is also the least free" (Asmus, McFaul, 2004).

Traditionally, *security* focused on defending territories, peoples or interests of nation states against others through political and military means, either individually or in concert. Conflict occurred when a threat was perceived. After the "empire of evil" collapsed, apprehension over territorial safety persisted but abated. Traditional "hard" concerns of security were complemented and sometimes overshadowed by unconventional "soft" threats[29]; too diffused, indeterminate and transnational to pin down to particular sources, agents, loci or objectives. The new threats not only menaced their targets but as ripples in a pond, created a risk for the whole social, political and economic fabric of modern life and the process of globality that held the entire world in its grip[30]. The question became less the plight of security in any particular locale but its impact on the systemic security of the world (*see*: Bostanoglu, 1996). As the world rapidly moved toward organic functional integration, global security had less tolerance for setbacks on the rule of law or political and economic liberalism because the modern way of mind and life required a predictable, controllable, manageable, safe and free world. Security thus metamorphosed into an indivisible, holistic, global concern. Its scope burgeoned out beyond territorial properties, military might and other classical determinants of power to encompass the vicissitudes at the interface between person and place, the domain of ideas, rationalities and mentalities or, to the realm of culture (Isen, 2007, forthcoming).

The modern / capitalist alliance assumed the right to take affirmative action to defuse critical situations, restore order, prevent frictions from graduating into confrontations; and as a last resort, to physically intervene and impose its "justice" on aggressors and violators of peace. The Gulf War and the emasculation of Saddam's expansionism, the suppression of Yugo-

---

[29] Whereas raw power, military might or similar topics of security are referred to as "hard"; threats where cultural and human elements play the significant role are called "soft". Soft security is concerned with resolving problems by establishing relationships and communication among societies and cultures as well as the political apparati[29] (*see*: Larabee, Green, Lesser, Zanini, 1998: 86).

[30] Militant ethnic and religious fundamentalism brewed along an axis that reached South Eastern Europe from the Asian Subcontinent. Russia was a paragon of instability. Caucasia resembled early 20th century Balkans. Former Yugoslavia turned to a genocidal bloodbath. In a watershed act of aggression, Saddam Hussein invaded Kuwait, setting forth a cascade of events that culminated in the occupation of Iraq; his subsequent deposement, capture, imprisonment and conviction. Secessionist movements gained impetus in a range of countries from Turkey to India and Indonesia. Poverty, homelessness, environmental deterioration, crime and other maladies could be seen with equal probability in urban North America or Europe as in Third World towns. Multinational crime rings amassed illegal fortunes that found their way into the international monetary system, while many illegal activities including terrorism were sustained by illicit gains from drugs or other contraband. Associated particularly with Islamic fundamentalism and believed to be sponsored by "rogue states", transnational terrorism came to represent an ultimate threat as a socialized, individualized, privatized and globalized *world wide warfare* that can be waged *by one against all*. The U.S., long harangued by attacks abroad, became a victim at home as transatlantic terrorism escalated to 9-11.

slavia *cum* Greater Serbia, the subtle demarcation of Israel's margins toward an eventual settlement with the already tame Palestinians, the initiatives to thaw the Cyprus impasse and the internationally sanctioned Afghanistan war were samples of global security campaigns in the last decade of the 20th century[31].

The GMEI / BMENAI does not represent a radical and sudden change in policy[32]. Two years before entering Iraq, Bush had already declared his intent[33] to restructure the dysfunctional politics of the Arab and more broadly, the Muslim world. "Stable and free nations do not breed ideologies of murder," he said[34] (Wittes, 2004). Culture was recognized as a *strategic* constituent of security, serving a function in the establishment of reliable socio-political systems. The BMENAI added modernist *enculturation* to the logic of global security. If preserving global equilibria with minimum risk depends on the generalization of certain modern material and cultural values, the BMENA societies had to be endowed with a quantum to render their preservation a common concern. Thus, economic, technological, political and cultural modernization was viewed as the safest, most functional, economical and longest lasting prospect of ensuring security.

VII. Khomeiny's Lesson: Loosen the Reins

Liberalization gained priority probably less from a fealty to good governance than the perceived disadvantages of unruly tyrannies "antithetical to principles of democracy and self-determination" (Achcar, 2004). After the Cold War, a wave of relative democratization washed over Eastern Europe and parts of Asia and Latin America. Middle Eastern and Muslim states were least effected, remaining the most autocratic in the world[35] (Fox, 2001). Yet, Middle Eastern peoples top worldwide polls in exalting democracy as "better than any other form of government" (AHDR, 2003: 19). Still, rhetorical complaints of oppression and non-liberty may not necessarily indicate

---

[31] The Palestinian situation displayed a period of regression after Bush and the electoral victory of Hamas, and the escalation of violence by Israel in the occupied territories. Cyprus recently developed into an impasse in Turkey's relations with the EU.

[32] *See* Isen, "The politics of being Mediterranean: What hope is there for peace in the North Eastern Mediterranean ?" presented to the Third Pan-European International Relations Conference and Joint Meeting With the International Studies Association; convention on Peace and Security in the Eastern Mediterranean Vienna, Austria, 16-19 September, 1998.

[33] Although the modern consensus received a blow when the neo-conservative U.S. polity quorum unilaterally bulldozed its way through diplomacy to the invasion of Iraq in the name of "preemption", even the Bush administration did not overlook the cultural dimension of security.

[34] Addressing the American Enterprise Institute on February 26, 2003.

[35] Studies find Muslim states outside the Middle East more autocratic than non-Muslim states but considerably less autocratic than those in the Middle East (See: Fox, 2001).

a desire for pluralist, inclusive, good governance. In especially religious circles, liberalism is highly suspect as a Zionist - Western ploy to weaken and subjugate the Arab world. Reformers are regarded as clients of colonialists (Alterman, 2004). Furthermore, extreme Islamist opposition employs the same democrat jargon of dissent, although what they convey by "freedom" may be contrary to what the liberals mean (Doran, 2004). Some American conservatives voice skepticism that Arab democratization can happen before profound changes in cultural and political institutions and attitudes occur. Huntington's (1996: 6-10) "democracy paradox" claims that in societies where democracy intersects with recrudescent identity politics, anti-Western and anti-democratic groups appealing to indigenous ethnic and religious loyalties and particularities may legitimately rise to power (Garfinkel, 2002; Achcar, 2004).

Incumbent regional rulers moved to consolidate their positions in this hiatus between the express popular wish for freedom and simultaneous suspicion of liberalism and liberals. The press[36], usually in tune with the regimes, decried the GMEI as an "outrageous imposition". Egypt's Husnu Mubarak called it "delusional". A Cairo editorial referred to "colonial echoes". Another concurred, though adding that Arabian "corruption and authoritarianism" paved the way for Western interference. Nevertheless, Arab governments from the Palestine Authority (then, under Yasir Arafat) to Libya, Egypt and Saudi Arabia launched self initiatives for a program of "controlled" liberalization[37].

Liberals emphasized that a process of mere elections[38] or controlled liberalization by virtue of quasi-democratic institutions with no real power is a long cry from democracy. Basic institutions as parties, free speech and press, right to organize, associate, assemble etc. were needed to enable citizens to operate in the political arena (Wittes, 2004). Arab liberals[39] seemed to be losing the "battle for the hearts and minds" of their people who view them as clients and collaborators of colonialists. Arab rulers, to whom China's

---

[36] For a digest of Arab press reaction to the GMEI *see*: http://www.islamonline.net/English/News/2004-02/25/article01.shtml.

[37] The 22 member Arab League unanimously voted in Tunis on 22 May 2004, to pursue reform and modernization, consolidate democratic practice, foster civil society and NGOs, widen women's inclusion, rights and status in political, economic, social, cultural and educational affairs and promised commitment to human rights, freedom of expression, thought, belief and the independence of the judiciary. In some states, including Saudi Arabia, limited access polls were held in which women were not allowed. The results tended to favor Islamist movements.

[38] As in Afghanistan and Iraq.

[39] *See*: Jon B. Alterman, head of the Middle East program at the think-tank, *Center for Strategic and International Studies (CISS)*, 2002. It must also be noted that the key role the BMENAI attributes to elites is another parallel with the 60's modernization theories.

"happy marriage" of open economy and closed politics was most attractive, realized perfectly that Washington's design for democratization was "long on vision and short in praxis". In the interim, the religious extremists continued to gain popular favor (see: Alterman, 2004; Wittes, 2004).

Nevertheless, Washington's ambitious prospect of reform moved cornerstones so that whether traditional balances are radically upset or timid self-reform schemes become the norm the status quo is susceptible to change. As a corollary, a failure of regional governments to effect some transformation is bound to wipe on the U.S. Therefore the political potential in Arab / Islam societies merits a quick glance: Islamists currently represent the main opposition to incumbent regimes. Only a nuclear Western style liberal movement exists. The clergy controlling the mosques possess ample chance to reach out to the community and an immense opportunity to organize and pilot political dissent. A new, not necessarily liberal class of elites has risen from religious, media or military backgrounds. With no political parties or organization, channels of communication controlled by the state, dissident groups have little chance for association outside the inviolate mosque (Alterman, 2004; Achcar, 2004).

The situation is reminiscent of Iran where Shah Reza Pahlavi suppressed all opposition to keep the Shi'ite religious hierarchy out and the communist TUDEH at bay. The fairly democracy oriented, secular middle class liberals, too, were denied access to politics despite their small numbers. Iran's human rights record was so foul that U.S. President *Jimmy Carter* threatened to stop arm shipments unless abuses were controlled. The Shah stuck to sluggish modernization and controlled liberalization until the opposition joined forces against the regime in the later 70's. Massive demonstrations were suppressed violently. In the mélee, the Shah had to invite Ayatollah Khomeiny, the leader of a mid-sized hardline Shiite faction back from exile. While Khomeiny arose as leader, protests assumed a religious tenor. By the time the Shah conceded to a moderate constitution, he was days from ouster. The radical *mullahs* toppled the 2500 year dynasty, declared an Islamic Republic, began to depose of moderates, and have since been the arch champion of anything anti-American and anti-semitic. Khomeiny nationalized business[40], held land reform and restricted foreign trade. The Islamic revolution thus not only immensely strengthened the already oil rich state apparatus of Iran but by instituting it as the sole estate, abolished potential

---

[40] The revolution's religious conservative, merchant and manufacturer power base also favored a protectionist economy and introverted politics.

power bases for any alternative social forces. The mullahs who effectively appropriated the mighty state controlled all aspects of the social-life-world.

Apparently though, in American political memory the Algerian experience[41] looms larger than the disaster in Iran. In Algeria, too, Islamic electoral victory can possibly be ascribed to socio-political conditions that resemble pre revolutionary Iran and are valid in almost every BMENA society: poverty, despondency and political oppression by an extremely mighty state.

VIII. Compulsory Democratization? An Evaluation

Cramped by the "democracy paradox" and marred with a credibility crisis in the region, among allies and at home, the U.S. needs demonstrable results. Effective reform implemented by incumbent regimes to forever oust Islamists would probably be "the" desirable solution. Yet, historical evidence renders it naive to expect structural change from autocracies unless they are externally *compelled* (*see* Wittfogel, 1981: 418-419, 422-423).

Peace, liberty and prosperity are issues of global stability. Independent of regional autocrats' discretion, security in the BMENA[42] is too vital for the global interests of the modern world to be trusted to chance or their slow goodwill. Therefore, the probability avails that sooner or later, openly or implicitly, crudely or subtly, the states in the region may begin to feel coerced to transform. As incumbent regimes are equally wary of bleeding popular power to Islamism, a chance exists that some will go along, albeit, grumblingly[43] (*see* Wittes, 2004). Democracy may not loom around the corner but the possibility of a universal recognition that world security can be achieved

---

[41] The Islamist party legitimately won 1991 elections in Algeria. The military moved in. The U.S. backed the putsch, and fearing Islamist victories elsewhere, struck democratization off its policy. Instead it encouraged the dubious baby steps dictatorships took toward reform. Islamist opposition deepened its roots in the vacuum (see: Wittes 2004).

[42] The apparent disagreements between Europeans and the U.S. on how to bring the pressure to bear on local rulers look more tactical than strategic, partly born of the possibly temporary mistrust on either side of the Atlantic. There is no way or reason for Europe to immunize itself against the fomenting chaos and forever act indifferently as the U.S. moves in. Either within the context of the European Union or through singular trials of major powers, Europe is likely to press its own imprimatur. The best chance Europe possesses in the area is contributing to a "fairer" solution than what America is likely to work out for Palestine, as sort of a counterweight to Washington's Israeli bias. And only then, in a second tier, the Afghanistan – Pakistan belt may also be considered for social restructuring.

[43] Induced liberalization may at least superficially and partially succeed: When the Emir was forced by the U.S. to loosen the reins in Kuwait, a liberal movement entered Parliament as an alternative to Islamists and the monarchists (Wittes, 2004). How well a sample of Mideast societies Kuwait constitutes is another question though, especially after its Western liberation from Iraqi invasion.

through some modernization in politics is not dim either[44]. In any case, in disputes between hegemonic powers and peripheral states, the question of who is "right" scantly matters. Any "solution" through collusive or coercive intervention does not necessarily have to be found equitable, fair, respectful to imperatives or even to the borders of "sovereign" nation states by local contestants. All such a settlement requires to be is practical, workable and applicable despite (inevitable) opposition[45].

IX. The Secularization of Religion by Politics

The "problem" in the BMENA was identified as a materialization of the controversy between modernity and *non*-modernity in a predominantly Muslim geography. In this conflict, though, Islam, much as it has been accentuated, argued, praised, reviled and defended, appears as less the context than the *pretext* of the debate.

Before continuing, a cliché, as often passed over as it is voiced, must be repeated here: "Islam" is an inadequate analytical category. Comprehensive categories assign their content a taken for granted, discreet, unproblematic epistemic unity, reducing the complexities of human experience to a singular linear narrative, pivoting on a central figure imbued with an automatic explanatory sovereignty, such as identity, religion or nation. Such *logocentricism* conceals the diverse and heterogeneous practices in Islam that find their cultural expressions and particularities in the way they assimilate and accommodate traditions and beliefs that shape practices of the faith (George, 1994: 200-201; Williams, 1996: 896). There is not a single creed binding over 20 Arab societies with Afghan militants, Egypt's Muslim Brethren or the secessionists Muslims in Philippines, Indonesia or Kashmir. Hatred often reigns between Sunnis and Shi'ites. The more secular Turks, the Pakistani

---

[44] If a little speculation is allowed, the resultant Arab / Moslem compromise is likely to be an *ersatz* Western democracy: formally a multi party parliamentary system, a fairly convincing but not too liberal rule of law favoring stability over freedoms as the basis of "controlled governance". Thus stability can be propped on multiple alternatives in the form of hitherto disallowed "opposition" parties and movements, instead of one ruling authority. In effect, this means that rather than civil social forces, factions representing particular traditional, regional, tribal, etc. interests will vie for the control of internally strong – internationally weaker state apparati. Bureaucracies, crowded by local elites as guardians of the state and the system, will wield unproportional strength. Tempered Islamists will have to be included as well, therefore, checks and balances will be in place to prevent any religiously based party from sliding into theocratic practices once in power – indeed early examples of the formula have revealed themselves in administrations formed in Iraq and formerly Afghanistan.

[45] In any case, an "applicable" solution often has sufficient domestic backing to make it work – the direst examples being the U.S. engineered military putsches in the 1960's and 70's that spread from Latin America to Greece, Turkey and Pakistan. Afghanistan's introduction to "democracy" despite not only Islamists but also local warlords' opposition is another example.

and Moroccans worship in mosques, as do 30 million Chinese Muslims or the Black Muslims of America – but they offer few similarities to be grouped together. Indeed, Muslims fiercely quarrel over what "true religion" is (*see*: Said, 2001, 2002; Doran, 2004). No geographical, political, cultural, theological and economic standard, idiosyncrasy or an objective criterion exists to group the BMENA countries as such – except Washington's strategic priorities, basic concerns and political visions, which may be shared only by Israel (Achcar, 2004).

The GMEI/BMENAI restricts the historic schism of modernity to a narrow cartography where Islam and political violence mingle with intense xenophobia, especially anti-Americanism and anti-Semitism. Although the language avoids allusions to religion[46], this eclectically abstracted cartography stands out as a meaningless stroke of the brush on the map if the "terrorism – Islam" linkage is extracted. This cartographic eclecticism inevitably reflects on Islam, the most empirically observable common cultural denominator, as a cause that hampers modernization. Thus, not in text but in context, the GMEI/BMENAI tacitly and implicitly reduces the cartographic to the cultural and, the cultural to the religious. It posits Islam[47] at the basis of the modernity conflict. In its political essence, GMEI/BMENAI appears as a further step in nation building: creating a *designer geography* where the apostate can be circumscribed and tamed.

Political culture in the BMENA is not generally attuned to a polyphony of crystallized, contesting discourses. Islam's *political* allure for dissent can be partly attributed to its profound morality and imperative references to social justice. "Justice" in Islam is a duty and liability of the ruling. Injustice can function as an effective rallying cause where the social harvest is asymmetrically distributed[48]. An absolutist cognitive style, the custom of referring to a hyperstatic wisdom also stimulate appeals to religious authorities for recourse against iniquity. Just as the *mullahs* did in Iran, the Islamic opposition can promise justice, a change of fortune and the *Qoran's* more egalitarian virtues as a reward for the "unheretical", *true* practice of Islam that they preach. On the other hand, beneficiaries of extant power structures cling to Islam's conservative discourse to legitimate their power and privilege as di-

---

[46] Except in a promise to provide legal aid to citizens in countries where Shariah, Islamic law based on Qoranic interpretations, is valid.
[47] Only Israel's majority is non-Moslem in the region.
[48] According to the 2002 UN Human Development Index and World Bank figures, the Arab world has a private wealth of $1,568 billion in the hands of 200,000 "men". In a geography of such wealth, access to basic services as health, education, housing and employment is worse than in the rest of the developing world. Poverty rate is on par with poor nations at about 20 percent (40 million): Not exceptional, that is, if the region's richness is ignored.

vinely ordained (*see*: Mardin, 1971: 234-236). Islam thus turns into a fulcrum on which political dispositions and temperaments compete. In the lack of convincing alternative discourses, Islam is expediently instrumentalized as the divine rationale of lay, mundane politics. Obversely, it is *secularized* through politic*ization*. Deconstructing and demonstrating the "power politics" behind Islamic discourses may be a step to disrobe it of political stamina and *de*-secularize it, meanwhile secularizing the practice of politics by segregating from religion.

In its hegemonic scheme, the U.S. occasionally had to deal with a problem or a problematic leader[49] in the Arab - Muslim world. However, these disputes stemmed from respective positions in Cold War politics and particularly the Arab-Israeli conflict. They had little to do with "Islam as ideology". America's scrimmage with Islam began when Khomeiny turned it into a fulcrum of radical and violent anti Americanism. The ayatollahs declared *jihad* over Palestine, dragging the strife into the realm of religion from that of politics. Terrorism, from which the PLO was extracting itself, again became a method with organizations like Hamas or Hizbollah, who were, rather than any state, the beneficiaries of Iran's avowed "revolution export". Iran *Islamized* the Palestine crisis and defied modernity in open preference of the traditional. From there on, any extremist political corps as Taliban or Al Qaeda could claim legitimacy invoking Mohammed's name.

X. The U.S., The West and The Good

American political epistemology tackled Islam as a problem. It was excessively studied and discussed relative to other ideologies, including modernity. Islamic intelligentsia, discontented with the presentation of the creed as pre-modern and violent launched a quest for cultural security that gained impetus after 9-11[50]. *Jihad* rhetoric was gradually restricted to extremists. Westerners, too, began to explore methods to incorporate Islam with Eurogenic culture. Pacifistic multi culturalist discourses of cultural relativism, reinterpreting[51] inter-cultural asymmetries as idiosyncracies rather than is-

---

[49] Long before Osama or Saddam, America had to contend with Egypt's Gamal Abdel Nasser, a founder of the Third World movement; Col. Qaddafy of Libya, Hafez Assad of Syria and the spiritual leader of the Iran Islamic revolution, Imam Khomeiny. Washington backed or turned a blind eye to putsches staged by younger Arab military elites against Kings who were relics of British and French colonial heritage. The new, "Baath" type regimes were republican, secular-*ish* and relatively left-ish. In the end, America's Israeli bias led to a mutual distrust. The U.S. turned to the more fundamentalist monarchies and sheikdoms (*see*: Kaplan, 1994; Pipes, 1991: 15-28; Bullard, 1958; 27-41).

[50] From which mainstream Muslims eagerly tried to distance themselves.

[51] For instance, Syrian-born Bassam Tibi of Göttingen University postulated Shariah as a "post-Qur'anic construction" and the medieval practices of killing apostates, stoning adulterers, secluding women, compul-

sues of conflict were phrased in an effort to construe an Islam compatible with modernity (Raines, 1996: 42-44; Cox, 2003). Instead of rejecting them outright, some traditionalist Islamic thinkers, still reluctant to relinquish customary privileges, re-interpreted key modern tenets as secularism, liberties, equality or gender parity in the light of doctrine (*see*: Modood, 2005, Mandaville 2001). Whether or how such hermeneutics may provide a niche for Islam as a counter-universal alternative is arguable but once again, Islam is hardly unique in such resistance (*see*: Raines, 1996: 42-44, Williams, 1996: 883, 885). Cultural security defines the recalcitrance of social particularisms in preserving and exercising their idiographic character and praxes in the face of transforming and usually modern dynamics (Larabee et.al., 1998: 4). Every *weltanschaaung* maintains enclaves of cultural security against the onslaught of new values[52].

With the sway of globality, pressures of adaptive change become a universal dynamic. Modernity may not be a teleological destiny but it does furnish basic universal paragons by which all cultures more or less define their particular notion of *good*[53]. Therefore, the right reflexes can be measured only by a culture's influence in determining the policies and acts that will constitute the evolving "better" world. If cultures lack adaptive flexibility, since they can contribute little to the universal aggregation of the criteria of good, "cultural security" resonates as *in*security.

The BMENA is cruising through a phase in its relations with modernity: When resistance is merely due to an alienation resulting from an ignorance of modernity, it can yield as novel standards and modes set. Yet, if resistance is vital for maintaining political, economic, cultural, physical and psychical structures, religion can be dogmatized critically to the extent its influence can halt the procession of globality. In Muslim and more generally non-modern societies, the concern with "cultural (*in*)security" is often motivated by a refusal to modify the highly asymmetric domestic structures of interests, power and authority. Just as any divine or secular[54] ecumenical

---

sory prayer, dress code, punishing alcohol, as customs created by jurists(see: Akyol, 2004). Extreme non modern praxes as public flogging, amputations or beheadings go hand in hand with traditional, premodern autocratic power schemata, as observed in the Saudi defense against The UN Committee Against Torture, on grounds that such penal practice has been an integral part of Islamic law for 1400 years (see: Sandall, 2003).

[52] To cite just one example, Christian fundamentalists in the U.S. propagate Biblical inerrancy campaigns to expel evolution theory from schoolbooks or to ban abortion.

[53] Not necessarily accepting but reinterpreting, opposing or rejecting them, too.

[54] Soviet Marxism or Nazi totalitarianism or their far smaller scale versions like North Korean *Jucheism* are comprehensive ideational systems possessing a power that can penetrate the most intimate privacies and sublate the individual to a collective symbolic entity: the nation, the laboring classes, a symbolized leader or a faith.

doctrine could have been, Islam has been converted into a totalistic discourse to consolidate extant power structures (*see*: Wittfogel, 1957: 87).

It is difficult to speak of a "religion state[55]" in history but a "state religion" is frequently appropriated into autocratic government for concentrating power and legitimacy in the ruler(s) or the ruling apparatus. Religion is important but the importance of an institution does not imply its autonomy. Religion in Near Eastern political culture is a mediating link between the rulers and the ruled (Mardin, 1971: 235). Faith as an "independent" force may rival the absolute potency of despots[56]. One of its functions, especially in undifferentiated societies, is to allow an alternative popular hermeneusis of polity that mediates discontent into discourses that integrate with mainstream, official religion (see: Mardin, 1971: 235). Thus, political authority fosters the dominant faith for maintaining absolute power and also controlling opposition. In all cases where Islam is ideologically associated with government, political and religious leadership is concentrated in one authority. Thus, both civilian, military and paramilitary bureaucracy and the ierocratic organization are controlled[57], affording the polity élite a total domination of society (Wittfogel, 1957: 90 , 92, 97; Mardin, 1971: 234-239). Therefore, in history, states have traditionally prevented Islam from developing into an independent organization like the Catholic Church[58]. Secularity is not necessarily concommittant with democracy but liberal governance is impossible in a state that employs religious dogma for total power. Throughout the BMENA, even relatively secular autocracies frequently refer to Islam for legitimacy– but autocracy is a style of government, not of ministering a faith (*see*: Fox, 2001; Wittfogel, 1957: 49-50, Mardin, 1971: 235-236).

XI. Problems of Political Gentrification

Lay daily problems cannot be solved with reference to divinity. Whether accompanied by liberal politics or not, secularity sprouts out of the life praxes of ordinary individuals. In a relatively diversified, pluralized social-life-

---

[55] Even in the case of "theocratic" Papal States Catholicism was the justification of worldly power rather than its extent.
[56] This is more or less the case in Saudi Arabia ruled by "shariah" where Islamists are the sole threat to the absolute monarchy. The political influence of Catholicism on pre-reformation European rulers is another example of divided popular loyalties.
[57] In "secular" Republican Turkey, a Directorate of Religious Affairs handles such affairs under the authority of the government. The Directorate in practice deals with affairs of the Sunni Muslims constituting the majority of the population.
[58] The similarity is obvious with Orthodox Christianity which has developed as a state religion in Byzantium and Russia.

world where interests are articulated in discreet, competing sectors and are not exclusive to the realm of state and government, modern business customs necessitate the eventual separation of the professional from the personal and the religious. Universal work and life patterns require rapid and independent decisions. If and whenever, with or without Western pressure for subsequent political liberalization, life and business patterns of "open economy" permeate quotidien practices in ways that deliver the individual from the stranglehold of the *political-cum-religious* collective, Islam may stop wielding such a comprehensive coercion.

Partial secularization as a result of economic modernization is a far cry from democratization. Till now, technical innovation[59] in the Near East has simply perpetuated extant power patterns rather than nurture a modern and liberal middle class to break the chain of autocratic – bureaucratic tradition of power, privilege and exploitation. In such constraints, relatively *technologized* autocracies end up adding a managerial and technical layer to the state's monopolistic administrative and clerical apparatus (*see*: Wittfogel, 1957). Especially considering that the ruling oligarchs either own or command the capital and management of technology, it becomes obvious that any serious transformation in spite of the polity apparatus can only be effected as a result of external influence[60]. Modernity is a compound of liberal geoculture[61] and capitalist economy. An iconoclastic displacement of traditional concepts and structures of power can be accelerated by the liberation of capital along with the liberation of politics. Only externally motivated political and economic influence can succeed in transforming Arab–Muslim societies by creating extraverted, attractive cultural dynamics into the social-life-world[62] besides religion.

Another issue of Islam is fatalist resignation. It is at once an excuse for popular socio-political apathy and a reason not to challenge authority (*see*: Mardin, 1971). Fatalism also is a rationale for poor, disenchanted individuals to seek what life has denied in the promises of extremists. For a considerable

---

[59] Purchased with oil revenues by autocrats to be used as they decree under their total control.
[60] *See*: Wittfogel, 1957: 423 about how only external interference can alter structures of total power in despotic autocracies.
[61] A geoculture roughly, is an ethos legitimating extant political economic structures. Capitalism's liberal geoculture propagates a scientific ethos to explain economic transformations and profits while liberal reformism contains popular discontent through some re-distribution softening the continuously increasing socio-economic polarization typical of capitalism. This system originated in Western Europe and expanded to incorporate the entire globe (Wallerstein, 1997, 1997a).
[62] Used in the Husserlian and Schutzian tradition to denote the intersubjectively constituted complex of domains of experience, both natural and cultural, within which individual experience is organized. Habermas insisted that the social life world has a free, communicative dimension outside the technical realm of rational control.

part of the population, livelihood is seldom the fruit of productive labor but often remuneration for submission and loyalty to the state, the ruler or the dissident religious pundit. Even a superficial glance at data shows how the rather non-productive Middle Eastern style of living is sustained by oil-dependent, monopolized economies. The ratio of oil in export revenues ranges between 70 to 90 percent. Nations without oil are among the poorest in the world[63]. All income is collected in the hands of limited oligarchies, their vassals or the treasuries of authoritarian governments. Rulers can seldom be held accountable for the way they spend petrodollars. The same mental problem that plagues Arab-Islam cultural and political time-space, namely, uniformity and lack of diversity, is the bane of economies, too. In at least the richer countries, poverty exists less in the shortage of means of subsistence than the narrowness of the cultural and economic social-life-world. Even oil exporters[64] face problems because of population growth, low crude prices, welfare, debt, but mostly, the failure to diversify their economies. Only by an infusion of intellectual capital to diversify productivity in *all* social activities can the social world be enriched and discourse of fatalism and poverty counterweighed to raise the quality of life. Self aware, confident individuals for whom faith provides no lay, quotidien imperatives but moral support require more than bread for a satisfactory existence[65] and are ready to explore new alleys of life and mind to enrich collective experience. Unlike China or India, BMENA does not possess almost endless cheap labor (*see*: CSIS, 2005). Therefore, any economic development has to be triggered by investment in human capital, which in the medium range, can be expected to upgrade the total quality of life. However, since that kind of individuality may challenge traditional, autocratic and patriarchal political authority, issues of Arabic- Islamic idiosyncracy and cultural security are likely to be raised to interfere with the American spearheaded *political gentrification* project when it comes to transforming "subjects" into citizens through *intellectual* modernization.

---

[63] Data from Energy Information Agency 2004 estimates. Oil producing countries export little else. Mines or ores in small quantities are other export goods. Lebanon enjoys a more diversified economy and the UAE boosts oil revenues with re-exporting. Kuwait and the Emirates are currently the only "wealthy" petroleum states.

[64] Algeria, Bahrain, Iran, Iraq, Libya, Oman, Saudi Arabia, Yemen.

[65] Ironically, regional despots, too, feel the shortage in qualified human capital. Saudi Arabia spends forty percent of its income on arms but because there are too few modern minds to be trained to use state of the art weapons, aircraft are grounded unless mercenaries pilot or service them (Sandall, 2003).

XII. The Voice Behind the Tiger's Roar

This brief trek through the politics of Islam absolves the religion of most of the vile associated with it, transferring the blame to autocratic power structures challenged by modernity. The polarization between the Arab – Islam time-space and the West is due less to any incompatibility of civilizations-redux-religions than the difference of pace in responding to the complex dynamics of globality. Islam, as but one form of non-modern discourses of time–space, is neither an autonomous source of evil nor a barbaric threat to Western civilization, *per se*. It crystallizes as an ideological paper tiger politicians marginal to modernity can hide behind and roar.

Culture appears at the interface of modernity and security for multiple reasons. "Problems" are identified and phenomena are assigned meaning according to culturally defined criteria. All relationships and communication as the fount of experience and meaning, find their expressions culturally. Cultural structures and phenomena are the place to search for revolutions or transformations from one *historical system* to another, because change that matters, effects cultural patterns, not instruments or institutions[66]. Such transitions occur when existing structures move away from equilibrium (Wallerstein, 1998: 81). The *zeitgeist* looks unusually right for an expansion of modernity toward new interpretations and experience of time-space regarding the BMENA. In the fray following the invasion of Iraq, the epistemology and politics of antinomy and clash, or Cold War mentality, resurrected. However, as the urgency of the GMEI /BMENAI witnesses, globality cannot favor segregation and confinement for long. The events insinuate a genre of global security that accommodates and amalgamates cultural differences rather than emphasize and escalate them.

In that context, a step to cleanse Islam of politics and leave it pure, as a faith that unites man to God, does not seem improbable as Islamic cultures are also besieged to come up with ways of melting their idiosyncrasies in the cauldron of globality. Thriving on dissent and originality, modernity has proved itself "a mongrel civilization par excellence" (Barzun, 2000: *xv*). The articulation of an *emic* culture into globality does not necessarily make either monolithic, unilinear or homogeneous. Modern culture is "at once support and conflict, tradition and objection"; an amalgam serving the survival of its motherlode, capitalism. In case of crises, culture rushes to the aid of the social order and thus plays an important part for the security of modernity

---

[66] Mussolini and Stalin held popular "elections" to fill their respective totalitarian Parliaments, just as Iraqis, Saudis or Afghans do.

(Braudel, 2004: 542-543). Even antagonistic agents have been functionally assimilated into that holistic structure of interaction which fosters "diversity in unity and unity in diversity" (Toynbee, 1962: 473-474). If Islam, as an alternative hermeneutics of time-space, proposes to become universal, it needs to present its cultural accumulation as a global consumer good (*see*: Williams 1996: 236); i.e., a system of knowledges that increases individuals' adaptive chances in everyday praxes of modern social life. It is only then that the "mongrel" can absorb and accommodate novel insemination.

Culture is a unifying and universalizing system that simultaneously creates a hierarchy of higher and lower tiers (Wallerstein, 2000a: 272, 275-282). Sociologists describe culture roughly as a society's way of *life*[67] (Barnard, 2003: 614- 615). Culture is used here to denote "*a way of mind*". All meaning generates from *inter-experience,* or the way persons experience one another. *Inter-experiential* evidence is wrought in the mind[68] into a picture of life and the world (Laing, 1967: 18-19; 1969: 23, 65). Collective methods and procedures of cognition and praxis are structured in time and space as cultures, representing the cogitative processes by which experience makes sense. Experience takes the mind on a cruise through cultures, which are comparable to roads: One follows a certain course, whether it is the best possible way or not. This lasts, even when other options are present, until an alternative route is recognized as "better". Thinking of cultures as *roads* facilitates understanding the skepticism about the prospects of Eurogenic democracy in the Islamic Middle East. The introverted security of these societies has played a significant role in their rejecting or failure to transit to modernity[69] or their inability to generate alternative historio-cognitive structures to cope or compete with it – although spatially and temporally they have been the closest esoteric culture to modernity.

XIII. A Designer Geography of Eclectic Opposites

A main difficulty in goading the region into transformation is creating a sense of history to bridge the societies' despotic past and present with a fu-

---

[67] Such definitions, numbering no less than 150, include as paragons norms, learned behavior and affective patterns, ideas, knowledge, attitudes, and artifacts; traditions, institutions, perceptions, habits or customs; actions interactions; means of ordering and interpreting the world, products of human work and thought, characteristics of communities or peoples (*see*: Barnard, 2003; 2003; Giannet, 2003; Murphy, 1986; Hofstede, 1980).

[68] "Mind" here is not dichotomous to "body" in the Cartesian manner. As the locus of meaning, where sense is born of experience, it comprises not only thought but also action and refers to the whole person capable of acting.

[69] Not as consequence of an inevitable historical trajectory but through their own will to become Westernized; as powerful and prosperous as the West.

ture of liberty (Wallerstein, 2000a: 273). Then, how can a theory of power be animated, to persuade or induce apathetic masses and regimes already secure in their power stanchions, to switch to a fast track of radical transformation?

Unless words are wiggled, the general adaptive superiority of modernity is to be conceded. "Cultural security" remains a meek excuse for retaining traits that fail to incorporate functionally with global values pioneered by the emancipative forces of modernity. Currently, almost all Arab – Islam despotisms feel threatened by religious radicalism. This inherent risk may instigate a compromise with modernity that allows rulers to keep a comparatively larger portion of their privileges intact. As all comprehensive *weltanschaaungen,* modernity, too, is a *mainstream* interpretation of time-space. It cannot pervade society totally. It lays down the principles of a historical – social system, like the rules of a game which every participant can play differently. Fernand Braudel (2001: 36-37) marked how the technical aspect of capitalism became a universal aspiration and that in the longer duration, technical identification may yield a global cultural similarity, as long as it exerts a pressure toward competitive capitalist economy and liberal governance – which, in the BMENA, looks next to improbable without foreign involvement. In case global pressures, coupled with the threat of extremism impel Islamic cultures to devise universally marketable ideas that can contribute to the definition of a "better" world, it may be possible to speak of Islam's cultural integration with modernity; or at least an articulation through modernization where an asymmetry nevertheless prevails and conservative pre-modern forces can continue to hold on to some of their mortgage on the society. In any case, since neither religion nor modernity as logocentrisms are autonomous from everyday life praxes, there will always be private corners for particularisms to survive – whether they collude or collide with the integrating processes of globality.

The collusion of Islamic and modern experiences of time-space – purported to be in collision – is a matter of a shift in the paradigms that carve facts out of experience. Half a century ago, Karl A. Wittfogel (1982: xlii, xliii) lamented how Europe's "great heritage" fell into "weak hands" when opinion leaders who entrusted the old continent's security to America's military might, "*which is enormous*", also succumbed to the American theory of power "*which is pathetic*".

On that note, this paper concludes in an ambivalent tone. On the optimistic side, the BMENAI shows that the U.S. vision of power has expanded to comprise the linkage between culture and security. It recognizes that a sustainable and productive coexistence in the same space-time dimension is *not* impossible through cultural intermingling and exchange of ideas.

As to the pessimistic conclusion, the BMENAI set off to create a *designer geography*. However, the epistemological tools, the knowledge and even the agency seem to be insufficient. The homage paid to culture may be viewed as an expansive shift; but preponderance in the way Washington relates to the world still rests with assumptions of material power, military coercion or political manipulation. The project is the brainchild of a perceived threat; its *Weltanschauung* is based on that "pathetic" theory of power. Instead of minimizing alienation, alter-*ization* and ostracism by constituting a community of interests in a new covenant among cultures, it sustains the primacy of force as a (false) modifier and unifier, while culture is supposed to serve as an "after-combat" weapon. As Jacques Barzun (2000: 521) warned, a campaign for change, too, can be perceived as a threat: "to replace by fiat one set of forms with another thought up by some improver, no matter how intelligent, ends in disaster".

References

Ali R. Abootalebi "Middle East economies: A survey of current problems and issues"MERIA- Middle East Review of International Relations, V. 3, No. 3, September 1999online http://meria.idc.ac.il/journal/1999/issue3/jv3n3a6.html.

Gilbert Achcar, "Fantasy of a region that doesn't exist, Greater Middle East, the U.S. plan" *Le Monde Diplomatique*, English Ed., April 2004.

Mustafa Akyol, "European Muslims and the Quest for the Soul of Islam" *New Europe Review*. November 16, 2004.

M. Shahid Alam, Is there an Islamic problem?", *Asian Affairs*, No. 16, Jan. 2002.

Gabriel Almond ve G. Bingham Powell, Comparative Politics: System, Process and Policy, Little Brown Pub., Boston, 1978.

Jeffrey C. Alexander, "Modern, Anti, Post and Neo", New Left Review, V.210, 1995.

Jon B. Alterman, "The False Promise of Arab Liberals" Policy Review, , No. 125 June / July 2004.

Galal Amin, "Colonial echoes" Ahram Weekly. 7 April 2004 (The) Arab Human Development Report, 2003.

Matthew Arnold, Culture and anarchy and other writings. Cambridge University Press, Cambridge, 1993.

Ronald Asmus, and Michael McFaul "Let's get serious about democracy in the Greater Middle East", *http://www.worldsecuritynetwork.com/showArticle3.cfm?article_id=9149&topicID=56* 09 March 2004.

Frederick M. Barnard "Culture and civilization in modern times" *The dictionary of the history of ideas*. The Electronic Text Center at the University of Virginia Library, 2003.

Jacques Barzun, From dawn to decadence – 1500 to the present 500 years of Western cultural life, harpers Collins Publishers, N.Y., 2000.

John T. Bonner, *The evolution of culture in animals*, Princeton University Press, 1983.

Burcu Bostanoğlu, "European Security : A Myth or Reality ? A Turkish Perspective", *Turkish Yearbook of International Relations*, 1996.

Burcu Bostanoğlu, *Türkiye-ABD ilişkilerinin politikası,(The polity of Turkish – U.S. relations)* İmge Yayınları, Ankara, 1999.

Thomas B. Bottomore, *Toplumbilim -Sorunlarına ve Yazınına İlişkin Bir Klavuz* (Sociology – Tr.Ü.Oskay), Ankara, 1977.

Fernand Braudel, Maddi uygarlık – dünyanın zamanı. (Civilisation matérielle, economie et capitalisme – Le temps du Monde). Trans. M. A. Kılıçbay. Imge, Ankara, 2004.

Fernand Braudel, Uygarlıkların grameri (Grammaire des civilisations). Trans. M. A. Kılıçbay. Imge, Ankara 2001.

Kenneth Neill Cameron, Humanity and society, a world history, Monthly Review Press, N.Y., London, 1977.

Pat Cox, "Liberalism in Christianity and Islam", Seminar at the European Liberal Democratic Representation, Brussels, 8 January 2003,
http://www.europarl.eu.int/president/speeches/en/sp0041.htm.

CSIS Middle East Studies Program: Stability and Instability in the Middle East: Economics, Demography, Energy, and Security / The Middle East has Failed to Compete in Attracting Investment, V.I http://www.csis.org/mideast/stable/1d.html.

Michael Scott Doran, "The Saudi Pa radox". Foreign Affairs, January – February 2004.

Richard Eder, "`Stolen Figs' tells of a journey through a land that feels like home" The New York Times, Sunday, Aug 03, 2003, P 19.

Jonathan Fox, Are Middle East Conflicts More Religious? The Middle East Quarterly, Fall 2001 Volume VIII, No. 4.

Adam Garfinkle, "The Impossible Imperative: Conjuring Arab Democracy" The National Interest. V. 1, N. 14. December 11, 2002.

Jim George, "Realist 'Ethics', International Relations and Postmodernism : Thinking Beyond Egoism - Anarchy Thematic" Millennium : Journal of International Studies, V. 24, No. 2, 1995.

Stanley Giannet, "Cultural competence and professional psychology training: creating the architecture for change". Journal of Evolutionary Psychology; August 01, 2003.

Ahmet K. Han, "Irak savaşı: Oyunun adı petrol mü?", Kartalın kanat sesleri – ABD dış politikasında yeni yönelimler ve dünya, ("Iraq war: is oil the name of the game?", Flapping wings of the eagle: new trends in U.S.A. foreign policy and the world) Ed. Toktamis Ates, Umit Yayincilik, Ankara, 2004.

Richard A. Higgott, Political Development Theory, Routledge, London, 1989.

Geert Hofstede, Culture's consequences: International differences in work-related values. Newbury Park, Sage, 1980.

Samuel P. Huntington, "The Clash of Civilizations?" Foreign Affairs, 72 1993.

Samuel P. Huntington, "Democracy for the Long Haul" Journal of Democracy, V 7, N 2. April 1996.

Galip B. İsen, "Terrorism, modernity, Islam and American politics: See no evil... How about the vile?", Siyasal Iktisat, (Political Economy) No, 1, V. 1, forthcoming.

Galip B. Isen, "Kum üzerinde siyasetin kumdan kaleleri: Zoraki demokrasi olur mu?" ("The sand castles of politics on the sand: can democracy be pushed down the throat?"), in: Ates (Ed.), 2004.

Galip B. Isen, " The politics of being Mediterranean : What hope is there for peace in the Northeastern Mediterranean ?" presented to the Third Pan-European International Relations Conference and Joint Meeting With the International Studies Association; convention on Peace and Security in the Eastern Mediterranean Vienna, Austria, 16-19 September, 1998.

Ronald D. Laing, The politics of experience. Routledge & Kegan Paul, London 1967.

Ronald D. Laing, The divided self. Pelican, Middlesex, 1969.

Stephen Larabee, Jerrold D. Green, Ioan O. Lesser, Michel Zanini, NATO's Mediterranean Initiative: policy issues and dilemmas, Rand, 1998.

John Macquarrie, Existentialism, PenguinBooks, N.Y. 1973.

Peter Mandaville, Transnational Muslim Politics:Re-Imagining the Umma. Routledge. London. 2001.

Peter Mansfield, A history of the Middle East, Viking, N.Y., 1991.

Kate Manzo, "Modernist Discourse and the Crisis of Development Theory", Studies in Comparative International Development, V. 26, No: 2 Summer 1991.

Şerif A. Mardin, "Ideology and religion in the Turkish revolution", Journal of Middle East Studies, No. 2, 1971.

Seumas Milne "They can't see why they are hated - Americans cannot ignore what their government does abroad" special report, The Guardian Thursday, September 13, 2001.Tariq Modood, Multicultural politics racism, ethnicity and Muslims in Britain. University of Minnesota Press, 2005.

Robert Murphy. Culture and Social Anthropology: An Overture. 2nd ed. Englewood Cliffs, NJ: Prentice Hall, 1986.

Marina Ottaway, Thomas Carothers "The Greater Middle East Initiative: Off to a False Start" Carnegie Endowment for International Peace Policy Brief, March 2004 / 29 http://www.ceip.org/files/pdf/Policybrief29.pdf.

Daniel Pipes, Tanri Adina (In Name of God) Yaprak Yayınları İstanbul, 1991.

Brent C. Smith, John C. Raines "The politics of religious correctness: Islam and the West. Cross Currents, Spring 1996, Vol. 46, N. 1.

Norman Rich, Great power diplomacy, 1814 – 1914, McGraw Hill, 1992.

Edward Said "Time for intellectual honesty - There are many Islams", Counterpunch. http://www.counterpunch.org/saidattacks.html September 16, 2001.

Edward Said, "Impossible Histories: Why the Many Islams Cannot be Simplified," Harper's Magazine, July 2002.

Roger Sandall "The politics of oxymoron", The New Criterion: a web special, http://www.newcriterion.com/archive/21/sum03/sandall.htm, Summer 2003.

Roger Sandall "When I hear the word 'culture' from Arnold to Anthropology". Encounter, V. 55, No. 4, October 1980.

Irvin Cemil Schick, Ertuğrul Ahmet Tonak, Geçiş sürecinde Türkiye (Turkey in transition), Belge, İstanbul 1998.

D. Michael Shafer, Deadly Paradigms The Failure of US Counterinsurgency Policy, Princeton University Press, Princeton N.J. 1988.

Taillander, "Middle-East connected anti-American terror attacks", The Middle East Review of International Affairs Journal (MERIA), V.5, #4, Dec. 2001, http://meria.idc.ac.il.

Dean C. Tipps, "Modernisation Theory and the Comparative Study of Societies : A Critical Perspective", Comparative Studies in Society and History, V.15, No.2, March 1973.

Arnold J. Toynbee A Study of History, V. XII. Oxford University Press, 1961.

Immanuel Wallerstein, "Eurocentrism and its Avatars: The Dilemmas of Social Science", Keynote Address at ISA East Asian Regional Colloquium, "The Future of Sociology in East Asia," Nov. 22-23, 1996, Seoul, Korea, co-sponsored by Korean Sociological Association and International Sociological Association http://fbc.binghamton.edu/ iweuroc.htm 1997I. Wallerstein, "Culture as the ideological battleground of the modern world-system", The essential Wallerstein, New Press (Dist. W.W. Norton) 2000 pp. 264 - 289, New York, 2000.

Immanuel Wallerstein, "The end of what modernity?", Theory and Society, 24, 1995.

I. Wallerstein, "Liberalism and Democracy: Fréres Ennemis ?" Fourth Daalder Lecture, Rijksuniversiteit Leiden, Interfacultaire Vakgroep Politieke Wetenschappen, March 15, 1997.

I. Wallerstein, "The Time of Space and the Space of Time: the Future of Social Science", Political Geography V. 17 No. 1, 1998.

Rhys H. Williams, "Politics, religion and the analysis of culture", Theory and society, V.25, No. 6, Dec. 1996.

Karl August Wittfogel, Oriental despotism – A study of total power, Vintage Books, N.Y., 1957.

Tamara Cofman Wittes "The promise of Arab liberalism". Policy Review. No. 125. July 2004.

PART V:
PROBLEMS OF TERRORISM
AND PERSPECTIVES
ON A MORE PEACEFUL DEVELOPMENT

Chapter 10
COUNTERING GLOBAL TERRORIST USE OF BIOLOGICAL AND NUCLEAR WEAPONS BY CIVIL MEANS

Clark C. Abt

I. Introduction and Overview

Given the growing threat of terrorist attacks on cities with biological and nuclear weapons of mass destruction, what is to be done? What is to be done to deter, defend against, limit, reduce, and defeat this unprecedented threat to the survival of cities, societies, and economies? And what is to be done better than what is already being done?

How serious is the threat of terrorist use of biological or nuclear weapons against city targets? How damaging and deadly? How likely? Previous studies by this writer and others in 2002, 2003, and 2004 have concluded that the potential deaths from a nuclear terrorist attack on a major city of several million could range between half a million and a million, and the effective removal of that city and its commerce and industry and housing from the national economy for decades. (See, for example, Abt, *The Economic Impacts of Nuclear Terrorist Attacks on the Freight Transport System in an Age of Seaport Vulnerability,* Abt Associates Inc., Cambridge, 2003). How likely? Nuclear terrorists already have the intention, potential capability, and opportunity to steal, buy, or make simple nuclear fission weapons of Hiroshima strength (10-15 Kilotons of TNT), and many opportunities for clandestine delivery to major target cities.

Less well known is the fact that a clandestine release in a crowded urban rail or air terminal of a suitcase full of aerosolized smallpox or plague could create a deadly epidemic killing millions as it is spread to other cities by interurban and international travelers. A local release of 100 pounds of weaponized anthrax in the circumferential highway around Washington D.C. could kill a million people within weeks, and put the entire city effectively out of action for years of cleanup. (The comparatively tiny anthrax attack, using a few ounces, on Washington, New York, and New Jersey killed only a handful but cost the better part of a billion dollars and over a year to clean up.) How likely? It has already happened on fortunately a small scale. The biological agents exist, as does the capacity to use them and probably the intent. (See Abt, Casagrande, Katz, *Urban Biological Preparedness: A Biodefense Assessment Workshop,* Abt Associates Inc., 2004, and Abt and

Casagrande, *The Economic Impacts of Bioterrorist Attacks on the Freight Transport System in an Age of Seaport Vulnerability,* Abt Associates Inc., 2003). The basic premise of this essay is that the US-led "war on terror" and war on Al Queda and Taliban in Afghanistan, and a combination of foreign and domestic terrorists, insurgents, and resistance fighter in Iraq have employed primarily military means, to the relative neglect of non-military civil means.

The chief distinction between military and civil means is not the use of force – both army and police use it – but the very different levels of violence and discriminating use of force in a usually symmetrically two-sided war of uniformed soldiers and artillery and tanks and airplanes and ships against a similarly armed and organized enemy, as distinguished from civil police in an asymmetric many-sided conflict against dispersed criminal law breakers usually trying to avoid direct conflict with the usually better armed and organized police that is lawfully authorized to use deadly force only as a last resort and in self defense.

Police may sometimes have to destroy property such as breaking down doors, but generally have the mission of protecting life and property from theft or destruction. The military have the mission of destroying enemy life and property to the extent necessary to defeat their enemy. This is why and how the laws of civil society regulate and highly constrain the police's legal use of force to protect legal property and persons against diverse small numbers of law-breaking criminals, while the laws of war constrain a military force only in its treatment of prisoners of war and non-combatants and use of in some cases mutually agreed outlawed weapons such as poison gas or torture (prohibitions often violated).

Obviously guerrilla wars and insurgencies are somewhere in between warfare and police protecting civilian life and property against criminals practicing lower levels of violence to get what they want (money, property, local control, sometimes revenge and removal of obstacles to theft and domination by murderous violence against other civilians or police.)

In a war, the object of each side is to destroy the enemy forces to whatever extent is necessary for the enemy forces and supporting civilian population, land and economy to "surrender" and stop fighting, granting to the war winner physical and legal control over the war loser's people, land, and property. In total war situations such as WW II there was no limit on the level of violence practiced and little distinction made between combatants and civilians as the destruction of entire city populations demonstrated – a kind of urban genocide. In a conflict of law-enforcing police and law-breaking criminals, a small minority of the population within a country are either police protecting the much larger number of citizens against a much smaller number of criminals, with an overwhelming majority of the citizens supporting the police against the criminals with information, authority, laws, arms, courts, and prisons.

Terrorism has been defined as violent action by a small group against a much larger one, making no distinction between combatants and civilians, with the intention of instilling fear in the larger population and acquiescence to terrorist political goals. Insurgencies and revolutions are rebellions against traditional authorities or foreign enemy occupation forces and their military and their police.

When civilians, civilian police, and military of one large fraction of a state's population fight for control of a country with a similarly armed and organized set of opponents, rebellions, revolutions and insurgencies merge into civil war, where the conflict is well beyond the capacities of civil law enforcement police, courts and prisons to manage and contain it, because the other side has its own laws and law enforcement and armed forces. Thus the debate about whether the "war on terrorism" is and should be managed as civil police actions protecting innocent civilians against criminals breaking national and international laws, or managed by military forces committed to destroying and defeating deadly enemies however asymmetrical their numbers and weaponry becomes moot when terrorists escalate the conflict within and across borders to the highest levels of mass violence against an entire population or population target. The conflict then becomes a mix of civil and military actions, ranging from police actions to full military warfare, involving both soldiers and civilians in all forms of violence as direct or indirect combatants.

The insurgents often do not consider the other side's civilians "innocent", and soon their opponents do not do so either, or only rhetorically, regretting the allegedly unavoidable "collateral damage" of non-military civilian loss of life and property. This is why some consider the undiscriminating destruction of a city by massive bombardment, whether with incendiary and high explosive bombs (Tokyo and Dresden) or with atomic bombs (Hiroshima and Nagasaki) in WWII, or with the planned destruction of each sides' forces and populations by "Counter-force" and "Counter-value" attack with nuclear weapons as in the avoided WWIII between NATO and Warsaw Pact examples of "state terrorism". (As defined by some in the Terrorism Working Group at the 54th Pugwash Conference on Science and International Affairs in Seoul, Korea in October 2004.)

Certainly when the most indiscriminatingly violent means of conflict with nuclear and biological weapons of mass destruction ("mass destruction" meaning the killing of tens of thousands to millions of people in a single attack) are threatened by state or non-state or transnational terrorists, all means of defense and counter-attack must be and are considered, including both civil police, fire, and public health and all forms of military force.

This is also the case when a conventional war such as that waged by US-led Coalition military forces against Nazi Germany and Imperial Japan in WWII and Iraq in 2003 results in the defeat and surrender of the enemy armed forces, deposing of the dictator and his government, occupation by the victorious armed forces and the occupier's civil administration of the defeated nation.

But in the case of Iraq and perhaps Afghanistan this first wholly military phase, however decisive in military terms, turns out to be indecisive in civil terms and merges into an insurgency resistance employing classic terrorist and guerilla war tactics. And worse, the occupation of Iraq (as in the smaller but chronic case of the Israeli occupation of Palestine and the West Bank) has generated worldwide recruitment of anti-Western Islamic fundamentalist terrorists dedicated to the indiscriminate use of weapons of mass destruction against America and allies. "Terrorists are not known to have ever stolen or built nuclear weapons, but they are trying to. In 1998, Osama bin Laden issued a statement titled "The Nuclear Bomb of Islam," declaring, "It is the duty of Muslims to prepare as much force as possible to terrorize the enemies of God." (from Graham Allison, *Nuclear Terrorism*, Times Books, 2004. p. 218).

That this did not occur at the end of WWII in Japan or Germany (with the minor exception of a few Nazi "Werewolves" holdouts in the Bavarian alps that could be handled by civil police) is a credit to the careful post-war planning and execution of non-military, civil means of police and law enforcement and civil administration to preserve post-war law and order and reconstitution of civil society, (and the complete and long since lost US monopoly of nuclear weapons in 1945.) Unfortunately for Iraq and America, this post-war civil administration planning and execution was not done in post(conventional) war Iraq in 2003, which has since swelled with the unemployed soldiers and civil servants its resistance to the primarily American military occupation in the form of a combination of terrorist attacks, criminal kidnappings, and violent and well-armed resistance to both Coalition forces and Iraqi police and reconstituted military and civilian aid workers, by at least five distinct adversary groups, including Al Caeda, and are now threatening 2-to-5-sided civil war if the 2005 elections continue to fail to unify and pacify the country under a popularly elected and not violently contested leadership.

Against state actors with territory at risk, the primarily military approach can be effective, as it was in WWI, WWII, the Korean War, and the first phases of the Afghan and Iraq wars since 9/11/2001. But against non-state terrorists and insurgents, especially those threatening to use catastrophic attacks of biological and nuclear weapons, military means however important are unlikely to achieve decisive results by themselves.

Deterrence – nuclear and conventional – worked in 40 years of Cold War against contenders threatening the use of both conventional and nuclear and biological weapons, because both sides had populations and territories at risk to the adversary's well protected and survivable retaliatory second strike forces. But the stable logic of two-sided deterrence tends to break down when there are many possible attackers as a result of nuclear weapons proliferation beyond known alliances of state actors with known loyalties and antagonisms, the so called "Nth Country Problem" in the nuclear strategy literature of the second half of the 20th Century.

Retaliatory deterrence is almost completely ineffectual against suicidal religious fundamentalist nuclear and biological terrorists who glory in becoming honored martyrs dying for their cause and reaping endless rewards in heaven if they die or if they live to fight again. Military action alone against such terrorists and their suspected locations tends to be sufficiently destructive of associated non-combatant women, children, elderly, and homes and workplaces to outrage the previously neutral and non-hostile population to mobilize the youth and the women into terrorist combat or combat support roles.

Military forces and their leaders and planners have little understanding or experience of psycho-social influence processes that might de-motivate the spread and escalation of terrorist insurgencies. Civil public health, education, and police professionals who do deal with violence prevention and youth crime every day using the minimum lawful force necessary to restrain the violent and diverse processes to demotivate violence and motivate peaceful and productive behaviors, the "peace officers" and clinicians and counselors, are too rarely consulted by occupying military forces attempting to pacify a militarily defeated but still resistant population. Democratic elections alone are not necessarily sufficient for pacifying an unwillingly occupied population, especially if law and order cannot be maintained to provide a fair and non-violent election process and its resulting elected government.

In fact there are many reasons to believe that military threats and actions against nascent and/or outlaw nuclear weapons states and trans-national nuclear terrorists, can be counterproductive and actually accelerate the very nuclear weapons development, proliferation and nuclear terrorist threats they are intended to deny. This may also be the case for purely military attempts to counter the threat of biological and conventional (high explosive) terrorism, as was the case in the justification of the military invasion and occupation of Iraq on the basis of Iraq's allegedly imminent threat of biological and nuclear weapons of mass destruction. (We consider these two- nuclear and biological weapons- truly the only weapons of mass destruction, capable of destroying an entire city in one day (or in a few weeks in the case of deadly biological weapons), killing millions and severely damaging national economies. Chemical and radiological weapons are orders of magnitude less destructive of life and property, capable of killing thousands much like conventional high explosive bombardments, and hence are not weapons of *mass* destruction).

The military response to the threat of mass terror from biological and nuclear weapons has been used intensely and extensively in Afghanistan and Iraq since 9/11/01, with mixed results. Some believe that the military response, particularly the invasion and occupation of Iraq and the unintended but unavoidable loss of many civilian women and children's' lives to military action has created many more enemies and murderous intentions of revenge than it has eliminated. Certainly the "war on terrorism" has expanded globally and intensified in terms of daily deaths on both sides. A horrendous escalation to biological and nuclear terrorist attacks now threatens the cities of the world and the economies and populations of the US, the EU, and directly or indirectly through their economies most of the world, and this enormous escalation in violence is not deterred or effectively defended against by military responses alone, not now and even less so in the future.

More effective means than military ones must be found to counter biological and nuclear weapons of mass destruction striking the population centers of the world. More effective counter-terror methods of deterrence and defense must be found, that cost less in lives (and perhaps resources) than military ones. There are many civil means that avoid the heavy "collateral" losses of lives and property and hostility-engendering effects inevitable in major military destructive actions, and by contrast are mainly productive and constructive of lives and property.

It is the thesis of this essay that the best civil means of countering terrorists threatening the use of weapons of mass destruction is the expanded capacity and use of international arms control diplomacy, development assistance, police, and public health. The dual benefits, in both war and peace, of international arms control diplomacy, foreign aid and development assistance, public health and public safety/police enhancement attract more universal popular support and greater economic productivity than purely military defenses, as well as providing more discriminating and humane responses to terrorist attacks that can greatly reduce casualties, costs, collateral damage, and incitements to adversarial recruitment of more terrorists (horizontal escalation).

Prevention of WMD terrorist attacks on cities by pacification of terrorist intentions or retaliatory deterrence seems impossible in the current situation of suicidal Islamic fundamentalist mass terrorists threatening the use of WMD as soon as they get them, which sooner or later is inevitable. However, since it is the stated intention of Al Caeda and Bin Laden to kill as many Americans and Europeans and do as much damage to their economies as they possibly can, a still uncertain degree of *deterrence of biological weapons mass attacks might be gained by demonstrating a capacity to greatly limit their damage.* For example, a mass release of aerosolized smallpox agent in a major air or rail transport terminal intended to create an epidemic killing millions probably cannot be prevented, but it might be deterred if a country can demonstrate its ability to promptly detect such a bioterrorist attack and prophylactically vaccinate most of its exposed population within the incubation period of the deadly contagious agent in time to render the attack mostly ineffectual (as Israel has done and the US and UK and other developed nations could do).

Deterrence by denial of intended lethality of a nuclear terrorist attack is more difficult than for a bioterrorist attack, but is not impossible. Denial of nuclear weapons to terrorists and rogue nations who might sell them to nuclear terrorists has been argued persuasively by Graham Allison in his book, *Nuclear Terrorism* (New York, Times Books, 2004). He urges a new international security doctrine of "Three No's: No Loose Nukes, No New Nascent Nukes, No New Nuclear Weapons States." These are the first and best lines of defense against nuclear terrorism. But they will take time to implement because they require much intensive diplomatic efforts to obtain international agreements on nuclear and pre-nuclear arms controls, and the broad public support needed to move political leaders to act. While these ultimately productive longer-term approaches are being pursued, more immediately executable second and third lines of defense should be implemented, such as export and import inspections and controls on the clandestine delivery of nuclear weapons to cities.

Another example: The much vaunted threat of a nuclear terrorist strike at a seaport or river port with a nuclear weapons smuggled into port in a cargo container, while costly to prevent entirely by 100% inspection of all containers at ports of embarkation (estimated to cost $10 billion per year in a 2003 analysis for the US Department of Transportation by this writer), might be so limited in damage potential as to deny its intended imposition of mass casualties and massive trade disruption, and thus contribute to its deterrence.

Because the nuclear terrorists are unlikely to have more than one or a very few weapons, they will tend to select a target offering maximum damage potential to population, government, and trade. The most lucrative targets could be made much less attractive by passive defense by dispersal and decentralization of the larger container ports into many smaller ones and remoting them from population centers, and the same for civil government functions. This might eventually even improve overall logistic, industrial, and government services efficiency. It is not so much de-urbanization as it is decentralization into dispersed linked networks offering fewer concentrated nodes making lucrative targets for small numbers of weapons of mass destruction.

The costs and fatalities and damage-reducing dual benefits of mostly military and mostly civil strategies to counter biological and nuclear terrorist mass attacks on US and EU cities have been estimated in previous studies summarized below, based in part on previous 2002-3 studies by the author of "The Economic Impacts of Biological and Nuclear Terrorist Attacks" for the US Department of Transportation, and of a 2004 "Biodefense Cost-Benefit Assessment" for the Ford Foundation.

It is the intention of this essay to identify much needed areas of policy research and scientific analysis of the most promising non-military, civil means of deterring, preventing, defending against, and limiting the deaths and damages of nuclear and bioterrorist attacks.

I don't believe we are on the point of blowing up the *whole* world with nuclear terrorism or responses to it. The likelihood of the US and Russia or China having a massive nuclear exchange creating nuclear winter or hundreds of millions of deaths is more remote than ever, and that particular horror has been contained for half a century and I strongly believe will continue to be for another fifty. Rather, we *are* very much threatened by one or a few nuclear terrorist attacks on major cities, for all the reasons accurately given in Graham Allison's recent book, *Nuclear Terrorism,* Steve Flynn's book and Foreign Affairs article *America the Vulnerable,* and in my 2003 reports on *The Economic Impacts of Nuclear and Biological Terrorist Attacks On The Freight Transport System in an Age of Seaport Vulnerability.* Such nuclear and biological terrorist attacks as are described could kill thousands to millions of people, but perhaps even more fatefully impoverish billions and destroy or grievously damage the world economy and all its trading partners.

We could prevent those catastrophes by expanding the Nunn-Lugar Cooperative Threat Reduction programs to secure Russia's "Loose Nukes" (which the Bush Administration has cut), and by building up our port inspection defenses (vs. nukes arriving in containers) and public health biodefenses (vs. bioterrorist attacks with deadly contagious diseases like smallpox and plague, or anthrax.) A civil, non-military, non-violent program of both kinds of defenses follow. This paper on civil (non-military) means of countering nuclear and bioterrorist attacks finds that such *civil defenses against catastrophic nuclear and biological terrorism may be more strategically cost-effective, politically and morally more attractive and unifying and less divisive, and cheaper, faster, and more humane than purely military defenses (such as preemptive bombardment offensives),* because they create valuable (and widely valued!) peacetime crime reduction, economic development, and public health benefits for all countries and peoples even if there are no terrorist attacks.

Promoting general and complete nuclear disarmament these days, to the neglect of nuclear and biological arms control cooperative actions and agreements, is I believe a case of the best defeating the good. We may be wasting valuable time and effort urging the ideal complete nuclear disarmament, distracting ourselves from the good that can and should be done to prevent the present greatest danger of nuclear proliferation and nuclear and biological terrorism. Making the general nuclear disarmament effort may discredit the even more urgently needed and currently feasible and affordable nuclear arms control and anti-terror efforts to protect our major cities from nuclear or biological terrorist attack and catastrophe. Liberals and conservatives everywhere can agree on the latter and move it, but not the former.

II. A Summary of the Economic Impacts of Bioterrorist and Nuclear Terrorist Attacks on Seaport-Based Transport Systems, Under Current and Improved Civil Defense Conditions

1. The Importance of Seaport-Based Transport Systems to the US and the World Economy: 20 % of the US economy depends on trade and transport, half of that (10%) (by value) by container ship. The US is 25% of the world economy ($13 Trillion).

2. The Biological and Nuclear Terrorist Threats to US & World Population and Economy: Weapons, Targets, and Aim Points. The Bioterrorist Threat of clandestine release of aerosols of weaponized deadly

contagious disease (smallpox, plague) in crowded air, sea, rail, or subway terminals infecting thousands, with the epidemic spreading to millions, killing 30 % of those infected who are unlikely to be prophylactically vaccinated within the one-week incubation period. The Nuclear Terrorist Threat of a Hiroshima-scale 10-20 Kiloton fission weapon or (in a decade) 1-5 Megaton Hydrogen bomb smuggled undetected into a major US seaport (New York, Los Angeles) or Washington, DC, in one of millions of cargo containers shipped or trucked into the US, and detonated at dockside or after being trucked into the city center.

3. Estimated Costs and Consequences of Successful Bioterrorist and Nuclear Terrorist Attacks Today (2005-7): Deaths and Damages under current (2006) inadequate defense conditions:

COSTS from 2006-7 Attack	Bioterrorist Attack (smallpox, plague)	Nuclear Terrorist Attack
Deaths	30,000 – 3,000,000	50,000 – 1,000,000 (NYC)
Property Damage - direct	$1-10 Billion	$ 50 - $500 Billion
Trade Disruption	$ 20-200 Billion	$ 100 – 200 Billion
Indirect cost (multiplier=2)	$ 42 - 420 Billion	$ 300 –1,400 Billion (1.4Trillion)
TOTAL Costs	Hundreds billions - Trillions	Hundreds billions- Trillions

4. Reduced Risks and Costs of Attack Damage with Improved Defenses feasible and affordable in 2007-2010:Improved non-violent Biodefense costing $10 Billion/year for 10,000 biodetectors installed in 100 cities for environmental surveillance and early warning.

5. Improved state and city public health biolab capacity promptly to identify and confirm pathogen released.

6. Pre-positioned in or near all major cities, vaccines and antibiotics for prompt prophylactic treatment on warning.

7. Command, control, inter-operable communications, and intelligence for first responder Vaccinated Vaccinators & Transport for prompt Logistic Support of (3).

8. Pre- and Post-Attack Weekly/Daily, perhaps hourly Public/Professional Education on all media on what do, and what not to do.

9. Active neutron scanners for 100% external inspection at each of 100 foreign POE's (Ports of Embarkation) for the US and 10 US ports trans-shipping into interior cities.

10. Tagging of all shipping containers and vehicles with internal reporting sensors, with videos taken on packing and relayed forward to POE command centers and US destination ports.

11. Standardization and enforcement of international standards of security of containers, cargoes, conveyances, and personnel.

12. Accelerated Cooperative Threat Reduction efforts to secure Russian, Pakistani, and other insufficiently secure stockpiles of nuclear weapons and fissile materials, and maintain secure or non-military employment of foreign nuclear weapons scientists.

COSTS of Attack + Cost of Improved Defense	2005-2007 BioAttack-Inadequate Defense	2007-2010 Improved Biodefense	2005-2007 NuclearTerrorist Attack, Inadeq.Defense	2007-2010 Improved Nuclear Defense
Deaths	30,000- 3 Mil.	1,000 – 3,000	50,000- 1 Million	5000-100,000 (Expected Value)
Property Damage, direct costs	$1-10 Billion	$0.5- 5 Billion	$50-500 B	$5-50 Billion
Trade Disruption	$20-200 Billion	$1-5 Billion	$100-200 B	$10-20 B
Indirect Costs (x 2)	$42-420 Billion	$3 – 20 B	$300 – 1.4 T.	$30-140 B(EV)
TOTAL Attack Costs	Hundreds of B.	$4.5 – 30 B	Low Trillions	$45-210 B
+ Cost of Defense	$1 B spent now	$10 Billion	$1-2 B ? in 2006	$10 Billion
TOTAL cost of Attack damage plus defense (excluding loss of life costs)	$43 – 421 B	$14.5- 40 Billion (est. 60 to 90% reduced costs of bioattack + biodefense)	$ hundreds of billions to low trillions	$55 – 220 Billion (est. 80% reduced costs of nuclear attack + defense)

Source: The Economic Impacts of Nuclear Terrorist Attacks on Freight Transports Systems in an Age of Seaport Vulnerability; Clark C.Abt, William Rhodes, and Tom Rich, Abt Associates Inc., Cambridge, Massachusetts. 2003, updated in 2006.

III. Countering Global Terrorist's Use of Biological and Nuclear Weapons by Civil Non-Destructive Means

Advantages of replacing military defenses with civil, non-destructive defenses:

- economically productive rather than destructive;
- politically more productive alliances, international agreements, and trade;
- scientifically more productive from dual R&D benefits shared by all;
- morally superior (adding to life and life quality, rather than taking life);
- consistent with most major religions' teaching;
- universally popular and a socio-psychological force multiplier;
- less costly;
- environmentally sustainable;
- proliferation and replication desired and desirable, rather than dangerous and shunned.

Defense against biological weapons of mass destruction is currently costly, difficult, and uncertain. If means of deterrence can be identified, even if incomplete and unassured, they can narrow the scope and intensity of bioattack threats, making biodefenses more feasible and cost-effective. Some combination of deterrence and defense is preferable to reliance solely on one or the other.

III.1. Prevention by Deterrence

1. *Deterrence of catastrophic bioterrorist attacks by the well-publicized threat of "blow-back"* of deadly epidemics to many countries allied with or sympathetic to the bioterrorists. For example, if the bioterrorists are suicidal Al Caeda fundamentalist Muslim extremists, they may not care about losing their own lives, but they are likely to be concerned about the great loss of life and worsened economic hardship of their supporting Muslim populations created by the almost inevitable spread of the smallpox or plague epidemic they initiated beyond the target city international transport terminal. The poorer populations will suffer the most. Muslim countries with their relatively weaker public health systems are also likely to suffer disproportionately from the international spread of the bioterrorist-induced epidemics, weakening the supporting populations and creating dissention among previ-

ous supporters of the bioterrorists. (It is not very difficult to trace the source of a large, well-organized bioterrorist attack.)

2. *Deterrence of catastrophic bioterrorist attacks by the well-publicized economic cost to trade-dependent countries of the shutting down of one or more major port operations for months to years.* The economic damage to trade-dependent poorer Muslim countries is likely to be disproportionately greater than that to the US and other major powers with large internal markets. (Over 80% of the US economy is domestic.)

3. *Deterrence by the moral reform of the would-be perpetrator of catastrophic bioterrorism*–a kind of ethical/ideological/religious deterrence: perhaps this would ultimately be most effective but most difficult to achieve without years of intense study and effort. We should be searching and seeking to find a benevolent reformist Muslim leader, perhaps some one like the Aga Kahn, who will passionately and charismatically confront the murderous fundamentalist Islamic jihadists and excite in them and their followers a great moral repugnance for what they consider doing to create suffering and death for others out of a distorted sense of justice and faith. I know of only one such Muslim reformer, the Pakistani-Ugandan-Canadian journalist Ms. Irshad Manji, and her book, *The Trouble with Islam.* If her views only became more popular among the Islamic masses, there might be sufficient moral force to demotivate murderous martyrdoms such as bioterrorist attacks. As decent citizens, humanists, and social and physical scientists, we should study the potential emergence of such Islamic moral leaders and support them, with all the educational, economic, psycho-social, political, and communications tools at our disposal. Where is our CIA of the mind and morals, valuing life and justice over religious or ideological faction? Why don't we at least look for our saints of peaceful counter-terrorism? Where is an Islamic Gandhi when we need him (or her) to deter catastrophically murderous moral outrages?

4. *None of the above approaches to deterrence of catastrophic bioterrorism can assure the world that they will be sufficient.* The long history of human conflict up to the present day gives no indication at all that there are not always present ruthlessly cruel fanatics of great ambition and persuasive skills who can mobilize the best science and technology and economic resources to attempt massive terrorist attacks on their enemies that bar their way to world power. Given the highly uncertain nature of deterrence in the current historical period, we must look to *denial of access* to the means, *ac-*

tive and passive defense against, and *mitigation* of the consequences of catastrophic bioterrorist attacks. We will see that fortunately these defenses against bioterrorism are not only much more effective than military ones, but also yield important peacetime benefits worldwide. (We cannot bomb all the potential bioterrorist labs in potentially hostile countries, we cannot search for, find and capture or kill all the world's potential bioterrorists.). These *peacetime "dual benefits" of biodefense* may stimulate more investment in better biodefenses by improving public health, and thus motivate yet more investment in better biodefenses as well. This has indeed been the case in the US since 9/11/01 and the 2001 anthrax attack. Upwards of $4 billion of new funds have been invested in biodefense, compared to small fractions of that (under $1 billion) of new money invested in improved defense against nuclear terrorism. Hopefully scientists and leaders of all technologically advanced nations will replicate. We do not consider the Bush Administration's roughly $10 billion annual investment in ballistic missile defense a serious, effective or efficient investment in defense against nuclear terrorism. There are so many easier, cheaper, means of delivering a nuclear weapon to the US than by a North Korean (or Chinese, or Iranian) ballistic missile: It could be delivered in one of the nine million containers coming into US ports each year, 95% of them not inspected before arrival. It could come in the trunk of a car coming across the Canadian or Mexican border. It could come in the bilge of an ocean-going yacht, it could come in by low-flying light plane. In sum, when deterrence is not enough to prevent bioterrorist attacks, we must look to other means such as prevention.

III.2. Prevention of Bioterrorist Attack by Denial of Access

The only military means of denying bioterrorists access to the means for making bioweapons is to destroy or capture and sequester all the world's bioweapons precursor biologicals and chemicals and lab equipments and microbiologists. This obviously will not happen, not least because the labs and fermenters and microbiologists capable of producing bioweapons are intrinsically 'dual-use', and essential to a multitude of legitimate and needed civilian biochemical processes for producing medicines, foods, beverages, plastics.

The civil means of denying or at least limiting access to dangerous pathogens is obviously more promising and less destructive. What are these?

For denial of access of bioterrorists to materials and equipment and knowledge needed to make biological weapons, there is scientific diplomacy, such as the Biological Weapons Convention, by which signatory nations (including the US and the USSR) promise not to produce, test, and deploy biological weapons. There are other international agreements about early warning and reporting of deadly infectious and contagious diseases, such as the UN/WHO and US/CDCP networks. But none of these measures have by themselves made it difficult to obtain the chemical and biological precursors to making biological weapons. There is now more attention paid, at least in the US, to regulating and limiting the ordering and purchase of particular strains of pathogens from the various university biomedical labs. Given the widespread distribution of natural plague and natural anthrax, only smallpox is difficult to obtain from the only two labs in the world that have them, one in Moscow and one in the US. One hopes that they will remain so.

Particularly with the advance of bioengineering genetics, it is only a matter of time before even such now rare and sequestered diseases like smallpox become available to bioterrorists willing to use them. Given the above described weakness of the deterrence, prevention, and denial of access of bioterrorists to bioweapons materials, we must turn to the more useful civil defenses of post-attack mitigation as the overall best way of civil biodefense.

III.3. *Prevention of Effective Bioterrorist Attack by Rapid Response Identification, Interception and Suppression-Active Civil Means*

Purely military means of intercepting a biological attack on the US by Soviet cruise missiles launched with deadly biological payloads may have had their place in the symmetrical two-sided Cold War of the 1950's, 1960's, 1970's, and 1980's, when both sides had quite similar classes of offensive and defensive weapons systems. For offensive Soviet and Warsaw Pact missiles, bomber aircraft, missile-launching submarines, and tanks there were corresponding US and NATO surface-to-air defense missiles and interceptor aircraft, hunter-killer submarines, and tanks, etc., and vice versa. But neither military superpower's massive conventional, nuclear, chemical, and biological weapons (abandoned by the US by order of President Nixon when he signed the Biological Weapons Convention, as did the Soviets but without abandoning them) have been much use against terrorists and insurgents, as demonstrated repeatedly by the defeat of overwhelming quantities of qualitatively superior military forces with underwhelming results for the US in Vietnam in the early 1970's, the Soviets in Afghanistan in the 1980's, the US in Iraq today, and Russia in Chechnia today, and both countries in their militarily muscle-bound but pathetically inadequate domestic civil defenses against great and small conventional terrorism and biological and nuclear catastrophic terrorism.

The military countermeasures to a military biological weapons attack on US military (and inevitably and unavoidably, civilian population targets) by Soviet cruise missiles launched with deadly biological payloads may have had their place in the symmetrical two-sided Cold War years, though now useless against dispersed and clandestine non-state bioterrorists.

Former Soviet bioweapons scientist Ken Alibek describes such a project in the 1980's at the Russian "Institute of Ultra-Pure Biopreparations" and its leader, a later defecting scientist named Pasechnik. "One of Pasechnik's most important projects was the modification of cruise missiles for the delivery of biological agents. The Leningrad scientists were asked to analyze the efficiency of aerosol clouds sprayed from a 'fast-flying, low-altitude moving object' containing one or more twenty-liter canisters as the missile passed over successive targets. The canisters would break apart on impact with the air. Cruise missiles have revolutionized warfare. With onboard electronic guidance and mapping systems that enable them to fly close to the ground and thus avoid most radar defenses, they can be launched from the air, land, or sea at great distances from their targets. Harnessing them for our use would dramatically improve the strategic effectiveness of biological warfare" (Ken Alibek, *Biohazard*, New York, Dell Publishing, 1999. P. 140).

Certainly the main *military* defenses against such strategic military missile bioattacks are low altitude surface-to-air missile barrier defenses and, failing that and the probably too late scrambled fighter-interceptor aircraft failing to shoot them down, preemptive counter-force bombardment of the launch sites might be tried.

But the military defenses against such a military bioattack are not really relevant, because here we are concerned with defending against bio*terrorist* attacks. A mutual bombardment of strategic missiles between superpowers is not our most pressing problem anymore, partly because of the long-standing and stable deterrent balance of terror, and partly because of détente. (However, military weapons systems have become an economic and a safety problem, because the enormous costs of securing and dismantling obsolete and excessive military forces and weapons have not been anticipated – perhaps willfully – and underestimated in life cycle cost analyses of new weapon systems, especially unconventional weapons, and specifically in nuclear weapons and nuclear power reactors. (See economic analyses of the high costs of environmental cleanup and security of the dismantlement of Russian and US chemical and nuclear weapons and retired nuclear power plants.)

Military defenses against non-state bioterrorists are ineffectual because neither are they deterred by having land and population at risk to retaliation, nor are there immediate prospects of détente like the NATO-Warsaw Pact and Russian-American ones. (Nor is there much of a long-term prospect of détente with terrorists who confront nations with an existential conflict in which one of them must disappear for the other to be satisfied, as in Arab and Israeli and Serb and Croat extremists devoted to completely destroying their adversaries.) Bioterrorists are unlikely to obtain or use a cruise missile to deliver their deadly biological weapons. Much simpler, cheaper clandestine means of delivery avail, such as aerosol spray bottles packed in briefcases. And military forces are of little use in intercepting a secret agent in New York or Washington's subway, carrying a briefcase filled with spray cans of deadly biological weapons. That is a job for the civil public health and police authorities.

Civil, non-military means of prevention of catastrophic biological weapons attacks by rapid response identification, interception, control and suppression of epidemics, and cleanup and mitigation of damage do exist. An active civil defense, currently called "Homeland Defense" in the US, has existed for two centuries in the US. Defense against natural biological "attack" or epidemics has long been the province of not primarily military medicine (which also has a long and useful history), but rather by civilian medicine and public health systems. The US Department of Homeland Security, organized in response to the 9/11/01 disaster, is nothing much more than the collection (and, one hopes, eventual integration) of previously otherwise distributed federal agencies. It consists of the old Customs Bureau, formerly in the Treasury Department; the Coast Guard and the Federal Aviation Authority (FAA), both formerly in the Transportation Department; and the Immigration and Naturalization Service (INS) formerly in the Department of Justice. Some small elements of the Public Health Service and the FBI have been incorporated, but the Departments of Health and Human Services and Justice, respectively, had sufficient political-bureaucratic power to retain these important elements in a comprehensive and effectively integrated biodefense within their own departments.

Today in the US, civil, non-military defenses involve elements of all the Federal government's departments, and state and many municipal departments of civil government as well. Outstanding in their contributions to the science of biodefense are also the US Departments of Energy (DOE), Health and Human Services (HHS) with its Center for Disease Control and Prevention (CDCP) and National Institute of Allergy and Infectious Diseases (NIAID), the Environmental Protection Agency (EPA), the Department of Agriculture (DOA), and the military medicine and R&D elements of the Department of Defense (DOD's DARPA and DTRA). The Department of

State has not been notable for much progress on expanding and enforcing the Biological Weapons Convention (BWC)[1] since 1972, but one of its subordinate agencies, the US Agency for International Development, has made outstanding and important contributions to advance public health and medical treatment through health systems reforms, technical assistance and training in developing nations and former adversary industrial countries such as Russia, Ukraine, Kazakhstan, and more recently, Iraq.

Iraq is a dramatic example of the intrinsic inferiority of military means of biodefense to civil biodefense. One of the justifications of the military invasion and occupation was the allegation of an imminent threat of biological weapons of mass destruction "ready on 30 minutes notice" according to UK Prime Minister Blair. The invasion accomplished nothing in reducing this threat, and in fact exacerbated it by dispersing the would-be bioterrorist capabilities and personnel, expanding recruitment for bioterrorist and other terrorist efforts throughout the Middle East, Europe and South Asia, and severely compromising the public health of the Iraqi people as medical facilities and personnel, water and sewer and electric power infrastructure were damaged and destroyed, first and inadvertently by the US-led coalition armed forces, and subsequently by Islamic terrorists drawn from the entire Islamic world and native Iraqi insurgents.

International non-military civilian agencies prominent in defenses against biological terrorism are the World Health Organization (WHO) and the Food and Agricultural Organization (FAO).

The basic functional elements of a comprehensive civil defense against bioterrorist attacks are fairly well understood, and have been implemented piecemeal for years as defenses against natural diseases and more recently, emerging new deadly infectious diseases such as AIDS, SARS, and new mutations of Avian Influenza (H5N1 "BIRDFLU"). These five elements are:

1. Detection, identification, and characterization of biological weapon pathogenic agents, for early warning. This is currently achieved mostly by syndromic surveillance at hospitals and physicians' offices taking days to weeks, which may be too late to contain the spread of an epidemic. New biodetector technology identifying large

---

[1] The BWC is officially known as the Convention on the Prohibition of the Development, Production, and Stockpiling of Bacteriological (Biological) and Toxin Weapons and on Their Destruction. 140 signatory nations have ratified it since 1972, including the US and the former Soviet Union. For more details on biological arms controls, see *Biological Weapons: Limiting the Threat*, Joshua Lederberg, ed., MIT Press, 1999.

terrorist releases of pathogens within hours is well advanced but has not been widely implemented.
2. Communication to first responders of national, state, and local public health services, and medical, hospital and clinic, fire, police, and transport workers of the bioterrorist attack nature, size, time, and location, so that (hopefully) preplanned defensive measures may be rapidly mobilized, including distribution of pre-positioned medicines and preparation of emergency quarantine facilities.
3. Prophylactic vaccination and antibiotic inoculation of the population exposed to the bio-weapon release within the incubation period of the pathogen, before they can transmit secondary infections to family and co-workers, and isolation of those exposed but not able to be reached by vaccination teams. (In Massachusetts, the Department of Public Health has made realistic plans in the event of an aerosolized smallpox, plague, or anthrax bioterrorist attack to vaccinate or inoculate with the appropriate antibiotics all six million residents within three days at some 500 high schools throughout the state mobilized for that purpose.)
4. Post-bioattack Logistic support for the rapid distribution of medicines, health workers, and associated medical, transport and public safety personnel and equipment, and food.
5. Pre-, Trans, and Post-bioattack public and professional education and communication, provided over all media in clear, consistent, accurate and authoritative ways what everyone should know, to do to protect themselves, and not do.

The theory of this effective and comprehensive biodefense has been well established in the last few years, but so far as is known by this writer only Israel has actually tested the complete approach successfully. Partial and scientifically flawed experimental tests in the US in 2002 and 2003 (Topoff I and Topoff II) have added little light and considerable cost to the systematic evaluation of civil biodefenses. In 2005 and 2006 in the US, more progress on pandemic preparations testing, evaluation, and training, was made by a variety of local and state-level "bottom-up" simulation exercises. (See, for example, the five BIRDFLUPLEX simulation exercises conducted in Massachusetts in 2006 by Clark Abt.)

The scientific community has made substantial progress in biodetector technology and vaccines and antibiotics. Production, distribution, and implementation of the five above essential elements of an effective biodefense in terms of equipments, personnel, testing, evaluation and training has proceeded slowly and haltingly, as the Department of Homeland Security lags in effective leadership of the effort and appropriate financial and intellectual resources mobilization to support it. It is unclear if the elections of 2006 and 2008 will much change this situation. Some say it will take a costly and partly successful bioterrorist attack on a major targeted city to impel the US bureaucracy and private sector to accelerate implementation of known and more effective civil biodefenses. In the meantime, the chief driver of biodefense improvements in funding the first line of defense is the intrinsically dual benefit of biodefenses in peacetime against natural deadly contagious diseases and emerging new ones such as SARS and potentially humanly communicable Avian Influenza.

III. 4. Mitigation of Bioterrorist Induced Deaths and Damages by Passive Civil Means

What if the distribution of biodetectors continues to fail to be funded adequately, so that there is no early warning initiating prompt enough prophylactic vaccination and antibiotic treatment of those exposed to a large bioterrorist release to avoid an epidemic?

What if, even if there is adequate early warning, medicinal stocks are insufficient or for lack of adequate logistic planning cannot be distributed to first responder public health and medical workers?

If there is adequate pre- and post-bioattack public education and communication by the electronic and print media, there is still the possibility of mitigating the deaths and economic damage from a bioterrorist-initiated epidemic. Although adequate backup quarantine facilities do not exist in most US locations or hospital wards, sufficient to accept thousands of local residents coming down with secondary infections of a bioterrorist-initiated (or natural) contagious disease, it is feasible for much of the urban and suburban population to "shelter at home" and thus protect themselves against infection, provided that they have been prepared for this possibility by having several weeks worth of food supply in their homes and apartments, or can be re-supplied by vaccinated drivers of food deliveries, including nurses, police, firemen, and vaccinated volunteers such as recent veterans of military vaccination programs.

In the advanced economies of the US, Europe and Japan, where many families have a private automobile and are not dependent on public transportation to do their food shopping, such vehicles provide an additional, relatively safe food re-supply system for those "sheltering at home" against a bioterrorist-induced deadly epidemic. As populations increasingly have professional work that goes on in offices can continue, mitigating the economic damage of an only partially contained epidemic.

IV. Costs Risks and Benefits of Current and Improved Prevention and Mitigation of Catastrophic Bioterrorist Attacks in War and Peace by Civil Means

A crude benefit-cost assessment of improved biodefenses against the three most catastrophic bioterrorist attacks on the most valuable and vulnerable urban transport centers (Washington DC and New York) was completed by the writer in 2004.[2] Potential economic and loss of life costs of the three most catastrophic types of bioterrorist attacks – smallpox, plague, and anthrax – were estimated from realistic scenarios, for current biodefenses and near-future improved ones. Fatalities from current potential mass bioattacks on US cities were estimated to range from a half to thirty million deaths; economic damage ranges from 200 billion to trillions.

The five essential elements of an effective biodefense were described and assessed for their current capabilities and potential for significant improvement:

1. bioattack early warning and agent identification by biodetectors at targets cities;
2. prompt (48 hour) initiation of exposure tracking and advance preparation and distribution of agent-specific vaccines /antidotes / prophylactic treatments for all expose;
3. timely (within incubation period) prophylactic and/or isolation treatment of all exposed to infection, together with trans- and post-attack survivable logistic support;
4. first responders' interoperable communications and logistic support linking warning, diagnostic, and treatment functions, and uncontaminated substitute facilities;
5. pre-, trans-, and post-bioattack public and professional education to teach productive responses and minimize panic.

Improved alternative biodefense strategies and programs were described, with potential benefits and costs in reduced deaths and damage. Additional

---

[2] A presentation by Clark C.Abt at the University of Southern California Center for Risk and Economic Analysis of Terrorism Events (CREATE) Symposium on the Economics of Terrorist Threat and Response, August 20, 2004.

national costs of now technically feasible and nationally affordable biodefense improvements range from under $1 to $10 billion per year. The least cost option for greatly reduced deaths and damages to a single prime target city multi-modal transportation hub such as New York, Washington, Boston, Los Angeles, London, Barcelona, Rotterdam, Marseille, or Hamburg was found to be under $100 million.

Collateral dual benefits to peacetime public health of improved biodefenses were found to add significant peacetime benefits as well as public support and governments' motivation of biodefense improvements. In terms of worst case bioattack costs avoided or reduced, net benefits ranged from one to tens of millions of lives expected to be saved, and hundreds of billions of expected reduced damage costs, or 10:1 to 100:1 benefit/cost ratios.

The primary policy issue for civil biodefense is that of effectiveness. National governments tend to be much more concerned with civil or military defense effectiveness than with efficiency, because it is even more important to survive than to thrive. But when competition for resources faces national leaderships, efficiency becomes important in allocating resources. Mathematically, the optimal allocation of resources among competing claims is in proportion to their marginal utilities, or relative efficiency or productivity for achieving a particular objective, which in linear and dynamic programming optimizations is called the objective function. For civil biodefense optimization, the objective function might be to minimize loss of lives, or to minimize economic losses, or some combination of the two. (Life loss and economic loss can be made commensurate by monetizing the value of lives lost, as the EPA does by assigning a value of $3 million, or alternatively and less commonly, rendering economic losses in terms of the lives lost to lack of economic investment in, for example, vaccine development and distribution.) The resource allocation decision problem for civil biodefense is still the same old defense economics questions: How much is enough? (to provide an effective defense against a given threat)? At what cost? To what and whose benefit and cost? Compared to what?

There are many illustrative analogies between the cost-effectiveness and efficiency issues that have faced health care analysts for fifty years. Socio-economic policy analysts began to apply cost-benefit analysis to law enforcement, environmental, education, public health and medical problems in the 1970's, with notable progress particularly in health and medicine (see, for example, Bunker, Barnes and Mosteller, *Costs, Risks, and Benefits of Surgery,* Oxford University Press, 1976).

The willingness of the public to spend on health care – the preservation of life against death, disease, and disability – is very great, in fact about three times what the US spends on military defense in so-called peacetime (more correctly called 'chronic limited-war-time' and 'acute war-on-terror-time'), or about 15 % of the US GNP (vs. about 5% on military defense, currently). In times of general and total world war, of course, the defense-to-health expenditure ratio – the 'Death-to-Life Investment Ratio' - is more than reversed. In WWII, the US spent 42% of the US GNP on defense in peak years, or about ten times current spending, while health care absorbed less than half the 16% of US GNP that it does today in 2006. This is mostly under-recognized good news for civil biodefense, because today the overlap between military defense and civil biodefense offers many opportunities for mobilizing public support funds for dual benefits of biodefense for public health and national and international security.

A civil biodefense is only as strong as its weakest link. Each link of an effective biodefense depends on the best possible understanding of the threat of known and realistically forecasted bioterrorist capabilities and intentions. There is little argument about Al Caeda's intentions to destroy the US economy. There is still much dispute about international terrorists' capability to do so, although with experience this is diminishing, in marked contrast with official optimism attempting to maintain biodefenses on the cheap, in an unfortunate overbalancing of biodefense effectiveness with business economics efficiency. On the grand strategy level it was argued in the last half century that the relative security productivity of deterrence vs. defense, and of active vs. passive defenses, and of military vs. civil defense, nations usually needed a mix of both, or various combinations of seemingly contrasting strategies. Deterrence was enhanced by effective defense; effective defense against the worst threats was enhanced by the constraints put on the enemy by retaliatory deterrence (an opportunity that scarcely exists today for biodefense strategy). (see Thomas C. Schelling's seminal *"Strategy of Conflict"*, 1960, and Herman Kahn's *On Thermonuclear War* (Princeton, 1960) for one of the best arguments for civilian civil defense for an overall effective military defense.) Active defense by interception of attacks was made more focused and efficient by combining it with passive defenses of hardening, hiding, and dispersal of targeted defenses and deterrent forces (see the important RAND Corporation Bomber Basing Study of the 1950's by Albert Wohlstetter).

On the tactical level, the main issue for military air defense was finding the best balance of investment in active and passive defenses, and within active defenses, what was the best balance between early warning, tactical warning, long-range interceptors for area defense (favored by the Air Force and Navy) and surface-to-air missiles for point defense (favored by the

Army), and the C3I linking them all into a coherent integrated system. Within each of these broad categories, there were choices of weapon systems and tactics to be made on the basis of simulation with war games, operational testing and evaluation with cost-effectiveness analysis. Would that the same expertise and experts provided the same analysis to the Department of Homeland's security mission against bioterrorist and nuclear terrorist threats today! Answered fairly well were the essential questions of how much was enough (to counter the threat) and how air defense resources could be most productively allocated among essential functions. The operational definition of strategy was the optimal allocation of resources of function, time, and space to achieve given objectives. This has unfortunately not yet been the case for biodefense, or for nuclear terrorist and counter-terrorist defense.

In civil biodefense, the functional analogies to military air defense are Active vs. Passive defenses such as hardening, hiding and dispersal of targets. For cities, there is no hiding or dispersal option available, but biodefense hardening of urban structures – offices, homes, schools, public buildings, transport terminals - is a definitely feasible technical and economic option (see, for example, *Urban Biological Preparedness: A Biodefense Assessment Workshop* by Clark Abt, Luba Katz, Dawn Revett, and Rocco Casagrande, Abt Associates Inc., August 30, 2004, and especially Appendix 5, "*Responding to the Threat: Building Science*" by Kevin M. Coughlan).

Analogous passive biodefenses could include "hardening" the target population with vaccines providing immunity to deadly contagious diseases, prepositioning of vaccines and antibiotics in population centers and neighborhood pharmacies, provision of dispersed isolation and quarantine sites to limit contagion if prior or prompt vaccination fails to protect against an unanticipated genetically engineered pathogens, major facilities and buildings reducing access to HVAC intake ducts and providing them with filters, and ultraviolet lights in subways and indoor transport terminals to kill pathogens These are all civil biodefense measures that also provide public health benefits of protection against natural communicable disease epidemics and emerging diseases.

Within active civil biodefenses, strategic warning with international disease surveillance and Biological Weapons Convention monitoring and enforcement is most useful and still under funded. Tactical Early Warning of mass bioterrorist attack at particularly dense and vulnerable population targets such as urban transport terminals can be provided with Biodetector networks for attack warning, pathogen identification and characterization, plume tracking, and exposure estimation (see *Urban Biological Prepared-*

ness: A Biodefense Assessment Workshop, ibid., and especially Appendixes 6 and 7. *"Novel Early Warning Systems I and II"*, by Tim Dasey and Fran Ligler of MIT Lincoln Laboratory, respectively).

Civil area and point target interception defense, by prophylactic vaccination or antibiotic treatment of targeted and exposed people, and isolation and/or quarantine against communicable disease threats is widely considered a preferred defense against Bioterrorist attacks, and also yields significant collateral benefits to peacetime public health (see "Urban Biological Preparedness: A Biodefense Assessment Workshop, ibid., especially "Technologies for Vaccination, Treatment and Cure of BW Agents" by Jeffrey D. Hermes).

Response and damage control, by medical treatment, cleanup and recovery of contaminated areas, and substitution of uncontaminated facilities and/or unaffected personnel for those killed or disabled. is an important mission of EMT's and firemen, for which they are trained and (often inadequately) equipped. Civil command and control and interoperable, interagency communications for integrating all these essential biodefense elements in both pre- and post attack phases is planned but still not adequately implemented or funded. Public education to maximize cooperative behaviors (such as civilian air raid wardens and shelter preparation and management.) has been discussed but still is inadequate, with much public and expert justifiable criticism of the Department of Homeland Security's color-coded terrorist threat warning system (Since eliminated). In sum, the technologies of civil biodefense and the functional protocols for their effective application have been successfully developed over the last few years, but they have not been generally implemented and made operational, because of a lack of vigorous political leadership and adequate funding. Nevertheless, despite many gaps, the US President was correct in stating in 2004 that the US is safer today in its defenses against bioterrorist attacks. However, his opponent Senator Kerry was also correct in saying we can and should do better.

Below is a preliminary benefit-cost assessment of the current state of US civil biodefenses, from threat definition and assessment to biodefense capabilities current and of potentially improved capability. (Military biodefenses are not considered here, and their assessments –if any- are classified and not publicly available).The overall situation is mixed and troubling. We focus on a very rough cost-effectiveness estimation of the five essential elements of biodefense identified, under currently inadequate and future improved biodefense conditions:

1. Early warning and agent identification by biodetectors at probable and high-value and vulnerable targets (urban transport centers); Tens of millions spent on R&D and very limited implementation, but full production and deployment at $5 billion cost, with savings of lives and economy in trillions not done).
2. Prompt mobilization of exposure/plume tracking and agent-specific antidote/prophylactic treatment resources (hundreds of millions spent on vaccine and anti-biotic stockpiles, but distribution logistics costing millions unevenly prepared, risking overall system effectiveness).
3. Capacity for prompt prophylactic and/or isolation treatment of all exposed, including the trans-attack and post-attack logistic arrangements that must survive the disruptive effects of the attack. (Tens to hundreds of millions spent on preparing first responders, but planning of timely in-crisis distribution and assurance of interoperable communications among all essential units and personnel, particularly at local levels, still incomplete, threatening effectiveness of the entire biodefense system.)
4. Trans- and post attack logistic support for all the above essential functions, including organization of substitute uncontaminated transport facilities, equipment, and personnel for public surface and air transport disabled or contaminated by bioattack (under 100 million spent, potential high cost to biodefense effectiveness of this gap in billions).
5. Pre-, trans-, and post-bioattack public and professional education to facilitate productive responses and minimize panicky or dysfunctional responses to both the bioattack and biodefense measures (only tens of millions have been spent on planning and programming, few nationwide education/training biodefense policies or practices have yet been tested or implemented, raising the potential costs by many billions and lives of all the above in the face of a fearful, confused, and conflicted public response). If training simulation exercises such as TOPOFF I and II are appropriately considered part of public and professional education, some $23 million was spent on the second of these with little useful results, as a result of defective design and lack of follow-up. Israeli preparations for bioattack response are believed to be a better example of effective preparation and public education. Compared to what? Consider the current $12 billion per year spent on military anti-ballistic missile defense, versus the

roughly $10 billion spent on biodefense vaccine development, in terms of overall cost effectiveness versus known threats.

Consider the tens of millions spent on biodetector R&D, versus the billions spent on vaccine and antibiotic development, in terms of relative and combined cost-effectiveness. (This is not an argument for spending less on the latter but for more on the former, to equalize the marginal utilities of each element and add to overall systems effectiveness more than to cost.)

Consider the billions spent on political and private industry advertising media to the perhaps tens of millions spent on public education about biothreats and biodefenses, both natural and man-made.

Consider the billions spent annually in California for earthquake defense and response in terms of added building and other construction costs, as insurance against a rare once-in-thirty years major earthquake, versus the small fraction of that spent in California (and most other states) on the unfortunately much less rare event of a very damaging biological attack or natural epidemic.

There is much more cost-benefit analysis to be done before these questions can be answered definitively, especially for likely bioterrorist-targeted countries other than the US. This is a major opportunity for economists and biological scientists to provide urgently needed benefit cost policy research on civil biodefenses. Here below, hopefully to stimulate such research initiatives, is a very rough cut cost-risk-benefit assessment of the present 2004-6 state of the US biodefenses against the most deadly bioterrorist threats against the most valuable and vulnerable American urban targets, and what it could be if improved in 2006-8 if the biodefense measures we understand today are implemented.

Most Valuable and Vulnerable to Bioterror Attack US City Targets:

- New York City and the Port of New York and New Jersey
- Washington, D.C. and inside the beltway to Baltimore & Dulles
- The City and Port of Los Angeles
- The City and Port of Chicago
- San Francisco and Bay Area from Berkeley to Oakland to Palo Alto
- Greater Boston and the Port of Boston
- Seattle and Tacoma
- The City and Port of Miami
- The City and Port of New Orleans
- The City and Port of San Diego.

Note that these ten top US urban population centers are all air-sea-rail-road transport hubs, and centers of commerce, industry, finance, and higher education. Most of them have subways with major airport, railroad, and bus terminal inter connections, making them ideal communicable disease biothreat targets. Because of their national/international air, rail, and ocean transport connections, a deadly epidemic created by clandestine mass release of deadly contagious agents at any one of them may be almost impossible to contain without early warning by biodetectors at transport terminals, to initiate prophylactic vaccination of those exposed.

Table 1: **2004 Costs of Most Deadly and Damaging Threats Executed Against any One of 3 Most Valuable and Vulnerable Targets, Including Costs of Current Biodefenses.**
Estimated Worst Costs, Direct & Indirect.

	Deaths	Damage[3]
Anthrax Mass Bioattack on Port of New York-NJ	1 million	$500 billion
Anthrax Mass Bioattack on Washington-Baltimore	1 million	$200 billion
Anthrax Mass Bioattack on Port of Los Angeles	0.5 million	$400 billion
Smallpox Mass Bioattack on Port of New York-NJ	3-30 million	$1 trillion
Smallpox Mass Bioattack on Washington-Baltimore	1-30 million	$1 trillion
Smallpox Mass Bioattack on Port of Los Angeles	1-30 million	$1 trillion

The 2002 Los Angeles Port Strike caused losses estimated at $5-10 billion per week from ocean trade disruption. Massive (100 pound) anthrax attacks are estimated to deny contaminated buildings, facilities and equipment to unvaccinated personnel (and possibly fearful vaccinated ones too) for a minimum of three months and a maximum of a year or more during fumigant cleanup and recovery operations. Capitol Hill cleanup of the *very small* 2001 anthrax attack cost $28 million in 3 months, and these are direct costs only and do not include disruption costs).

Costs of current domestic (non-DOD) Biodefenses, including R&D and production of biodetectors, vaccines, antibiotics, first responder equipping

---

[3] Direct and Indirect Damage Costs do not include costs of lives lost (variously estimated at half a million to $3.5 million each- the latter is a figure used by the EPA), but do include the economic costs of domestic and international trade losses from the denial of facilities, vehicles (planes, ships, trucks, trains) and operating personnel (especially for smallpox) at the cities struck *and their communicating cities in the US, Europe, Asia, and Latin America.*

and training, public education, C3I, and planning, testing and evaluation are probably in the range of $15-20 billion per year, with vaccine development having the largest and probably adequately funded share at some $10 billion. Those regarding the risk of mass bioattack low might find even this amount excessive, palliated perhaps by the dual benefit of vaccine development to public health defenses against emerging diseases. Others- this writer included- find the amount disproportionately small when compared to the risks and costs of a massive bioattack in the hundreds of billions, compared to the $10 billion per year spent on ballistic missile defense.

Table 2: **2000-2005 Risks of Most Deadly and Damaging Threats Actually Being Executed Against One or More of 3 Most Valuable and Vulnerable Targets.**
Direct and Indirect.

	Deaths	Damage[4]
Anthrax Mass Bioattack on Port of New York-NJ	1 million	$500 billion
Anthrax Mass Bioattack on Washington-Baltimore	1 million	$200 billion
Anthrax Mass Bioattack on Port of Los Angeles	0.5 million	$400 billion
Smallpox Mass Bioattack on Port of New York-NJ	3-30 million	$1 trillion
Smallpox Mass Bioattack on Washington-Baltimore	1-30 million	$1 trillion
Smallpox Mass Bioattack on Port of Los Angeles	1-30 million	$1 trillion

Risk Probability of mass smallpox attack is controversial. While enemy intentions to cause maximum deaths and economic destruction are clear, *enemy capabilities* for making aerosolized smallpox agent and delivering it in massive amounts (briefcases full of modified spray cans of aerosolized smallpox delivered clandestinely by vaccinated bioterrorists to crowded indoor transport terminals in major transportation hub cities) are not. The two known repositories of live smallpox virus are in the US and Russia.

Given the "Loose Nukes" problem of the still too insecure storage of nuclear weapons and fissile materials in Russia and the risk of terrorist theft or purchase, we are not confident that the risk of bioterrorist purchase or theft of smallpox from the Russian stockpile is low, particularly over a period of years. (See Ken Alibek's book, *Biohazard, ibid.*). However, the risk is obviously lower, in any one year, than that for anthrax capability. But even with a 10% per year probability of capability acquisition, that cumu-

---

[4] See previous footnote.

lates to 100% in only 7 years. Accordingly, we estimate a risk probability of 0.7 over the next 4 years, too high for comfort.

V. Benefits of Current 2004-5 Inadequate Biodefenses & Benefits of Feasible 2006-08 Improved Biodefenses

The benefits of the cumulative national biodefense effort, including Biowatch and Biosense and many other programs at HHS, DOE, DOD, EPA, DOT, and DHS, are best expressed in terms of the estimated reduction in Risk and Cost of the most deadly mass bioterrorist attacks on the most vulnerable and valuable of the enemy's demonstrated intended city targets. The US has only begun to develop, deploy, and operate the best possible biodefenses of which we are presently capable against the known enemy intention and capability for destroying or very severely damaging the American people and economy. Considerable progress has been made since the 9/11/2001 wake-up call. Even current biodefenses can save many lives.

Table 3: 2004 Worst Case Cost Reduction Potential of Current 2004-5 Biodefenses*.
In terms of costs avoided. Direct and Indirect.

	Deaths	Damage
Anthrax Mass Bioattack on Port of New York-NJ	1 million	$500 billion
Full implementation of current biodefenses:	10,000	$100 billion*
Anthrax Mass Bioattack on Washington-Baltimore	1 million	$200 billion
Full implementation of current biodefenses	1,000	$50 billion*
Anthrax Mass Bioattack on Port of Los Angeles	0.5 million	$400 billion
Full implementation of current biodefenses	3,000	$100 billion
Smallpox Mass Bioattack on Port of New York-NJ	3-30 million	$1 trillion
Full implementation of current biodefenses	1-3 million	$500 billion
Smallpox Mass Bioattack on Washington-Baltimore	1-3 million	$1 trillion
Full implementation of current biodefenses	10,000	$100 billion*
Smallpox Mass Bioattack on Port of Los Angeles	1-30 million	$1 trillion
Full implementation of current biodefenses	1-2 million	$400 billion

*Assumes biodetectors in D.C. Metro, 300 million smallpox vaccine supply

Table 4: Benefits of Feasible 2006-8 Improved Biodefenses*.
In terms of costs avoided. Direct and Indirect.

	Deaths	Damage
Anthrax Mass Bioattack on Port of New York-NJ	1 million	$500 billion
Full implementation of **2006-8** biodefenses:	100	$50 billion*
Anthrax Mass Bioattack on Washington-Baltimore	1 million	$200 billion
Full implementation of **2006-8** biodefenses	100	$50 billion
Anthrax Mass Bioattack on Port of Los Angeles	0.5 million	$400 billion
Full implementation of **2006-8** biodefenses	100	$50 billion
Smallpox Mass Bioattack on Port of New York-NJ	3-30 million	$1 trillion
Full implementation of **2006-8** biodefenses	100	$10 billion
Smallpox Mass Bioattack on Washington-Baltimore	1-30 million	$1 trillion
Full implementation of **2006-8** biodefenses	100	$10 billion
Smallpox Mass Bioattack on Port of Los Angeles	1-30 million	$1 trillion
Full implementation of **2006-8** biodefenses	100	$10 billion

Note: *2006-8 improved biodefenses are assumed to include
- at least hundreds of operational biodetectors with high sensitivity and very low false alarm rates to Class A biothreats, deployed in major city subways, air and rail and ocean transport terminals;
- C3 real-time linking of deployed biodetectors to public health and other first responders, at all levels nationally and internationally;
- prompt prophylactic vaccination or anti-biotic treatment of exposed/infected population(within 3 days of agent release detection);
- attack-survivable logistic support for first and last responders and preparation of alternative transport facilities during 3-month cleanup;
- pre-, trans-, and post-event timely, accurate, authoritative, effective public education of all language population groups by all media.

This is all do-able for a roughly $10 billion annual budget, yielding a probable benefit/cost ratio of avoided costs to improved biodefense costs in the range of 10:1 to 100:1. Corrections, amplifications, and comparisons to other homeland security and national defense investments are invited.

VI. Countering Global Nuclear Terrorists by Civil Means

First, important facts that show the threat to be countered by civil means: Facts and Judgements about Potenetial Nuclear Terrorism (quoted or paraphrased from *Nuclear Terrorism* by Graham Allison, Times Books, 2004). Making fissile materials requires roughly $1 billion and a decade of effort.32 countries have a total of 3,200 tons of weapons-grade fissile material, enough to make 240,000 nuclear weapons.More weapons-grade fissile material is still being produced today, by India, Pakistan, North Korea, and possibly Iran. The US stopped in 1992.It would take several years to secure the world's supply of fissile material if it was made as high a priority as the war on terrorism, and would cost $30-50 billion.If a terrorist group started with fissile material, it could make an elementary nuclear weapon in less than one year. Having a nuclear reactor helps in building a nuclear weapon. Several states have used civilian nuclear reactors as a cover to make nuclear weapons. The spent-fuel waste produced by a civilian reactor contains plutonium that can be used to make a bomb.

There are sizable global supplies of uranium and plutonium. The global supply of uranium will not be exhausted in the foreseeable future. Plutonium is a by-product of the fission process in nuclear reactors, and would thus run out only when uranium did.Weapons-grade uranium-235 is extracted out of uranium ore mined from rock that is crushed, chemically soaked, and filtered into a coarse powder ("Yellowcake), widely available from annual global production of about 64,000 tons. It takes hundreds of tons of yellowcake to make enough weapons-grade fissile material for a bomb. Uranium ore is processed into reactor fuel (LEU or Less Enriched Uranium) or weapons-grade bomb fuel (HEU or Highly Enriched Uranium) by separation techniques such as gaseous diffusion and gaseous centrifuge enrichment.

To extract weapons-grade plutonium-239, plutonium-239 is chemically separated from spent reactor fuel by removing spent fuel rods from a nuclear reactor, chopping them up, and then dissolving them in nitric acid. The resulting liquid is further separated into plutonium, uranium, and radioactive waste.At least 28 states have sought nuclear weapons in the last 60 years, including the current 9 known owners of Britain, China, France, India, Israel, Pakistan, Russia, the US, and North Korea. The 19 others who at one time sought them but have either relinquished them (like South Africa, Belarus, Kazakhstan, and Ukraine) or stopped seeking them include Argentina, Australia, Belarus, Brazil, Canada, Egypt, Germany, Iraq, Italy, Japan, Kazakhstan, Libya, Romania, South Africa, South Korea, Sweden, Taiwan, Ukraine, and Yugoslavia. Four states had nuclear weapons and then relinquished them. South Africa has six or seven in the 1980's and dismantled them just prior to the transfer of power to the post-apartheid government. Ukraine, Kazakhstan, and Belarus together had more than 4000 nuclear weapons on their territories when the Soviet Union dissolved, and agreed in 1994 to return them to Russia.

As of 2002, there are some 20,000 nuclear weapons in the world. The largest nuclear bomb produced to date was produced by the Soviets with an estimated yield of 100 megatons, or 6,500 times the yield of the bombs dropped on Hiroshima and Nagasaki. The US produced the smallest confirmed nuclear weapon, the "Davy Crocket", with a yield of 0.25 kilotons (= to 250 tons of TNT) and weighing only 50 pounds. States develop nuclear weapons for a combination of reasons: security, prestige, and domestic bureaucratic politics. If all the resources needed to design a working nuclear bomb are readily available, isn't nuclear proliferation inevitable? No. President Kennedy in the early sixties predicted that by 1970 there would be 15-20 nuclear weapons states. Although there are over 40 states capable of making a bomb, as of today, only eight have nuclear weapons. The record shows that nonproliferation works when it is given serious attention and resources. Factors that prevent states from seeking nuclear weapons include: Inadequate national resources, technological constraints, the international nuclear taboo, international treaties, domestic politics, international inducements, security assurances, aid, threats of sanctions and coercion, and limited strategic utility of nuclear weapons.(C.C. Abt would add: high absolute cost, increased vulnerability to preemptive nuclear counterforce attack, increased overall defense and security costs, and increased environmental and political risks.) States secure their nuclear weapons with a combination of barriers, guards, surveillance cameras, motion sensors, personnel background checks, and locks built in to the actual nuclear weapons. The US and most nuclear powers employ all these protections. Unfortunately, because of Russia's enormous nuclear stockpile and lack of funds, its nuclear facilities have been left inadequately protected.

The US over the last 59 years has lost an estimated 11 nuclear weapons, out of tens of thousands produced. Russia has denied that any of its nuclear weapons have gone missing, although it admits that some fissile material has been lost or stolen. Moscow's assurance that "all nuclear weapons are in place" is wishful thinking, since at least four nuclear submarines with nuclear warheads sank and were never recovered by the Soviets. Terrorists are not known to have ever stolen or built nuclear weapons, but they are trying to. In 1998, Osama bin Laden issued a statement titled "The Nuclear Bomb of Islam," declaring, "It is the duty of Muslims to prepare as much force as possible to terrorize the enemies of God." No state has ever sold a nuclear weapon to a terrorist (so far as is known in 2004), although the potential for such a sale exists.

Terrorists could acquire HEU or plutonium. There have been dozens of documented thefts and sales of fissile material to potential terrorists who were subsequently captured. Russia's substantial amounts of poorly secured HEU and plutonium remain a prime target for theft. Terrorists could deliver a nuclear weapon or the fissile material required to build one, into the US undetected. HEU and plutonium are easy to conceal and give off faint radiation signals, and thus could be smuggled into the US almost as easily as illegal drugs. (For more information, the single best source is the Nuclear Threat Initiative; http://www.nti.org. At NTI, the best publication on nuclear terrorism is Controlling Nuclear Warheads and Materials: www.nti.org/cnwm.)

Deterrence of a transnational nuclear terrorist attack on a city will not work, because transnational nuclear terrorists do not have real estate or population at risk for retaliation. Deterrence of state-based nuclear terrorism is deterred by threat of retaliation to the aggressor's homeland.

Prevention of nuclear terrorist attacks by denial of nuclear materials, technology and weapons by civil means is the best hope for avoiding a nuclear terrorist attack on a city, and the grievous loss of life and disastrous economic consequences entailed. Needed are diplomacy and scientific exchanges cooperatively creating International Nuclear Arms Control and Disarmament Agreements such as the NPT, CTB, Missile Control Regime, IAEA, and nuclear and related defense technology conversion to civilian economy in energy production. The most direct and obvious way to deny by civil, non-military means the many (from Al Qaeda to Hezbollah) global would-be nuclear terrorists with both motive and capacity to seek access to nuclear weapons and weapons-grade fissile material is to deny transnational terrorists access to the sources. Currently the Nuclear Terrorists' easiest sources of nuclear weapons or weapons-grade material are the under-secured Russian stockpile and the small North Korean stockpile. Soon – if Iran continues to refuse to give up its nuclear weapons potential based on its power reactor technology and associated fuel enrichment and reprocessing, Iran will also become an easy source for nuclear terrorists. Others may soon follow.

The threat of nuclear terrorism is sufficiently serious to have prompted military denial by Israeli bombardment of Iraq's civilian reactor with military potential in the 1980's, U.S. bombardment and dismantlement of Iraq's nuclear program in the 1990's, and US air-ground invasion and occupation of Iraq in 2003, on the (incorrect) presumption of an imminent Iraqi nuclear weapons capability. The continued threat of nuclear weapons denial to trans-national terrorists by military means by the American military-economic superpower's current policies of unilateral preemptive defense, regime change, preventive war, disdain for UN and allied nations' authorization and nuclear arms reduction, insulting statements about "the axis of evil" leaderships, disrespectful refusal of bilateral negotiations, and renewed development of new nuclear weapons ("deep penetration bunker busters" and a new generation of even smaller and more portable nuclear weapons for special forces use, also ideal for terrorists!), all threaten the North Korean and Iranian leaderships into resisting IAEA inspections enforcing NPT (because risking precision targeting of nuclear facilities), pushes them into leaving the NPT, and accelerates their nuclear weapons and other military programs designed to deter threatened US regime change, military action, economic blockade, and denial of development and humanitarian aid.

The Bush Administration's continued *threat of military means of nuclear weapons denial to trans-national terrorists* who might seek them from nascent or new nuclear weapons states such as Iran and North Korea is thus highly counterproductive of not only peaceful and productive conflict resolution, but also of the very nuclear non-proliferation and nuclear terrorism it was originally intended to prevent! Clearly, an *alternative strategy of civil, non-military denial of nuclear weapons technology and materials to would-be nuclear terrorists* seeking them from new or nascent nuclear weapons states such as North Korea and Iran is called for.

Because of the military potential of civilian nuclear energy, the legitimate needs of North Korea and Iran and many other LDC's for diversified, independent, and economically and environmentally sustainable energy sources to redress shortages impeding economic development *must be supplied by civil means other than civilian nuclear power*. (See Albert Wohlstetter et al, *Swords into Plowshares: The Military Potential of Civilian Nuclear Energy,* University of Chicago Press, 1977, and for a more up to date authoritative statement, see *A Fresh Examination of the Proliferation Dangers of Light Water Reactors*, by Victor Gilinsky et al, The Nonproliferation Policy Education Center, Washington, D.C., September 30, 2004).

Non-nuclear, environmentally superior, economically competitive energy sources and associated technological capabilities exist *today* in the form of renewable energy –solar, wind, water, and tidal-generated electric power, operational on many sites in Europe, Asia, Africa, and Americas. A program to accelerate the application of renewable energy technologies in North Korea and Iran by international cooperative technology transfer, training, technical assistance and investment in North Korea and Iran renewable energy projects is believed to be the best *non-military, civil means* of substituting a higher economic value, high tech prestigious, peaceful, environmentally sustainable and practical source of energy faster, cheaper, and better for the potentially dangerous and more costly development of civilian and inevitably potentially military nuclear technology in these and other developing and newly industrialized but still substantially-non-nuclear weapons states.

Concerning ways to motivate North Korea (and possibly Iran) to abandon its quest for nuclear weapons and the threat of their possible export or accession by terrorists, some of the following concepts were discussed with participants and South Korean speakers at the 54th Pugwash Conference on Science and World Affairs in Seoul in early October 2004, which the South Korean government graciously hosted.

We discussed the problem of persuading the North Korean leadership to halt its development of nuclear weapons, while helping the people to avoid starvation and working toward a less threatening and more peaceful and productive relationship. Several suggestions were discussed that might be useful for the coming six-nation negotiations, summarized below. They are grouped under the headings of Strategic Objectives, current military programs intended to achieve those objectives, possible non-military replacement and defense industry conversion programs and incentives for North Korea to halt or reverse development of nuclear weapons and associated capabilities (such as long-range ballistic missiles), and a suggested benefits, costs, and risks analytical framework.

Three important assumptions about North Korean leadership concerns and preferences helped formulate these proposals intended to diplomatically and non-militarily non-threateningly persuade North Korea to abandon nuclear weapons capabilities: (1) North Korea has a serious energy shortage, impacting adversely all aspects of its economy including agriculture, and looks to exports to pay for imported oil and nuclear power to generate electricity and provide the dual-use capacity for producing both power and weapons. (2) The leadership feels increasingly insecure, internally from the disenchantment of its impoverished population, and externally from its isolation from neighbors and the perceived hostility of the United States whose current leadership has insultingly named it a part of "the axis of evil", threatening it by violent "regime change" as it threatened and carried out in Iraq. (3) Any economic incentives to peaceful cooperation, technology trade, and halting nuclear weapons development would best be in the form of cash directly to the leadership so that it can appear strong and benevolent to its people in purchasing from outside and distributing inside North Korea whatever goods and services needed, the higher level the better, so as to appear the gift of that leadership and not outsiders.

China's foreign ministry might welcome and seriously entertain the kind of four-way entrepreneurial defense science and technology conversion workshops suggested, that might bring to North Korea economic advances, reduced interest in nukes, cooperative scientific enterprises with commercial value to all four parties, and a general strengthening of trust and reduction of tensions.

There would also be benefits to China, where there is strong interest in reducing dependence on coal generating greenhouse gases and global climate change, and its high transportation cost for the non-coal producing three quadrants of China. Increased use of economically competitive photovoltaic curtain walls on high rise buildings can generate most of a building's electricity needs at very little additional capital cost, and store the daytime surplus in the extant grid. Also, cladding the hills too steep to farm south of Beijing with photovoltaic solar power panels could produce enough electricity to satisfy Beijing's daytime needs, greatly reduce unhealthy air pollution there from coal and costly oil consumption, and create much employment for unemployed rural labor - all at lower capital costs and shorter lead times than building additional nuclear power plants (which generally cost 3-4 billion dollars and take ten years or more to build). China could readily become a world leader in environmentally and economically sustainable renewable energy technology and production, and help create such an industry in North Korea as well. A joint effort with the US, the two Koreas, and possibly Japan where photovoltaics production and building-integrated solar systems are quite advanced might be beneficial to all the nations concerned with oil and electric power and investment capital shortages and air pollution problems.

If these concepts could be promoted, supported with accurate and persuasive economic analysis, and implemented in the near future to support scientific cooperation among the four countries for environmentally sustainable economic growth, it might satisfy North Korea's needs for electric power, economic development and cooperation, improved agricultural productivity through solar pumped irrigation, a more viable export technology than weapons to pay for continued imports, the respect and prestige in the international political, scientific and economic community its leadership craves, and all the while working against nuclear proliferation.

It may be unlikely that North Korea will agree to give up its nuclear weapons in exchange for a US non-aggression pact, and the US is unlikely to trust NK to do so sans unacceptably intensive inspections that could be used for targeting intelligence and to promote regime change. In short, a persuasive case exists that lack of mutual trust is a major obstacle to North Korea's giving up its nuclear programs in the current climate of the Bush Administration. It might still be difficult in a possible Kerry Administration. It may be concluded that trust-building measures would be most welcome by both North and South Korean governments as well as China. This prompted the suggestion for confidence building of a joint defense science and technology conversion workshop hosted by China with both Koreas and the US participating, "Swords into Ploughshares". There are the successful precedents of the Hong Kong China defense conversion conference in 1993, where South Africa first renounced its nuclear weapons, and the series of Russian-American Entrepreneurial Defense Technology Conversion workshops for Russian and American nuclear weapons physicists and other scientists produced in Boston, Moscow, and Livermore Labs from 1991 through 1994 under the Nunn-Lugar Cooperative Threat Reduction program for the US Departments of Energy and State.

The contents of such a Korean-Chinese-American series of Defense Technology Conversion workshops would be education and training in the peaceful and economically productive applications of defense R&D and production - with emphasis on nuclear, missile, radar, and tank technology, on national or joint enterprise public-private basis, producing viable peaceful business plans for conversion products for export by North and South Korea. Examples could include radiation medicine, industrial scanners, radiation food and water purification, solar photopholtaics and wind turbine manufacture and application, agricultural machinery produced by tank plants, and manufacture of inexpensive lightweight all-electric trucks and passenger automobiles together with solar electric-powered battery recharging stations for export worldwide to oil-short LDC's. Worldwide markets may be very interested in buying such a North Korean export product, particularly if developed jointly with world-famous South Korean automobile technology expertise and quality and quantity production know-how.

The participants in such an All-Korean-Chinese-American entrepreneurial defense technology conversion workshops would be 20 to 30 senior scientists and engineers from all four countries, with industry leadership experience or potential. Workshops could be held alternately in Seoul, Beijing, and at designated sites in North Korea as trust was developed. It would be a high prestige operation, showing respect for the best scientists and engineers in all four countries and establishing long-term professional bonds of cooperative endeavors and economically productive friendships. Best of all, it would not cost very much -probably under a million dollars a year - and could possibly be privately financed by charitable foundations if governments did not want to spend much on it. It could also evolve and expand into an export-oriented technical job creation program addressing North Korea's needs for export income, employment, and the respect of the international community for its achievements.

Comments are sought on the usefulness of this proposed program for the upcoming negotiations and for South and North Korea and China's international relations and environmentally sustainable and strategically safe economic growth in general.

A similar non-military civil diplomatic approach to Iran for its nuclear technology program conversion to civil renewable energy projects yielding faster and less contentious economic returns and avoidance of IAEA. EU and US punitive economic actions should be investigated and its economic benefits and risks analyzed.

VII. Mitigation of Deaths and Damages from Nuclear Terrorist Attack by Civil Means

Unlike the very different mitigation potential of civil public health and medical measures to mitigate the consequences of a catastrophic terrorist attack on a population center, it is much harder to mitigate the deaths and damages from a nuclear terrorist attack. Prevention is by far the best response, and very probably the most cost-effective.

However, something can be done fairly economically if public and first responder education and training is improved significantly. Assuming that for the next few years the main risk of nuclear terrorism is from a relatively primitive fission weapon of Hiroshima-scale destructive power (15 Kt.) that would most likely be a surprise surface burst without warning from a cargo container ship in harbor or at dockside or from a container-carrying truck or weapon-carrying car, the deadly fallout radiation plume will far exceed the area of most destructive blast and fire damage. While there is little that can be done to mitigate blast and fire damage short of rebuilding low-rise and underground windowless hardened concrete structures providing blast shelters – hardly an acceptable practical solution for urban populations – much can be done to provide protection from radioactive fallout beyond the smaller heavy blast and fire damage zone at relatively low cost and inconvenience.

Basement and interior building fallout shelters provide substantial protection from radioactive fallout, with the amount of protection a function of the mass of material between the fallout and the individual. For those in the path of the fallout plume and with access to private cars or buses, and with good wind direction data and radio broadcasts of the path of the cigar-shaped fallout cloud, there may be time enough for many in its path to simply evade it. A quiet but thorough public education campaign, advance preparation of radio and TV advisory reports, and location and signage of urban fallout-shelters (such as large school, hospital, and office building basements) could greatly mitigate urban radioactive fallout exposure and radiation sickness resulting from a nuclear terrorist surface burst.

Seaport-Based Transport Systems are critically important to the U.S. and the World Economy. Today a third of the world economy, and a quarter of America's, depends on safe international commerce and trade, most of which since the last thirty years is transported across the oceans and land borders in standardized steel cargo containers carried by ships, trucks, and rail. It is this enormous worldwide container traffic that constitutes the major nuclear terrorist attack delivery vehicle threat.

Thirty percent of the world economy and 20 percent of the U.S. economy—$2 trillion—depend on trade. The transport of world trade is absolutely dependent on the shipping portals at seaports, land borders, and airports. The major seaport cities, together with their usually co-located international airports, constitute both the most valuable and vulnerable targets of catastrophic nuclear terrorism. The world's seaports have some 72 million containers moving through them every year (7-8 million in the United States alone), in any one of which a 60-to-600-pound nuclear weapon could be delivered to the seaport and detonated before unloading, wreaking havoc with the world economy.

The conjunction of three trends—*globalization* of industry, trade, and transport; *nuclear weapons technology diffusion and proliferation*, and the threatening rise of *globally dispersed, WMD-armed, undeterred terrorism*—today present an unprecedented threat to the United States and all trading partners, and the whole world economy. The recent accelerated growth of this offensive threat to peace and otherwise rising world prosperity has not been matched by a parallel strengthening of effective civil and military defenses of international law, law enforcement, and policing and freedom of the seas. Nor have there been significant advances in the counter-threat capabilities of the relevant institutions, the United Nations, Interpol, and the defense departments and intelligence agencies of all the nations whose economies are put at risk by nuclear-armed international terrorists.

International terrorists have asserted their intention to acquire nuclear weapons, and have an increasing capability of secretly purchasing, stealing, or making a nuclear fission weapon from fissile material stolen or bought from the many insufficiently secured stockpiles, today primarily in Russia but also increasingly in several other nuclear-capable countries. Currently a

Hiroshima-scale 10-20 kilotons/fission weapon (or, in a few years, a 1-5 Megaton Hydrogen bomb) could be smuggled undetected into a major U.S. seaport (NY, LA) or the DC Capital in any one of millions of cargo containers shipped or trucked into the into the United States every year – thousands daily - and detonated dockside or after being trucked into the city center.

The catastrophic nuclear terrorists' priority targets are the major U.S. population, commercial, government, and transportation centers. The top three are New York, Washington DC, and Los Angeles, as has been repeatedly demonstrated in the last decade before 9/11/2001. Clearly the centers of American economy, government, and urban society are targeted by the terrorists for strategic bombardment and destruction, and are likely to continue to be their targets for the foreseeable future.

The aim points for nuclear weapons detonation, within the priority target cities, are either dockside at container ports (so they don't risk inspection of container delivery vehicles after unloading), or the centroid of the most valuable targets accessible by container-bearing truck, such as the 14th Street Bridge in DC, or midtown Manhattan.

Assuming the main current nuclear terrorist threat of a cargo container-delivered 10-20 Kiloton fission weapon, several plausible scenarios were examined to estimate the economic impacts of a nuclear attack on two major seaport cities and the government center of Washington, DC. First the destructive radii from the probable aim points of the weapons were plotted on maps of three likely targets, New York, Washington DC, and Boston. (Boston was selected as fairly representative of an important seaport with city center adjacent to the container port, similar to Baltimore, Charleston, Miami, Oakland, and Seattle.) Loss of life and property estimates are based on the density of population and property value in the destroyed or severely damaged area.

The losses attributable to trade disruption were estimated on the basis of the extent and duration of disruption of ocean, truck, and air cargo transport at the target and corresponding sites that might be shut down in response to such an attack (as they were for a week after 9/11) significant indirect economic costs were estimated by a conservative multiplier times the direct costs. Only one-year costs were estimated for the United States, and did not include either global or long-term costs, which are believed to exceed substantially the immediate U.S. costs estimated. Uncertainties in the determining variables are reflected by the estimates being given as ranges rather than point values.

The economic impact of even a single nuclear terrorist attack on a major U.S. seaport would be very great. In the three plausible scenarios examined, a successful attack would create disruption of U.S. trade valued at $100-200 billion, property damage of $50-500 billion, and 50,000 to 1,000,000 lives could be lost. Global and long-term effects, including economic impacts of the pervasive national and international responses to nuclear attack, though not calculated, are believed to be substantially greater.

The Vulnerability of the Trade and Transportation Sectors of the U.S. Economy to disruption and destruction by Nuclear Terrorism remains high in 2004. This vulnerability to great costs is preventable and avoidable. Currently available and affordable technology and systems could be deployed within two to three years that would dramatically reduce the likelihood and destruction of a container-based nuclear terrorist attack.

Current civil defense efforts by the Customs Bureau, the Coast Guard, and local and national police are aimed in the right direction but are inadequate in scope, speed and intensity. The U.S. Customs strategy of intelligence-based sampling of a small fraction of the flow of millions of containers a year can be too easily countered by terrorists and their supporters. Terrorists can evade or deceive the data and intelligence collection and intelligence information analyses of suspicious cargoes, conveyances, and personnel handlers, by shielding and decoying the weapons from external gamma-ray detector screening, by saturating the inspection process with higher peak traffic loads than can be carefully screened by current methods without seriously impeding the flow of trade, and by leaving most foreign container ports unsecured and without uniformly high inspection standards. A nuclear weapon loaded on to a container in a foreign port has a very high probability of passing undetected through the foreign port of embarkation. A terrorist who can get a nuclear device into a container is virtually assured of achieving at least a dockside detonation in the US, and greatly disrupting world trade and economies.

The technology and the organizational and procedural designs exist which could greatly reduce the risk of deaths and damages from nuclear terrorist attack on seaport-based transport. The key technology is the shielded pulsed-active neutron interrogation device, or scanner, augmenting the currently partially deployed gamma ray scanners. Expertise in this technology exists in government labs, university research labs, and private industry firms. An effective system of defenses built around this technology would include: Forward deployment of customs inspection to foreign container ports of embarkation for the United States, 100 percent external scanning of all U.S.-bound containers, using fixed drive-through installations, mobile truck-mounted scanners, and scanners on lift cranes; Augmented container transport intelligence information systems, including the use of tamper-resistant electronic reporting seals on containers; and Strengthened personnel security.

The annual cost of a solution for effectively screening 100 percent of U.S.-bound containers at Ports is estimated to be about $100 Million per major port, or $10 billion for 100 ports. The likelihood of a successful nuclear terrorist attack using cargo container transport can be greatly reduced by such an improved defense system. Analysis shows that the improved defenses can reduce the terrorist's chances of evading detection of this means of weapon delivery at the port of embarkation to a fraction of what it would be without such civil defenses, and the chances of successful container transshipment to an inland target are even more reduced.

However, an effective defense must encompass overseas freight export operations. There is broad agreement among government officials and independent analysts on the ideal attributes of a global containerized cargo system secure from nuclear weapons attack by means of container-borne delivery. All Researchers speak of "extending the borders out," "controlling and monitoring the entire supply chain from origin to destination," securing individual containers, conveyances, and crews handling them with various security and identity clearances, collecting information from all sources, including financial and transportation and personnel records, and data mining it to gain early warning of suspicious cargoes and to gain more efficient sample selection of those containers to be taken off line and opened for rigorous internal inspection. Needed is universalization and enforcement of international standards of container security with fast-track rewards for cooperation and compliance, and denial of port access rights for the recalcitrant, careless or willful violators. There is an increased need for inter-agency intelligence information sharing and coordination, and for public-private cooperation and burden sharing.

Currently there is little or no agreement, domestically and internationally and between government and industry, regarding how much improved transport security will cost, who is in charge of what aspect and the whole system, and what will be the burden-sharing arrangements. Competition among agencies, governments, and industries for control and benefits, and to avoid costs continues apace.

At this writing, U.S. Customs must be given credit for having done the most to improve the security of the container transport system, but with their still very constrained resources they have not been able to mobilize the cooperation (which sometimes must be dearly bought) in inspection and cargo intelligence of more than 25 of the 50-100 major container ports abroad shipping to the United States, nor have they been given adequate budget and mandate to procure and operate the best and latest external screening and scanning equipment. Progress on this effort is also retarded by current diplomatic disputes between the United States, France, Belgium, and Germany, and the recent SARS crisis in major Chinese and Southeast Asian ports. Only time will tell whether it will be politically feasible to obtain the worldwide cooperation and burden sharing required for an effective and affordable defense of the seaport-based transport system against nuclear terrorist attack.

Clearly the momentous and challenging organizational and political implications of the key design principles of the overseas-deployed layered defense-in-depth port security systems approach require further detailed operations analyses and technology and systems benefit cost analyses and evaluations: Worldwide container port deployment of U.S. Customs inspectors staffing operation of U.S. standard inspection devices and procedures. Thousands of inspectors and scanning equipment operators must be recruited, trained, and deployed to foreign ports.

Cargo crime is currently estimated to cost the trading countries of the world some $650 billion per year in losses. The recommended improvements in container cargo security costing $10 billion per year could easily pay for themselves by a mere 2 percent reduction in cargo crime losses, which seems highly likely. Insurance rates are also expected to come down, providing added savings.

The recommended cargo tracking systems can improve freight transport efficiency and the productivity of ports, trade, and production dependent on just-in-time deliveries to minimize inventory costs.

Offensive military capability maintenance costs might be significantly reduced, to the extent that an improved preventive civil defenses of U.S. seaports and homeland populations reduce policy pressures for preventive and preemptive attacks on threatening WMD proliferators, in the (now mistaken) belief that deterrence and cost-effective defense against nuclear terrorist attacks is impossible.

Currently, American seaports are dangerously vulnerable to nuclear terrorist attack, especially by means of a cargo container carrying nuclear weapons or materials. If it occurred today, such an attack could destroy an entire container port along with adjacent, densely populated urban areas, and catastrophically disrupt the entire seaport-based import/export supply chain. Although numerous U.S. government-sponsored studies have examined the vulnerability of U.S. seaports to terrorism using weapons of mass destruction, no comprehensive solutions to the specific threat of nuclear terrorism have yet been devised.

U.S. seaports handle thousands of cargo containers every day. Despite the great risk that a standard-size container might carry a smuggled nuclear weapon, only a tiny fraction of containers can now be inspected without crippling the flow of trade. To mitigate this risk, the U.S. and foreign customs and law enforcement agencies have so far relied on improving existing procedures for inspecting cargo contents, conveyances, documentation, and associated personnel. These procedures, which employ statistical sampling methods, are only partially effective against the illegal drugs, arms, and other contraband for which they were originally developed; they are woefully inadequate against the threat of nuclear terrorists using just one of the millions of cargo containers transiting the United States as a delivery vehicle.

Improved strategies and technologies could significantly reduce the risks of catastrophic damage to the U.S. economy, seaports, and their associated container-based freight transport systems as a result of nuclear terrorist attack. The civil defense proposed here employs technology currently in development and testing, costs less than $10 billion annually, involves minimal disruption to the flow of goods through seaport-based transport, and would dramatically reduce the risk of catastrophic human and economic losses from a nuclear terrorist attack using shipping containers as delivery vehicles.

The economic impact of even a single nuclear terrorist attack on a major U.S. seaport would be very great. In three scenarios examined in this paper, a successful attack would create disruption of U.S. trade valued at $75-175 billion and property damage of $45-170 billion. The scenarios suggest that 20,000 to 150,000 lives would be lost: applying DOT conventions for valuing a statistical life, this catastrophe would be valued at $60-450 billion. The terrorist can achieve destructive values in this range through either dockside detonation of the nuclear device at the U.S. port of debarkation or through detonation at an inland target after transshipment of the device.

The U.S. Customs strategy of intelligence-based sampling of a small fraction the flow of millions of containers a year can be too easily countered by terrorists and their supporters. Terrorists can evade or deceive the data and intelligence collection and intelligence information analyses of suspicious cargoes, conveyances, and personnel handlers, by shielding and decoying the weapons from external gamma-ray detector screening, by saturating the inspection process with higher peak traffic loads than can be carefully screened by current methods without seriously impeding the flow of trade, and leaving foreign container ports unsecured without uniformly high inspection standards.

Analysis suggests that a nuclear container loaded on a container in a foreign port has a 98 percent probability of passing undetected through the foreign port of embarkation. That means that a terrorist who can get a nuclear device into a container is virtually assured of achieving at least a dockside detonation. The terrorist's probability of success is somewhat lower if the aim point requires transshipment, but his chances of success are still estimated to exceed 75 percent. Advanced inspection technologies are available and could be exploited now.

The technology and the organizational and procedural designs exist which could, if fully applied to this problem of container port security, greatly reduce the risk of deaths and damages from nuclear terrorist attack on seaport-based transport. The key technology is the shielded pulsed-active neutron interrogation device, or scanner. Expertise in this technology exists in government labs, university research labs, and private industry firms. Leading organizations were, respectively, Lawrence Livermore National Laboratories (LLNL) of the U.S. Department of Energy, the MIT Lincoln Laboratories, and American Science and Engineering. There are no doubt other worthy organizations that have much to contribute. The assistance of scientists at LLNL is particularly indispensable, since many of them are experienced in both nuclear arms control and stockpile security bearing directly on the detection of hidden weapons.

An effective system of defenses built around this technology would include: forward deployment of customs inspection to container ports of embarkation shipping to the United States, 100 percent external scanning of all U.S.-bound containers, using fixed drive-through installations, mobile truck-mounted scanners, and scanners on container lift cranes; augmented container transport information systems, including the use of tamper-resistant electronic reporting seals on containers; and strengthened personnel security.

The Annual Cost of a Solution for Effectively Screening 100 percent of U.S.-Bound Containers at 100 Ports is $10 Billion. A comprehensive installation of the best and latest nuclear detection and screening technologies, in sufficient numbers to permit parallel drive-through and/or drive-by and crane-lift operations to avoid any costly delays in inspection or loading of container ships, could be procured for around $100 million per average major container port. If it is considered desirable to outfit the 100 most important container ports, the annual cost of an effective preventive civil defense screening of 100 percent of containers at the selected ports comes to $10 billion per year.

The Likelihood of a Successful Nuclear Terrorist Threat Can be Greatly Reduced by an Improved Defense System. An improved civil defense of container ports can greatly reduce the terrorist's chances of evading detection at the port of embarkation, and the chances of successful transshipment to an inland target.

An effective defense must encompass overseas freight export operations. There is broad agreement among government officials and independent analysts on the ideal attributes of a global containerized cargo system secure from nuclear weapons attack by means of container-borne delivery. All serious reports and researchers speak of "extending the borders out," "controlling and monitoring the entire supply chain from origin to destination," securing individual containers, conveyances, and crews handling them with various security and identity clearances, collecting information from all sources, including financial and transportation and personnel records, and data mining it to gain early warning of suspicious cargoes and to gain more efficient sample selection of those containers to be taken off line and opened for rigorous internal inspection. Needed is universalization and enforcement of international standards of container security with fast-track rewards for cooperation and compliance, and denial of port access rights for the recalcitrant, careless or willful violators. There is an increased need for interagency intelligence information sharing and coordination, and for public-private cooperation and burden sharing. Necessary but Complex Negotiations with the Governments of U.S. Trading Partners Have Just Begun Concerning this Kind of Comprehensive Anti-Nuclear-Terrorist Defense of Port Cities, and They Have a Long Way to Go and Require Top Level Attention to Make Progress. There is little or no agreement, domestically and internationally and between government and industry, regarding how much improved transport security will cost, who is in charge of what aspect and the whole system, and what will be the burden-sharing arrangements. Competition among agencies, governments, and industries for control and benefits, and to avoid costs continues apace with no evidence of increased resolution.

Design control and financing of the International port defense system by organization of an international multi-governmental public-private partnership of all stakeholders, under U.S. leadership, and with individual national and private corporation members having veto powers over their own participation in the system, at the risk of being denied the special fast-track treatment and other commercially advantageous privileges of membership. This is essentially a legal law enforcement and technologically explicit international trade and tariffs and arms control agreement that will require many months, possibly years, of diplomatic, technological, economic, and commercial negotiations. The most expeditious beginning of this approach has been made by U.S. Customs C-TPAT program, and this should be fully supported, extended, and expanded.

Biological and Nuclear Arms controls are a lot cheaper, safer, and morally superior to biological and nuclear arms races. The power of the civil is to the military, as the moral is to the physical (Napoleon), as three is to one. This is even more so for civil and military biodefense against catastrophic bioterrorism, and civil and military nuclear defense against nuclear terrorism.

Economists and other social and physical scientists should exert more applied research efforts to prove the above verities and communicate them to national and transnational leaderships across the political spectrum, so that they become universal principles for peaceful, just, humane, and productive resolutions of human conflicts.

Chapter 11
HETERODOX ECONOMICS
AND RADICAL NON-INTERVENTION
-THESES-*

Wolfram Elsner

This paper presents a few exploratory themes for a strictly non-interventionist approach to international affairs. While recognizing the value of positive strategies and programs that envision constructive international development programs, the focus is on the simple injunction to do no harm and ideas concerning:

- the region as the appropriate and adequate space for institutional action, cultural growth and change, and to develop collective capacities;
- the exclusive and power-based character of the current global system;
- the corresponding imperial character of any power-based, violent or military intervention.

Also the article refers to the heterodox economic concepts of inter-regional cultural diversity and historical time.

I. The Adequate Space of Agency

The region, however specified, is the adequate and most appropriate space for acticm and the most effective source of institutional and cultural change. It has an action capacity that can be gained only through collectively learned institutions of coordination and cooperation. Collective learning is intense with largely tacit knowledge that endows socio-economic processes with specific efficacy. In regional intcractions, dense, face-to-face contacts constitute a large portion of all interactions. The basis of collective capability, readiness and inclination to learning, change and innovation, in the widest sense, is located within a region. Localization and relocation thus mean bringing agency to, or back to, or leaving it where the problems are and where people are aware of them and can learn from them.

II. The Current Global System

---

* This was an invited statement at a panel on war and peace at the first conference of the International Confederation for the Advancement of Pluralism in Economics (ICAPE), held at the University of Missouri-Kansas City, 2003. It was reprinted in the ECAAR newsletter (now: EPS Quarterly), Nov. 2003

II. The Current Global System

The current global system is an unregulated, exclusive, unimbedded and power-based mechanism. Its logic is a "deliberate destruction of collective action" (Pierre Bourdieu), "undermining the public interest" (Lori Walach). As such, it is predominantly re-distributive rather than welfare-enhancing for the whole socio-economy. It encourages a hierarchical unification, with the homogenization and subordination of cultures, rather than a diversification among regional, national and local cultures. This weakens any inherent problem solving capacity leading to a reduced ability to absorb shocks, and a loss of resilience in the whole global system.

Being power-based, hierarchical and excessively competitive the global system shows signs of becoming an authoritarian system that is prone to violent, mainly militaristic, intervention as far as international relations are concerned. One might say, "normal" imperialism is back, operating at a higher level.

III. The Problem-Aggravating Character of Any Power-Based Intervention

Against this background, any power-based, violent or military intervention is incapable of solving any problem (even if it appears capable of doing so). Any imported or exported solution is, and cannot help but be, more disastrous in the long run than any endogenously learned solution, however incomplete. Violent interventionism may force adaptation in the short run, but will impede adaptability in the long run (Gemot Grabher/David Stark), since it destroys the basis of real experience, local or national cultural learning, learned trust, openness to change, willingness and inclinations to innovate.

IV. The Role of Virtual Reality to Justify Military Interventionism

Given these facts about the existing power system, there is no basis for anything like a "just war" or violent "humanitarian intervention" and there can be no moral/ethical justification for such an intervention. Under existing circumstances, any violent intervention must turn into a vehicle of imperialism at some stage, if not from the outset.

The historical experience of Europe in WWI and WWII suggests that "the first victim of a war is the truth" which also applies now more than ever. While WWI was still going on, Lloyd George clearly stated that if people knew the truth, the war would end immediately. In the Nuremberg trials after

WWII, Nazi-leader Hermann Goring said frankly that any government of any political orientation with a well-working mass media apparatus could make any person support any military intervention within weeks: Just tell them "we are under attack" or "they killed some of us."

In the war against Iraq, justifications were largely based on a massive structure of false information. Now the half-life of such misinformation has greatly decreased. Instead of thirty years for the release of documents, now false claims can be frankly admitted as soon as they have fulfilled their immediate purpose.

V. Regional Cultural Diversity and Global Problem-Solving Capacity

Real and sustaining problem-solving capacity can only be built on regional cultural diversity, rather than some variant of universalism or cultural/ethical essentialism where there is just one standard or a set of commensurable standards of truth. Most of the current problems in regional, national or local cultures stem from decades, even centuries, of hierarchical unification, foreign interventions and forced foreign influences on local economic and social conditions.

Diversity and equality based intercultural interactions, in contrast, require protection of diversity for regional development and largely endogenously learned problem-solving drawing on the direct experiences of those involved.

VI. Problem-Solving and Historical Time

Finally, real problem-solving requires recurrent interaction, trust-building, collective learning, institutional development and change within regional spaces. Such processes are inherently sequential, path-dependent and time-consuming, which rules out any short-run interventionist solution. Heterodox, institutional and evolutionary economists can contribute to understanding problems of conflict resolution and development by using their well-elaborated theoretical concepts relating to structural power and violence, cultural diversity, path dependence and real, historical time.

I have not argued that nothing can be done from the outside to address regional conflicts. Imported weapons can be kept from areas of conflict or non-violent interventions can be offered. I see the approach outlined here as realistic, pragmatic, implementable, and as an expression of real courage, spirit and individual and collective strength.

Chapter 12
OVERCOMING WAR AND EMPIRE
BY INCENTIVIZING JUSTICE AND DEMOCRACY

Lucy Law Webster

The international interventions of the past decade in Kosovo, East Timor, Afghanistan and Iraq have posed peace and law and human rights in strange forms of tension against each other. In fact international humanitarian law and peace are congruent, but the only forms of international intervention that would be legitimate have not as yet been tried. This relates to the lack of creative evolutionary approaches to social science and policy. The essay shows the limited legitimacy of recent interventions, explains why such non-humanitarian actions are no longer appropriate and how international law and civic action can be used to build peace and to transform the power that tends to encourage empire and imperialism into power for democracy.

I. A Critique of Collective Security as Envisioned in the United Nations System

Collective security as envisioned when the UN Charter was written was intended to allow strong states to protect weak states whenever there would be aggression by one against the other. But there have been relatively few acts of invasion across neighboring borders; the Iraqi invasion of Kuwait that was reversed by the Persian Gulf War was an exception. Most wars occur within states as civil wars between factions or insurgents against incumbents. This fact is based on economic power relationships that deserve more attention from economists and more action to create incentives for peace to replace the historic incentives for war. Almost any international intervention whether fully endorsed or just barely tolerated by the UN Security Council leads to power gains and losses within the country in conflict and internationally and results in some measure of outside control and imperialism even when the motive is humanitarian. It is sometimes said that collective security is what the P5 permanent members of the Security Council do to poor nations. And now we have seen the invasion of Afghanistan and Iraq led by the world's only superpower. The fact that the first of these wars is deemed legal (the United States was attacked by people based in Afghanistan) and the second is much less widely viewed as legal obscures the main issues. Both wars can be seen as callous acts of empire by the people attacked, and consequently there is no effective demonstration of the value of avoiding the types of behavior that led to these wars. Instead of reducing terrorism, more people have seen reasons to become terrorists to resist what they perceive as the hand of empire.

Collective security involves collective punishment; whole nations suffer for the actions of their leaders. Often, as in the Gulf War of 1990/1991, the leaders do not suffer at all; in which case there is no disincentive to start other wars, whether wars against weaker segments within a state, or wars to liberate or protect the weak. The use of military force, even when endorsed by Security Council mandate, requires the violent imposition of order as defined by and administered by global powers whether they are sensitive to the local and regional culture or not.

II. The Need to Replace Military Globalism with the Democratic Rule of Law

Such military globalism feels like imperialism to the people whose lives and homes and cultures are attacked and it looks like imperialism to millions of people worldwide who value human rights and cultural autonomy. The historical evidence indicates that norms of humanitarian law and democracy can be built up within a region, and even create a magnet for imitation as has happened in the European Union. However there is no evidence that such norms can be imposed from the outside unless there are strong indigenous roots that an outside force can then endorse. Whoever would impose democracy probably does not understand it. Democracy requires voluntary participation and a history of common learning and interactive mutual respect. This is unlikely to be forthcoming when soldiers of major military powers impose order according to norms that are at best globally recognized primarily by international elites and are at worst the norms of industrialized states acting against less industrialized, less "modern" or less Westernized nations and peoples.

III. The Responsibility to Protect the People

Nevertheless, when militias supporting states such as Serbia or Indonesia attack the people of Kosovo or East Timor, I would assert that the international community has a responsibility to protect the people attacked and that the UN Security Council has a duty to act. Such action is needed to demonstrate the disutility of war crimes and genocide. To sustain this principle it would be important to respond whenever the government of any state abrogates its sovereign responsibility to protect the people within its borders either because it is unable or unwilling to do so. However it matters greatly HOW the international community responds. The widespread outcry against the human rights abuses in Darfur shows that the norms are widely respected by citizens throughout the world, but the lack of effective action to stop the genocide shows that there is currently no effective way to protect the international norms that are identified by the statute of the International Criminal Court. The purpose of this essay is to indicate how protection could be provided without war—without action that contradicts the essential objectives of the action taken.

This is a multi-stage process. In any given time period it is important to respond to gross violations of human rights in whatever ways best serve the needs of the people persecuted, and to do so in a way that creates the least possible violence and the least possible motivation for additional future violence. Concomitantly, pre-violence time periods should be identified to introduce programs that mitigate the causes and the incentives for abuse and that demonstrate its counterproductive effects, to show that crime does not pay, even for heads of state who have often experienced immunity from censure. Preventive action can avert both human rights violence and any military response. A systematic program to remove the incentives for violent conflict can bring practice into line with stated norms. Current practice recognizes standards that are important, but often not honored in practice.

The "best-practices" criteria for international humanitarian action can be specified as follows:

- There must be a just cause relating to a supreme humanitarian need.
- Force should be used very carefully for specific testable objectives, but it should be available early to be used proactively to stop violence as soon as it appears.
- The action taken should be consistent with the ends sought and meet the test of proportionality.
- The decision to intervene and the type of force used should have a high probability of achieving a positive humanitarian outcome both for the case at hand and in its impact on future norms.

IV. The Case Histories of Kosovo and East Timor

In Kosovo, and also in East Timor there was a clear humanitarian need for international action. In both instances earlier humanitarian intervention could have prevented extensive crimes against people and property. The impending violence that attracted international attention in Kosovo in 1998 had been anticipated for several years as the Belgrade government removed ethnic Albanian Kosovars from public employment, and much of the displaced leadership established a peaceful informal parallel civil administration, while others became new recruits into the Kosovo Liberation Army. When action was taken by the international community it was not only too late to have any preventive value, but it was also disproportionate and disjunctive in relation to the problems faced by the people persecuted by Serb militia and Yugoslav army personnel. The bombing by NATO was inconsistent with the stated humanitarian goals. It made it easier for Milosevic to dislodge people from their homes, not harder. The probability of achieving a positive outcome in Kosovo when the intervention took place must be assessed in relation to the goals set, whether explicit or hidden. The humanitarian goals claimed were not effectively met because of the extensive displacement and destruction of lives and property, and the ambiguous stability for Kosovo of the resulting peace. If the goal was regime change and bringing Milosevic to court, those objectives were achieved.

In East Timor the efforts at intimidation of pro-independence citizens provided clear signals that, if people were not intimidated before and during the ballot, there would be retribution after it. This was clearly presented as a serious possibility to the UN Security Council prior to the August 1999 ballot asking people to choose between autonomous incorporation into Indonesia or independence. Nonetheless between the announcement of the ballot results on September 4 in New York (September 5 in Dili), and the time the Security Council voted to set up a multinational force under Chapter VII of the Charter (Resolution 1264, September 15, 1999), almost two-thirds of the population had fled their homes and villages to escape the murder and pillage of militia units opposed to independence. The intervention force approved by the Security Council in September 1999 succeeded in mitigating a humanitarian disaster. The fact that it arrived too late to save the lives and homes of many is a result of the fact that the Security Council did not find a way to act except by a coalition of the willing led by Australia, which would not act without the agreement of Indonesia. Australia was the only major state to have recognized Indonesian sovereignty in East Timor following the Indonesian invasion and occupation of East Timor in 1975. But there was no way to act except to wait for Australia to wait for Indonesia. This demonstrates the lack of international peacekeeping capacity. The United Nations should have its own standing force ready to move in to protect the people without waiting for major states to do so. The best model would be a directly recruited force responsible to the UN Secretary General without the encumbrance of real or perceived imperial attitudes or ambitions.

V. The Potential Importance of Civil Society Engagement

The most essential basis for a legitimate system of global responsibility to protect would engage the active participation of local and regional communities. The past half century of professionalization and international institutionalization of development planning has created a culture in which outsiders arrive in problem areas to suggest and guide and sometimes to impose solutions. Should the historic experience and knowledge of the local people and the cultural region not be given similar respect? The past 200 years of economic growth has served some nations well, but it now seems clear that many nations might have developed in a manner that would have better served their people had the paths chosen been more firmly grounded in their own history. Now there are disturbing disjunctions. Should the salary of an engineer recruited as a driver for a "development expert" be higher than the salary of a construction engineer? How can community development become development of the people, for the people and by the people? How can democracy grow from existing historic roots? These are urgent questions to address if participatory development is to engender local power for democracy. More local and regional leadership is needed to nurture power from the cultural roots of nations and peoples.

The sources of terrorism lie in the alienation that arises in the people who are most disenfranchised at the bottom of an undemocratic world system where military imperial power is imposed on nations that are themselves deeply undemocratic, excluding their citizens from effective participation. Terrorists are recruited in countries that lack modern education and constructive opportunities where there is a backdrop of extreme poverty and a sense of anger at insults to the nation, the religion and the culture. Terrorists arise when it feels more empowering to participate in commitments to destroy than to participate in building.

A major commitment is needed throughout the system of United Nations agencies, by individual governments, and by networks of NGOs to redeploy "development assistance" away from the experts and to give it to the people. All children deserve access to and engagement in modern education and experience of their own historic culture and of world community values as well as access to food, clean water, shelter and basic health services. If this is not available, the security of the entire world is put at risk. Locally generated community development can provide the key to bringing basic cultural and economic services to villages and cities throughout the world. People must be engaged in their own development and in their own security.

There is an unused tool available for locally-based community development in the largely hortatory commitments made by almost all governments throughout the world to various norms of international law and programs of action generated by a range of UN bodies and conferences. In the hands of the people this body of commitments can become a powerful tool—either for direct action or for putting pressure on ones own government to fulfill its stated obligations. If local civil society groups were proactively involved doing what is needed to enhance implementation, they would not only achieve some of the objectives identified such as better access to clean water and sanitation, but they would build their own power to achieve and to protect themselves from any future economic exploitation or violation of their human rights. Such self-generated action can be coordinated with the work of international networks of Non-Governmental Organizations that could provide resources when invited and help connect with broad networks of governments and with the UN Security Council. The goal is to put the Security Council on call to serve the people, especially people in communities at risk of violence and exploitation.

VI. Empowering the People for Self-Rule and Democracy

The goal is to forge local and worldwide networks in support of UN norms as a counterweight to the power of the sorts of militias that played truly devastating roles in Kosovo and in East Timor. In most countries at risk of violence and human rights abuses, as well as those at risk of extreme poverty, there are many civic groups that can better mobilize themselves to act if they see an overarching strategy for self-enhancement. The goal is to empower local communities that are embedded in their own cultures to use the global norms that fit their needs.

In parallel with local action, international NGOs that respect cultural autonomy can, when asked, assist in monitoring human rights interests by keeping records of violations and making these available to the UN High Commissioner for Human Rights or to officials of the International Criminal Court. The role and the responsibility of individuals before international law is expanding. A major step forward is represented by the International Criminal Court, making individuals as well as states responsible under international law. This is the best way to end the collective punishment inherent in war and in traditional forms of interstate action for collective security. It is the responsibility of the world community to protect people when the state in which they live will not or cannot prevent war crimes, crimes against humanity or genocide. But it is not the duty of anyone to do this in a way that leads to violence or undermines justice. Concepts of justice vary, but the ideas in the Universal Declaration of Human Rights are widely recognized. Almost none of the norms of the Universal Declaration have been denounced, but many remain unobserved. The citizens of every nation can insist that they be protected according to these norms by effective international law. If it is known that people are watching, potential wrong doers will be deterred. Local and global networks of civil society groups and of governments can monitor the implementation of agreed norms of humanitarian law.

VII. Asserting the Sovereignty of the People

Civil society within countries at risk of conflict and international civil society groups can use preventive diplomacy to avert violence. It is easier to visualize how this could have worked in Kosovo or East Timor than in Afghanistan under the Taliban or Iraq under Hussein, but that is largely a matter of timing and sequencing. By engaging in the implementation of the less controversial parts of the many plans of action and other agreements that states have endorsed, thousands of aware citizens can be ready to prevent the importation of illicit arms, the exploitation of labor or the violation of human rights. In Afghanistan there were some opportunities for this before the Taliban achieved effective control, although such opportunities were almost certainly inadequate once state violence against descent was decisive in most parts of the country. This was also true in Hussein's Iraq, as was the case in Hitler's Germany.

The price of freedom is early vigilance. That is the point of the strategy of proactive, locally-based engagement suggested here. The big news is that now, unlike the 1930s, there is a network of civil society groups committed to protect the human rights of people everywhere, and to respond to cries for help. There is also a network of middle-power states that is equally committed to protect the citizens of every nation from genocide, war crimes and crimes against humanity even when such crimes are committed by a citizen's own government. These are the groups and the nations that understand that collective security by means of war is essentially dysfunctional and counterproductive, but that there are now institutions and norms that make it possible to replace the rule of war with the force of law. As more and more states sign onto a law-based mode of international action, the role of imperial, war-based power will shrink. If the nations using the soft power of law are supported by civil society, that mode of action will prevail. Above all, if civil society within the countries and communities at risk of exploitation and violence uses its own ability to communicate and grow, it will be able to act in concert with the states and citizen networks that actively seek direction from the people who most need their support. Such direction from below will undermine the power of empire. Empires depend upon authoritarian decisions imposed from above with military force. The value of such force can be replaced with effective law-based action implemented by the people and by the United Nations.

VIII. Taking Action to Establish New Norms for Future Expectations

It is important to assess how different forms of international action can contribute to the expectations of individuals, and the norms that affect state practice. What is done successfully in one case will become a model for the future. Rightly or wrongly, states will feel constrained to act within the precedents set. Thus each case becomes a precedent and a model for future action. The most benign form of intervention in defense of human rights would be to send in UN Marshals to apprehend individuals who commit crimes against humanity, war crimes or genocide. This could be done with almost no violence if there were strong convictions within the nation concerned that these crimes should be stopped and prevented in the future. Civil society support of UN action would be of critical value to underpin successful interventions by UN Marshals, so that a pattern of such interventions would deter future violations.

We have seen that individuals and networks of non-state actors can be very powerful. A combination of high technology, lethal weapons and borderless communications means that a wide range of people and groups can act decisively to do harm. It will not always be practical to bomb the country that harbors terrorists, and such action generates new terrorists. Modes of international action must be developed that engender relatively peaceful responses by states and by individuals. The efficacy and legitimacy of any given action should be assessed in terms of its long-term impact, not just in terms of what it achieves initially. A democratic response to any challenge to peace and human rights is required by the people from within nations and cultural regions to uphold their own civic values, their own cultural norms and the peaceful global norms that have been endorsed by the United Nations and by governments worldwide.

About the Authors

Clark C. Abt, Ph.D. Distinguished Professor of Management, Cambridge College, Cambridge, Massachusetts and Chairman Emeritus and Founder, Abt Associates Inc.

Liliane Bensahel, Doctor in economics; Researcher in economics at the University Pierre Mendès France of Grenoble and former Director of Espace Europe (a federal structure of research centres in social science).

Jurgen M. Brauer, Professor of Economics at Augusta State University's College of Business Administration; he holds an economics undergraduate degree from the Free University of Berlin and a doctoral degree in economics from the University of Notre Dame; he taught at St. Mary's College and at the University of Notre Dame; he has been a Peace Fellow of the United States Institute of Peace and is a member of the academic honour societies of *Sigma Xi* and *Phi Kappa Phi*.

Fanny Coulomb, Senior Lecturer at the University of Grenoble and vice-director of CESICE, a research centre on international security and European cooperations.

John Paul Dunne, Professor of Economics in the School of Economics, University of the West of England, Bristol; his research interests include econometrics, defence and peace economics and political economy.

Wolfram Elsner, Professor of Economics, Structural Research and Economic Policy, Faculty of Economics and Business Studies, University of Bremen, Germany; previously University of Cologne and University of Bielefeld; head of the Planning Division of the Ministry of Economic Affairs of the State of Bremen, and Director of the Bremen Economic Research Institute; former Bremen State Official for Industrial Defence Conversion; member of the Council of the European Association for Evolutionary Political Economy (EAEPE); chair of the German chapter of Economists Allied for Arms Reduction (ECAAR).

Jacques Fontanel, Professor of Economics, Vice-President of international relations at the University of Grenoble and Director of PEPSE, a research centre on economic and social policies.

María García-Alonso, Lecturer in Economics in the Department of Economics, University of Kent; her interests are in industrial organisation, international trade, defence and peace economics and international relations.

Gulay Gunluk-Senesen, Professor of Public Economics in the Faculty of Political Sciences, Istanbul University, Turkey; she studied Economics in Bogazici University; her research interests include defence economics, input-output modelling and gender issues.

Michael D. Intriligator, Professor of Economics at the University of California, Los Angeles (UCLA); he is also Professor of Political Science, Professor of Public Policy in the School of Public Policy and Social Research, and Co-Director of the Jacob Marschak Interdisciplinary Colloquium on Mathematics in the Behavioural Sciences, all at UCLA; he is also a Senior Fellow of the Milken Institute in Santa Monica and the Gorbachev Foundation of North America in Boston; he has received several distinguished teaching awards.

Galip B. Isen, Professor of social sciences at the Istanbul Bilgi University, Faculty of Communication in Istanbul, Turkey. He focuses on the psychological, cognitive and cultural aspects of social and political phenomena, with a special interest in terrorism and violence, the affairs of the Mediterranean and how the modern *Weltanschauung* affects the interaction of cultures.

Christos Kollias, Associate Professor at the Department of Economics, University of Thessaly; he has held posts at the Technological Education Institute of Larissa, the Centre of Planning and Economic Research and the University of Crete; his research interests include defence economics, public sector economics and political economy; he also serves on the editorial board of *Defence and Peace Economics*, *European Review of Economics and Finance* and *Review of Economic Sciences*.

Paul Levine, Professor of Economics in the Department of Economics, University of Surrey; his general research interests are defence economics and conflict; macroeconomic policy; growth theory; migration of labour; regulation of networks.

Luc Mampaey, Senior Researcher at GRIP (Groupe de Recherche et d'Information sur la Paix et la sécurité, Brussels) where he is the head of the

Luc Mampaey, Senior Researcher at GRIP (Groupe de Recherche et d'Information sur la Paix et la sécurité, Brussels) where he is the head of the Arms Production and Trade Project; he is a commercial engineer (HEC St. Louis, Brussels) and holds a special degree in environmental management (Université Libre de Bruxelles, ULB-IGEAT); he is at present a doctoral student in Economics at the University of Versailles-Saint-Quentin-en-Yvelines (Lab. C3ED).

Andrew Michael, Senior Lecturer in Economics and Business at the School of Business, Intercollege, Cyprus; he has an MA in Economics and is currently working on his PhD in Business Administration; his current research interests are in political economy, defence economics, and job satisfaction.

Susana–Maria Paleologou, Lecturer at the Department of Economics, University of Ioannina, Greece; she was a staff member of the Council of Economic Advisers at the Hellenic Ministry of Economy and Finance; her current research activity concentrates in the areas of defence economics, electoral-partisan business cycles and applied econometrics.

Claude Serfati, Maitre de conférences of economics and project leader on Globalisation, Governance, and Sustainable Development at C3ED, University of Versailles-Saint-Quentin-en-Yvelines. His main research topics are on globalisation (interrelations between productive and financial activities, security issues and global governance) and arms industry, with special reference to science and technology policy. He is author of numerous books and articles on these topics, some of them available in English and German.

Ron P. Smith, Professor of Applied Economics in the Department of Economics at Birkbeck College, University of London; his research interests include econometrics, defence and peace economics and political economy.

Lucy Law Webster, Secretary of the Board of Directors of Economists for Peace and Security, and the EPS UN Representative; she also works as Senior Fellow of the Institute for Global Policy, which is part of the World Federalists Movement; her background includes 14 years in the UN Secretariat, mostly as a Political Affairs Officer in the Department of Political Affairs; she has an MSc in International Relations and is working on an MA in Global Political Economy and Finance at the New School University, New York.

Bremer Schriften zur Konversion
hrsg. von Prof. Dr. Wolfram Elsner
(Konversionsbeauftragter des Senators
für Wirtschaft und Häfen der Freien
Hansestadt Bremen)
Schriftleitung: Dipl.-Ök. Marion Salot

Carsten Sieling
Regionale Strukturpolitik und Konversion
Eine vergleichende Untersuchung von
Konversionsstrategien in Bremen und
Lancashire
Infolge rückläufiger Rüstungsgüternachfrage Ende der achtziger Jahre sind eine Reihe europäischer Regionen unter besonderen strukturellen Anpassungsdruck gekommen, verbunden mit einer starken Gefährdung von Arbeitsplätzen. In dieser Situation wurde die Idee der industriellen Rüstungskonversion als Ansatz für regionale Strukturpolitik entdeckt und bis Ende der neunziger Jahre in einer Vielzahl regionaler Aktivitäten angewendet. Die vorliegende Arbeit diskutiert die theoretischen Grundlagen für eine konversionsorientierte regionale Strukturpolitik und evaluiert die Praxis dieses Ansatzes am Beispiel zweier Regionen. Im Ergebnis werden Stärken und Schwächen von Konversion und regionaler Strukturpolitik verknüpft mit Empfehlungen für eine Weiterentwicklung und Spezifizierung strukturpolitischer Instrumente.
Bd. 8, 2000, 304 S., 25,90 €, br.,
ISBN 3-8258-4301-1

Joachim Schuster
Die internationale Rüstungsindustrie
Perspektiven für die Rüstungsproduktion und Konversion nach 2000
Bd. 9, 2000, 128 S., 17,90 €, br.,
ISBN 3-8258-4722-5

Noemi Bußkamp
Konversion und ihre betriebswirtschaftlichen Effekte
Das Beispiel der industriellen Rüstungskonversion und ihrer Förderung im Lande Bremen 1992–2000. Gutachten der Firma Cap Gemini Ernst & Young Mittelstandsberatung erstellt im Auftrag des Senators für Wirtschaft und Häfen der Freien Hansestadt Bremen
Die industriepolitische Konversionsförderung im Lande Bremen in den Jahren 1992 bis 2000 galt und gilt, gemessen an der Anzahl der geförderten Projekte und der Intensität ihrer regionalen Einbettung, als europaweit besonderer Fall einer öffentlich begleiteten regionalen Umstrukturierung. Grund genug, am Ende des Prozesses auch zu fragen, was der darin enthaltene Teil der betrieblichen Förderprojekte für Wirkungen im Hinblick auf Arbeitsplatzsicherung, Organisationsmodernisierung und Steigerung der Wettbewerbsfähigkeit hervorgebracht hat. Vor diesem Hintergrund hat der Bremer Wirtschaftssenator eine externe Evaluierung aus Sicht der Unternehmensberatung und Wirtschaftsprüfung an die Fa. Cap Gemini Ernst & Young vergeben. Die hier vorgelegten Ergebnisse erlauben in vielfacher Hinsicht Einblicke in den betrieblichen und sektoralen Strukturwandel, den Umgang mit Innovationen und Marktschließungsstrategien sowie das Interaktionsverhältnis unternehmerischer und öffentlicher Akteure. Sie liefern aber auch Kriterien für eine erfolgreiche Umsetzung und Förderung von betrieblicher Konversion und sind somit sowohl für die öffentliche Verwaltung als auch die betriebliche Praxis von großem Interesse.
Bd. 10, 2002, 152 S., 17,90 €, br.,
ISBN 3-8258-4723-3

Wolfram Elsner (Ed.)
International Restructuring and Conversion of the Arms Industries and the Military Sector
Industrial, Regional and Sociocultural Aspects. Proceedings of the International Conversion Conference, Bremen, April 2001
The decade of the nineties saw a rapidly changing political world, a sudden and severe change of political conditions for the state-dependent industries, sectors and regions and, consequently, increased research on and

LIT Verlag GmbH & Co. KG Wien–Zürich
Auslieferung Österreich: Medienlogistik Pichler-ÖBZ GmbH & Co KG
IZ-NÖ Süd, Straße 1, Objekt 34, A-2355 Wiener Neudorf, Postfach 133
Tel. +43 (0) 2236/63 535 - 290, Fax +43 (0) 2236/63 535 - 243, e-Mail: bestellen@medien-logistik.at
Auslieferung Deutschland: Fresnostr. 2 48159 Münster
Tel.: 0251 – 62 03 222 – Fax 0251 – 23 19 72
e-Mail: vertrieb@lit-verlag.de – http://www.lit-verlag.de

resuming of this unique experience. The international 2001 Bremen conference was a kind of comprehensive convention of all the relevant researchers, the trade unions and companies, other regional and national agents and their European networks – a central event to approach a comprehensive balance of the rich experience made. The present volume, therefore, represents settled experience, sector analyses, spatial and company case studies and perspectives for proactive change management in the coming decade. The conference brought to the fore not only recent alternative views from European and U. S. perspectives but also a clear message for all relevant agents to openly face and proactively address the structural challenges in the field in this decade. There is no justification for a reluctant or reactive approach to the issues of peace, disarmament and corresponding industrial and regional restructuring. The present volume is a major source for an ongoing debate on the political and economic issues of peace, (dis-)armament, and related structural change in "21".
Bd. 11, 2002, 482 S., 25,90 €, gb.,
ISBN 3-8258-5761-1

Wolfram Elsner; Marion Salot
Industrielle und regionale Konversion im Lande Bremen 1992 – 2000
Abschlußbericht 2001
Bd. 12, 2002, 160 S., 20,90 €, br.,
ISBN 3-8258-4725-x

Wissenschaftliche Paperbacks
Politikwissenschaft

Hartmut Elsenhans
Das Internationale System zwischen Zivilgesellschaft und Rente
Gegen derzeitige Theorieangebote für die Erklärung der Ursachen und die Auswirkungen wachsender transnationaler und internationaler Verflechtung setzt das hier vorliegende Konzept eine stark durch politökonomische Überlegungen integrierte Perspektive, die auf politologischen, soziologischen, ökonomischen und philosophischen Ansatzpunkten aufbaut. Mit diesem Konzept soll gezeigt werden, daß der durch Produktionsauslagerungen/ Direktinvestitionen/ neue Muster der internationalen Arbeitsteilung gekennzeichnete (im weiteren als Transnationalisierung von Wirtschaftsbeziehungen bezeichnete) kapitalistische Impuls zur Integration der bisher nicht in die Weltwirtschaft voll integrierten Peripherie weiterhin zu schwach ist, als daß dort nichtmarktwirtschaftliche Formen der Aneignung von Überschuß entscheidend zurückgedrängt werden können. Das sich herausbildende internationale System ist deshalb durch miteinander verschränkte Strukturen von Markt- und Nichtmarktökonomie gekennzeichnet, die nur unter bestimmten Voraussetzungen synergetische Effekte in Richtung einer autonomen und zivilisierten Weltzivilgesellschaft entfalten werden. Dabei treten neue Strukturen von Nichtmarktökonomie auf transnationaler Ebene auf, während der Wiederaufstieg von Renten die zivilgesellschaftlichen Grundlagen funktionierender oder potentiell zu Funktionsfähigkeit zu bringender, dann kapitalistischer Systeme auf internationaler und lokaler Ebene eher behindert.
Bd. 6, 2001, 140 S., 12,90 €, br.,
ISBN 3-8258-4837-x

Klaus Schubert
Innovation und Ordnung
In einer evolutionär voranschreitenden Welt sind statische Politikmodelle und -theorien problematisch. Deshalb lohnt es sich, die wichtigste Quelle für die Entstehung der policy-analysis, den Pragmatismus, als dynamische, demokratieendogene politisch-philosophische Strömung zu rekonstruieren. Dies geschieht im ersten Teil der Studie. Der zweite Teil trägt zum Verständnis des daraus folgenden politikwissenschaftlichen Ansatzes bei. Darüber hinaus wird durch eine konstruktiv-spekulative Argumentation versucht, die z. Z. wenig innovative Theorie- und Methodendiskussion in der Politikwissenschaft anzuregen.
Bd. 7, 2003, 224 S., 25,90 €, br.,
ISBN 3-8258-6091-4

LIT Verlag GmbH & Co. KG Wien – Zürich
Auslieferung Österreich: Medienlogistik Pichler-ÖBZ GmbH & Co KG
IZ-NÖ Süd, Straße 1, Objekt 34, A-2355 Wiener Neudorf, Postfach 133
Tel. +43 (0) 2236/63 535 - 290, Fax +43 (0) 2236/63 535 - 243, e-Mail: bestellen@medien-logistik.at
Auslieferung Deutschland: Fresnostr. 2 48159 Münster
Tel.: 0251 – 62 03 222 – Fax 0251 – 23 19 72
e-Mail: vertrieb@lit-verlag.de – http://www.lit-verlag.de

Beiträge zur Konversionsforschung
hrsg. von Prof. Dr. Ulrich Albrecht (Freie Universität Berlin)

Ernst Buder (Hg.)
Möglichkeiten und Grenzen der Konversion von B-Waffen-Einrichtungen
Die Konversion ehemaliger biologischer Waffen (BW)-Institute sind ein entscheidender Schritt zur biologischen Rüstungskontrolle. Die Autoren des Buches stellen die BW-Konversion in den Zusammenhang mit definitorischen Aspekten und internationaler Gesetzgebung und ziehen Lehren aus der Konversion konventioneller, nuklearer und chemischer Rüstungseinrichtungen, Besonderes Gewicht wurde auf die Konversion ehemaliger sowjetischer BW-Einrichtungen gelegt, die heute bereit sind, sich in die westliche Wissenschaftsgemeinschaft durch Hinwendung zur Gesundheitsforschung, insbesondere durch Erforschung von Prophylaktika, Diagnostika und Therapeutika gegen gefährliche Infektionskrankheiten, einzuordnen.
Bd. 7, 2000, 304 S., 25,90 €, br.,
ISBN 3-8258-4499-4

Herbert Zeretzke
Betriebsbezogene Prozesse und Projekte der zivilen und ökologischen Konversion und Innovation
Natur und Finanzsystem treffen im menschlichen Aktionsfeld, im Produktionssystem, aufeinander. In ihm wird entschieden, ob sich Persönlichkeit entfaltet, oder sie degeneriert: als Manager, Arbeitnehmer, Gewerkschafter. Hier werden Kriege begünstigt und vermieden, Ressourcen nachhaltig verwendet und verschwendet, Innovationen realisiert und verhindert. Kultur, Religion und Säkularisierung prägen die Beteiligten. Der Autor reflektiert seine vielschichtige Praxis während weltgeschichtlicher Umbruchphasen durch die Innen- und Außensicht des Akteurs in einem Kieler Produktionsbetrieb.
Bd. 8, 2004, 600 S., 49,90 €, br.,
ISBN 3-8258-8325-6

Studien zur Gewaltfreiheit
hrsg. vom Institut für Friedensarbeit und Gewaltfreie Konfliktaustragung

Uwe Painke
Ein Stadtteil macht mobil
Gemeinwesen gegen Gewaltkriminalität. Neighborhood Safety in den USA
Mit gewaltfreien Mitteln Gewaltkriminalität stoppen? – Ein aussichtsloses Unterfangen? Dieses Buch zeigt, daß es geht. Mehr noch: anhand von Praxisbeispielen aus den USA wird konkret aufgezeigt, wie wirksam ein solcher Weg selbst unter schwierigsten Bedingungen großstädtischer Gewaltkriminalität sein kann. Zugleich zeigt das Buch erste Ansätze und Schritte auf, wie ein solches Konzept auch in Deutschland umgesetzt werden kann. "Ein Stadtteil macht mobil" richtet sich dabei nicht nur an Menschen, die beruflich mit Kriminalitäts- und Gewaltprävention zu tun haben. Denn die Frage, wie Staat und Bürger/innen mit dem Problem krimineller Gewalt umgehen wollen, ist so brisant, daß sie Menschen aus allen Bereichen unserer Gesellschaft bewegt.
Bd. 3, 2001, 504 S., 20,90 €, br.,
ISBN 3-8258-5600-3

Burkhard Bläsi
Konflikttransformation durch Gütekraft
Interpersonale Veränderungsprozesse
Welche gewaltfreien Verhaltensweisen können zur Veränderung von Konflikten, zur Überwindung von Gewalt beitragen? Auf der Grundlage von Interviews mit neun Personen, die über Jahrzehnte Erfahrungen im gütekräftigen Vorgehen gegen Gewalt gesammelt haben, legt der Autor die erste empirische Analyse der Gütekraft-Forschung vor. *"Lasst tausend solcher Studien blühen!"* Johan Galtung, Dr. h. c. mult., Professor für Friedensforschung, Versonnex.
Bd. 4, 2001, 206 S., 10,90 €, br.,
ISBN 3-8258-5731-x

LIT Verlag GmbH & Co. KG Wien – Zürich
Auslieferung Österreich: Medienlogistik Pichler-ÖBZ GmbH & Co KG
IZ-NÖ Süd, Straße 1, Objekt 34, A-2355 Wiener Neudorf, Postfach 133
Tel. +43 (0) 2236/63 535 - 290, Fax +43 (0) 2236/63 535 - 243, e-Mail: bestellen@medien-logistik.at
Auslieferung Deutschland: Fresnostr. 2 48159 Münster
Tel.: 0251 – 62 03 222 – Fax 0251 – 23 19 72
e-Mail: vertrieb@lit-verlag.de – http://www.lit-verlag.de

Schriftenreihe zur Konfliktforschung
des Zentrums für Konfliktforschung und des (ZfK) der Philipps-Universität Marburg und des Arbeitskreises Marburger Wissenschaftler für Friedens- und Abrüstungsforschung (AMW)

Johannes M. Becker
Militär und Legitimation
Eine vergleichende Studie zur Sicherheitspolitik Frankreichs und der Bundesrepublik Deutschland
Bd. 20, 1997, 85 S., 4,90 €, br.,
ISBN 3-8258-5575-9

Gert Sommer; Rüdiger Zimmermann (Hg.)
Gewaltfreie Konfliktaustragungen
Bd. 21, 1998, 120 S., 4,90 €, br.,
ISBN 3-8258-5576-7

Gert Sommer; Jost Stellmacher; Ulrich Wagner (Hg.)
Menschenrechte und Frieden
Eine Zusammenstellung aktueller Beiträge und Debatten
Bd. 22, 1999, 550 S., 15,90 €, br.,
ISBN 3-8258-5577-5

Johannes M. Becker; Gertrud Brücher (Hg.)
Der Jugoslawienkrieg – Eine Zwischenbilanz
Analysen über eine Republik im raschen Wandel. Mit Beiträgen von Johannes M. Becker, Peter Becker, Gertrud Brücher, Jürgen Elsässer, Hermann L. Gremliza, Dieter S. Lutz, Tobias Pflüger, Werner Ruf, Hajo Schmidt, Gert Sommer und Erich Schmidt-Eenboom
Der Jugoslawienkrieg markiert für die Bundesrepublik Deutschland einen entscheidenden Einschnitt in ihrer Geschichte. Die Nach-Kriegsgeschichte nach dem Zweiten Weltkrieg, die diesem Land nach der faschistischen Kriegs- und Vernichtungspolitik des "deutschen Reiches" eine gewisse Sonderrolle zuzuweisen schien, ist nun offenkundig beendet. Das vereinte Deutschland ist ein normaler interventionistischer Staat geworden, das Stigma "Auschwitz" ist abgeschüttelt und mit ihm das Gefühl für eine besondere Rolle im Finden und Praktizieren von Außen- und Sicherheitspolitik. Dieser Krieg markiert auch weltweit die neue Ausgangsbasis von Sicherheitspolitik nach dem Zusammenbruch der Warschauer Vertrags-Organisation (WVO) am Beginn der 90er Jahre. Die USA, und in ihrem Schlepptau die NATO, diktieren derzeit unilateral das kriegs- oder friedenspolitische Geschick der Erde.
Bd. 23, 2001, 216 S., 25,90 €, br.,
ISBN 3-8258-5520-1

Konflikttransformation
hrsg. vom Berghof-Forschungszentrum für konstruktive Konfliktbearbeitung (Berlin)

Petra Haumersen; Helmolt Rademacher; Norbert Ropers
Konfliktbearbeitung in der Zivilgesellschaft
Die Workshop-Methode im rumänisch-ungarischen Konflikt
Eine deutsche Nichtregierungsorganisation veranstaltet wenige Jahre nach dem Sturz Ceausescus eine Serie von insgesamt 7 Workshops zum Konfliktmanagement mit Rumäninnen verschiedener ethnonationaler Herkunft. Ziel ist es, zivilgesellschaftliche Bearbeitungsmöglichkeiten des interethnischen Konflikts zwischen der rumänischen Mehrheit und der ungarischen und anderen Minderheiten in Rumänien zu fördern. Welche Überlegungen gingen dem Vorhaben voraus' Was passierte im Verlauf der Workshops? Welche Methoden wurden eingesetzt und haben siel bewährt? Welche Lehren lassen sich allgemeiner für da' Engagement externer Akteure in interethnische Spannungsfeldern aus den gemachten Erfahrungen, ziehen? Darüber gibt das um Anschaulichkeit und praktische Nutzbarkeit bemühte Buch von Dr. Norbert

LIT Verlag GmbH & Co. KG Wien – Zürich
Auslieferung Österreich: Medienlogistik Pichler-ÖBZ GmbH & Co KG
IZ-NÖ Süd, Straße 1, Objekt 34, A-2355 Wiener Neudorf, Postfach 133
Tel. +43 (0) 2236/63 535 – 290, Fax +43 (0) 2236/63 535 – 243, e-Mail: bestellen@medien-logistik.at
Auslieferung Deutschland: Fresnostr. 2 48159 Münster
Tel.: 0251 – 62 03 222 – Fax 0251 – 23 19 72
e-Mail: vertrieb@lit-verlag.de – http://www.lit-verlag.de

Ropers, Helmolt Rademacher und Petra Haumersen Auskunft. Alle drei Autorinnen waren Mitglieder des Leitungsteams dei Workshops und stellen ihre Reflexionen für die theoretische Diskussion und praktische Nachahmung zur Verfügung.
Bd. 1, 2002, 296 S., 17,90 €, br.,
ISBN 3-8258-5465-5

Oliver Wolleh
Die Teilung überwinden
Eine Fallstudie zur Friedensbildung in Zypern
Die Annäherung zwischen den Volksgruppen in Zypern ist schwierig und voller Hindernisse. Oliver Wolleh hat über einen Zeitraum von fünf Jahren das Geflecht von friedensbildenden Bürgergruppen in Zypern untersucht. Er fragt nach den Möglichkeiten und Grenzen dieser Aktivitäten und wie sich die Handlungsspielräume der lokalen Gruppen durch die Unterstützung internationaler und ausländischer Akteure erweitert und verengt haben. Dabei ist eine systematische Evaluierung entstanden in deren Zentrum die Begegnung und der Dialog in der Pufferzone stehen.
Bd. 2, 2002, 432 S., 20,90 €, br.,
ISBN 3-8258-5464-7

Ekkehard Forberg; Ulf Terlinden
Hilfe, die nicht vom Himmel fällt
Gewaltprävention in der Entwicklungsarbeit von NGOs
Die Kriege in Somalia, Sudan, Ruanda, Burundi, Kongo und Angola sind bekannte Beispiele für die Bruchlandungen des internationalen Konfliktmanagements „von oben". Unter Entwicklungs-NGOs, die in solchen Konflikten immer wieder zu stummen Zeugen der Gewalteskalation werden, lösten sie eine - wenn auch zögerliche - Reflexion der eigenen Tätigkeit aus. Wie können sie als nicht-staatliche Akteure von außen dazu beitragen, dass Konflikte auf dem afrikanischen Kontinent ohne Gewalt ausgetragen werden? Geleitet von dieser Frage wird die komplexe Wirklichkeit jener Entwicklungsorganisationen untersucht, die sich der Herausforderung stellen, in Konflikten eine konstruktive Rolle zu übernehmen. Anhand zahlreicher Beispiele hinterfragt die Studie die Praxistauglichkeit der vorhandenen Konzepte und prüft, inwiefern diese in der entwicklungspolitischen Arbeit von NGOs umgesetzt werden. Kritisch reflektieren die Autoren zugleich die Rolle, die Gewaltprävention in der Entwicklungszusammenarbeit einnimmt bzw. in Zukunft einnehmen könnte: Handelt es sich um eine legitime Einmischung in Konflikte oder vielmehr um die zeitgemäße Garnierung althergebrachter Hegemonialpolitik? Durch eine genaue Problemanalyse werden die Chancen und die Veränderungskraft deutlich, die mit rechtzeitiger Gewaltprävention „von unten" verbunden sind. Ein ermutigendes Plädoyer, inspirierend für Praktiker und Theoretiker der Entwicklungspolitik.
Bd. 3, 2002, 224 S., 15,90 €, br.,
ISBN 3-8258-5933-9

Giovanni Scotto
Friedensbildung in Mostar
Die Rolle der internationalen NRO
Internationale Nicht-Regierungsorganisationen haben eine wichtige Rolle im Friedensprozess in Bosnien-Herzegowina gespielt. Diese Untersuchung beschreibt die Arbeit internationaler NRO in Mostar und analysiert ihre Auswirkung in der Transformation des Konfliktes in einer Stadt, in der die Teilung entlang ehtnischer Grenzen nach dem Ende des Krieges nicht überwunden werden konnte. Internationale NRO konnten dabei in Zusammenarbeit mit lokalen Kräften einen wichtigen Beitrag für die Brückenbildung leisten. Die beobachtete Stärkung der Zivilgesellschaft sowie die verbreitete Bereitschaft, sich auf den Dialog jenseits der Konfliktlinien einzulassen, sind zwei wichtige Zeichen dafür, dass in Mostar Frieden eine Chance hat.
Bd. 4, 2004, 280 S., 19,90 €, br.,
ISBN 3-8258-7852-x

LIT Verlag GmbH & Co. KG Wien – Zürich
Auslieferung Österreich: Medienlogistik Pichler-ÖBZ GmbH & Co KG
IZ-NÖ Süd, Straße 1, Objekt 34, A-2355 Wiener Neudorf, Postfach 133
Tel. +43 (0) 2236/63 535 - 290, Fax +43 (0) 2236/63 535 - 243, e-Mail: bestellen@medien-logistik.at
Auslieferung Deutschland: Fresnostr. 2 48159 Münster
Tel.: 0251 – 62 03 222 – Fax 0251 – 23 19 72
e-Mail: vertrieb@lit-verlag.de – http://www.lit-verlag.de

Dialog
Beiträge zur Friedensforschung

Österreichisches Studienzentrum für Frieden und Konfliktlösung (Hg.)
Die Weltunordnung von Ökonomie und Krieg
Von den gesellschaftlichen Verwerfungen der neoliberalen Globalisierung zu den weltumspannenden politischen Ansätzen jenseits des Casinokapitalismus.
Projektleitung: Thomas Roithner
Der vorliegende Band stellt die globalen Zusammenhänge zwischen Ökonomie und Krieg in einen breiteren Kontext und bedient sich dabei eines umfassenden Friedensbegriffs – über den Zustand von Nicht-Krieg hinausgehend –, wie auch der Untertitel des Buches signalisiert. Die „Weltunordnung von Ökonomie und Krieg" wird aus Sicht der Friedens- und Militärwissenschaft, der Wirtschaftswissenschaften, der Philosophie, der Kommunikationswissenschaften, der Gewerkschafts- und Friedensbewegung, der Entwicklungspolitik, des Journalismus sowie der Politik diskutiert. Mit Beiträgen von Elmar Altvater, Jörg Becker, Heinz Fischer, Thomas Fues, Erich Kitzmüller, Friedrich Korkisch, Peter Lock, Hildegard Goss-Mayr, Hans Holzinger, Jörg Huffschmid, Gerald Mader, Birgit Mahnkopf, Bernhard Mark-Ungericht, Angela Riedmann, Werner Ruf, Thomas Roithner, Hans Sallmutter, Hermann Scheer, Peter Strutynski, Jakob von Uexküll und Andreas Zumach.
Bd. 49, 2. Aufl. 2006, 304 S., 12,90 €, br., ISBN 3-8258-9723-0

Österreichisches Studienzentrum für Frieden und Konfliktlösung (Hg.)
Konstruktiver Pazifismus im 21. Jahrhundert
Symposium zum 80. Geburtstag von Dr. Gerald Mader
Im Pazifismus gab es immer zwei Orientierungen: Die in der kritischen Öffentlichkeit prominenteste war der Anti-Militarismus – mit dem Slogan: „Die Waffen nieder!" Weniger publikumswirksam, aber langfristig umso bedeutungsvoller waren und sind jene Versuche, die jenseits aller berechtigten Kritik zu einer positiven Friedensperspektive gelangen wollen. Denn nicht nur gilt es, die den Frieden verhindernden und ihm entgegenwirkenden Strukturen, Verhaltensweisen und Mentalitäten abzubauen bzw. zu überwinden. Ein besonderes Anliegen von Pazifismus muss sein, Bedingungen aufzuzeigen, die friedensförderlich sind und überdies dauerhaften, also nachhaltigen Frieden begründen. Dieser Herausforderung stellen sich die AutorInnen dieses Bandes.
Bd. 51, 2006, 176 S., 9,90 €, br., ISBN 3-8258-9835-0

Kieler Schriften zur Friedenswissenschaft
Kiel Peace Research Series
hrsg. von Christian Wellmann

Vadim Poleshchuk
Advice not welcomed
Recommendations of the OSCE High Commissioner to Estonia and Latvia and the response
Bd. 9, 2001, 120 S., 12,90 €, br., ISBN 3-8258-5700-x

Hanne-Margret Birckenbach; Christian Wellmann (eds.)
The Kaliningrad Challenge
Options and Recommendations
The Kaliningradskaya Oblast, Russia's Baltic exclave which soon will turn into an island amid the enlarged EU and NATO, constitutes a twofold challenge to European politics: Due to its economic, social, historical, geographical, strategic and cultural peculiarities the detached region may become a source of instability. However, due to the same peculiarities the region also bears the potential to serve as a pilot-region for an EU-Russian partnership. To meet the latter perspective all actors concerned need to engage in a dialogue-based, co-ordinated, and problem-solving approach. The book provides recommendations to a

L IT Verlag GmbH & Co. KG Wien – Zürich
Auslieferung Österreich: Medienlogistik Pichler-ÖBZ GmbH & Co KG
IZ-NÖ Süd, Straße 1, Objekt 34, A-2355 Wiener Neudorf, Postfach 133
Tel. +43 (0) 2236/63 535 - 290, Fax +43 (0) 2236/63 535 - 243, e-Mail: bestellen@medien-logistik.at
Auslieferung Deutschland: Fresnostr. 2 48159 Münster
Tel.: 0251 – 62 03 222 – Fax 0251 – 23 19 72
e-Mail: vertrieb@lit-verlag.de – http://www.lit-verlag.de

wide range of actors on how to approach the Kaliningrad challenge in a proactive manner. It starts by presenting a policy paper which was drafted by a group of Kaliningrad experts from eight countries. The Paper is then complemented by 14 issue-oriented chapters which provide in-depthreasoning on the suggestions made by the group.
Bd. 10, 2003, 304 S., 25,90 €, br.,
ISBN 3-8258-6650-5

Leonid Karabeshkin; Christian Wellmann
The Russian Domestic Debate on Kaliningrad
Integrity, Identity and Economy
The book investigates into the domestic background of Russia's policy with respect to its Baltic exclave, the EU and NATO encircled Kaliningrad region. Based solely on Russian sources, the book strives for deepening the understanding of Russia's Kaliningrad policy by non-Russian actors and of why it quite often appears to be unsuitable, eruptive or offensive. The policy issues studied in-depth concern identity formation, economic development and the visa regime. Common to all is that the respective federal policies are strongly affected by worries about the territorial integrity of Russia and the possibility of alienation of the exclave from the mainland. The book concludes with lessons to be learned on how to respond constructively to the mode of Russia's Kaliningrad policy.
Bd. 11, 2004, 104 S., 12,90 €, br.,
ISBN 3-8258-7952-6

Emma J. Stewart
The European Union and Conflict Prevention
Policy Evolution and Outcome
The book examines the evolution of EU conflict prevention as an internal EU process and as an area of external cooperation with the UN, OSCE and NATO. Conflict prevention has emerged as a prominent EU policy in the post-Cold War era. Yet, how suited is the organisation to practice conflict prevention, and what does the record of cooperation with other key European organisations tell us about the EU's external priorities? The book critically analyses the EU's policy and outcomes to date, concluding that conflict prevention is underdeveloped by the EU, and is in danger of being marginalised in favour of shorter-term crisis management. Moreover, EU external cooperation reinforces this: the priority is cooperation in crisis management with the UN and NATO, rather than longer-term cooperation with the OSCE.
Bd. 12, 2006, 280 S., 24,90 €, br.,
ISBN 3-8258-9114-3

Ulrike Kronfeld-Goharani (Hg.)
Friedensbedrohung Terrorismus
Ursachen, Folgen und Gegenstrategien
Der Terrorismus der Neuzeit, transnational organisiert und global ausgerichtet, ist zu einer ernsthaften Bedrohung des Weltfriedens geworden. Der vorliegende Sammelband möchte einen Beitrag zur Fortführung der Debatte über die verschiedenen Formen des Terrorismus leisten und befasst sich mit ausgewählten Aspekten des Problems terroristischer Gewalt. Aus dem Blickwinkel verschiedener Disziplinen wird das Phänomen des Terrorismus beschrieben. Es wird nach den Ursachen gefragt und auf Gefahren aufmerksam gemacht. Auswirkungen und Folgen werden betrachtet und Möglichkeiten zur Bekämpfung des Terrorismus diskutiert.
Bd. 13, 2006, 312 S., 29,90 €, br.,
ISBN 3-8258-9264-6

LIT Verlag GmbH & Co. KG Wien – Zürich
Auslieferung Österreich: Medienlogistik Pichler-ÖBZ GmbH & Co KG
IZ-NÖ Süd, Straße 1, Objekt 34, A-2355 Wiener Neudorf, Postfach 133
Tel. +43 (0) 2236/63 535 - 290, Fax +43 (0) 2236/63 535 - 243, e-Mail: bestellen@medien-logistik.at
Auslieferung Deutschland: Fresnostr. 2 48159 Münster
Tel.: 0251 – 62 03 222 – Fax 0251 – 23 19 72
e-Mail: vertrieb@lit-verlag.de – http://www.lit-verlag.de